THE WOMAN WHO
THOUGHT TOO MUCH

Joanne Limburg was born in London in 1970, and studied Philosophy at Cambridge. She is the author of two poetry collections. *Femenismo* (Bloodaxe, 2000) was shortlisted for the Forward Best First Collection Prize; *Paraphernalia* (Bloodaxe, 2007) was a Poetry Book Society Recommendation. She lives in Cambridge with her husband and son.

'Judicious and elegant, lucid and spry, Joanne Limburg uses her uncommon gifts to anatomize an all-too-common disorder. She brings a sort of glee to the process: for all the unhappiness she describes, this remains a joyous read.' **Kate Clanchy**

'Joanne Limburg's *The Woman Who Thought Too Much* is about that most intimate and destructive of civil wars – the fight against one's own thoughts and obsessions. Brave, witty, intelligent, wise, and honest, it is the story of a lifelong battle with neurosis, but it transcends pathology, uncovering the extraordinary underside of all our "ordinary" consciousness. Her unremitting candour liberates us all.' **Raymond Tallis**

'Limburg's clear, unsentimental poet's eye... conveys with great skill... the identity issue of separating the disorder from the person. Moving and compelling, full of dark humour and insight.' *Sunday Business Post*

'Reading this will compel some readers – I'm one of them – to ponder their own hang-ups. There are no easy answers, but this book offers some hope... Limburg is a talented writer, and poet... Revealing, honest and thought-provoking.' *Time Out*

'Weighty in places, both intellectually and emotionally, but Limburg renders her autobiographical tale with charming gusto and boundless energy while referencing everything from medical journals, Freud and Dante, to Hollywood films and Prefab Sprout. A lovely read, expertly crafted and imbued with wry humour. These very personal and extraordinary accounts of a difficult life feel markedly different from the norm.' *The List*

THE WOMAN WHO THOUGHT TOO MUCH

A Memoir of Obsession and Compulsion

Joanne Limburg

Atlantic Books
London

First published in Great Britain in 2010 in hardback and export and airside trade paperback by Atlantic Books, an imprint of Grove Atlantic Ltd.

This paperback edition published in Great Britain in 2011 by Atlantic Books.

3 5 7 9 10 8 6 4 2

A CIP catalogue record for this book is available from the British Library.

ISBN: 978 1 84354 703 7

Printed in Great Britain

Atlantic Books
An imprint of Atlantic Books Ltd
Ormond House
26–27 Boswell Street
London WC1N 3JZ

www.atlantic-books.co.uk

THE WOMAN WHO
THOUGHT TOO MUCH

Contents

Author's Note

As I am aware that few people would choose to be a character in someone else's memoir, most names have been changed. In some cases, a few other details have changed along with them.

Shame

48. At certain moments I am tempted to tear off my clothes in public.

The Padua Inventory

––––––

It's not catastrophes, murders, deaths, diseases, that age and kill us; it's the way people look and laugh, and run up the steps of omnibuses.

Virginia Woolf, Jacob's Room

Shame is an inescapable part of being human: without it, there would be little to stop us assaulting attractive strangers and defecating on tube trains. In other words, it acts as an internal social regulator, and most of the time, for most people, it does an unobtrusively good job.

But shame can also be a bully. Nastier by far than guilt, which is merely the feeling that one has *done something* wrong, shame is the feeling that one is *being someone* wrong. When we feel guilty, we want to make right the wrong action; when we feel ashamed, we want to hide the wrong self away – or obliterate it.

There are quite a few of my own selves I would obliterate, if I could: the unsuccessful, soiled selves that could never quite act or speak or look as they should; that drag shaming memories around with them. The youngest of these is myself in middle school. She is being told off in front of everybody, and her peers are enjoying it.

The ironic thing about this particular public shaming is that it never would have happened had I not been trying to avoid that very thing. By that time, I had already spent several years as one of the class weirdos, what with my precociously serious manner, my penchant for long words, and my awkwardness at games. Sometimes I did manage to join in with the other girls for a while, playing skipping, or elastic, or ball and stocking, but more often I was turned away. I can remember spending countless break-times walking round and round the perimeter of the playground all alone, head down, doing my best to look self-contained.

I didn't feel the way I was trying to look: I felt lonely, and vulnerable with it. My school wasn't a rough place by any means, but children are pack animals by instinct, and can't seem to help attacking the solitary beasts. One day, for example, I was sitting on a bench, staring thoughtfully into the sky, when a couple of girls came up to me and shouted angrily in my face, 'You're *mad*!' I didn't know who they were, and I certainly hadn't done anything to them, but all the same my solemn, introverted presence was an offence to them. It bothered the teachers too: every parents' evening, my mother and father would come back to tell me the stale news that I was doing very well at my schoolwork, 'but was a bit of a loner'.

At lunchtimes, the rule was that all children had to queue for the dining hall in twos. The dinner ladies would count off so many pairs at a time and then bring their arms down like car park barriers to hold the rest of the queue back for a few minutes, before letting another few pairs in. Looking back, I suppose this must have been the easiest way for them to manage the flow of child traffic through the dining hall, but at the time the main purpose of the whole ritual seemed to be to humiliate the friendless. More often than not, I had no partner, and the penalty for this was to be sent to the back of the queue. Again and again and again. So it was hardly surprising that, after a while, I gave up trying to get into the dining hall altogether.

Running parallel to the school's main building was a row of

single-storey, post-war prefabs. There was a long strip of uncut grass and weeds between the two which was safe and quiet. Nobody played there, because nobody was allowed to, so that was where I went every day to eat my packed lunch. I didn't tell anyone what I was doing, and the nettles had nothing to say about it.

But I had been spotted. Donna had stolen my friend Nathalie from me and turned her against me. Lately they had spent a lot of time together on the long path between the prefabs and the playing fields, playing catch with a big, heavy football; I remember that it was heavy because every time I walked past them it hit me on the head. When we played netball, it always seemed to be Donna who marked me; who stuck her hands up my T-shirt because, she said, they needed warming up; who followed me about the court asking endless questions about myself to which there were only wrong answers. She couldn't get enough of my blood, and when I came out of my private dining place one day and bumped into her, ready and waiting with a whole gang of girls, I knew I had handed her a victory on a lunch plate. 'What are you doing, Joanne?' she asked in that syrupy tone I had come to dread. 'Were you eating your lunch there?' I must have said something back, but I don't remember what: I spoke into my chest in those days, and I had a stammer to boot.

So, she told on me. Our usual form teacher, Mrs Hall, was a kind woman and probably would have dealt with the matter quietly, but unfortunately for me she was away on holiday, so I had to face Mrs Greenbaum instead. She was one of those teachers who, as far as I could tell, had entered the profession solely for the opportunities it gave her to snap children's heads off, the more publicly the better. By the time I came back into the classroom after break-time, Donna had already spent a good ten minutes telling on me, embroidering wherever possible, and working Mrs Greenbaum up beautifully. Donna had told her that she had found me eating in the *toilets* – how dirty! How disgusting! She had even looked into the toilet after I had gone, she said, and seen a Marmite sandwich floating in the water, with the initials 'JL' scratched into it.

Perhaps Mrs Greenbaum wasn't listening to the details, or perhaps she was just an extraordinarily credulous woman, but whatever the reason, she took Donna at her word and laid into me: I was naughty; what I'd done was filthy; the headmaster was going to be *furious*. She finished by using me as a teaching aid to help the class rehearse their proverbs.

'What do they say?' she asked. 'When in Rome . . .'

'. . . DO AS THE ROMANS DO!' chorused the good children.

What could I do? My efforts to hide my soiled self had ended up with it being waved around in front of everybody, as if it were – I don't know – a urine-soaked monogrammed sandwich. However I played it, I was different and that difference was felt as a stigma.

According to Erving Goffman, who wrote the book on stigmas and their management,[1] an individual can be said to carry a stigma when there is a discrepancy between his or her 'virtual identity' – his term for what one is expected to be – and that person's actual identity. A stigma is something which marks that person as outside the norm, and not in a good way. When it is revealed, its appearance might be said to interrupt the flow of easy social intercourse; it makes everyone, stigmatized and 'normal' alike, feel uncomfortable.

Some stigmas, such as obvious physical disability, or severe facial disfigurement, or a skin colour which differs from the norm, are impossible to hide, and any individual thus stigmatized faces a stark choice when it comes to the management of that stigma:

1. Erving Goffman, *Stigma: Notes on the Management of Spoiled Identity* (Prentice-Hall, Inc., New Jersey, 1963)

either they shun society altogether, or they go out into it with their 'spoiled identity' on show and take the awkward consequences. If your stigma is not immediately obvious, you have a third option: to 'pass' as normal, to fail to mention it, whatever it is, and hope that you don't get 'outed'. Since Goffman was writing, in the 1960s, a fourth option has become increasingly popular: you out yourself. You give a newspaper interview; you go on a chat show; you write a book. But if you have any sense, you'll think hard beforehand about how much you have to lose.

The Mental Health Foundation addressed this dilemma in 2000, in a report it called 'Pull Yourself Together! A survey of the stigma and discrimination faced by people who experience mental distress'. One respondent wrote: 'when I tried to kill myself 2 years ago I walked out of A&E on Saturday morning and went to work on Monday as if nothing had happened because I was scared to let anyone know.'

The report goes on to say: 'There were many more reasons why people could not tell work colleagues than why they could . . . the most frequently reported reason for not telling work colleagues was fear of discrimination, stigma and prejudice.' They have good reason for their fear: there are psychiatrists who advise their patients against disclosing their histories on application forms.

When it comes to covering up one's mental health problems, sufferers from obsessive-compulsive disorder (OCD) and its 'spectrum disorders'[2] lead the field. This is a characteristic that Freud noted about a hundred years ago, when he commented that 'many more people suffer from these forms of obsessional neurosis than doctors hear of'.[3] He guessed that the prevalence of these kinds of disorders must be vastly underesti-

2. Body dysmorphic disorder, bulimia, trichotillomania, compulsive skin picking, etc.
3. Sigmund Freud, *Obsessive Actions and Religious Practices* (Standard Edition, Volume 9: pp. 115–28, 1907)

mated, and current received wisdom suggests that he was right. Thanks to some rapid developments in research and treatment which have taken place over the last thirty years or so, the perception of OCD has shifted from that of a rare condition with a poor prognosis to its current status as a very common condition which can respond extremely well to the right treatment.

Despite the better prognosis and treatment, the average sufferer copes alone with the condition for an average of eleven years before seeking appropriate help. They know they've got a problem; in many cases, they don't realize that their problem has been classified as a treatable illness, but, illness or not, they know they feel ashamed of it, and that they'd better keep it hidden.

The very nature of their symptoms contributes to their sense of shame. There are two components to obsessive-compulsive disorder: obsessions, which are intrusive and distressing thoughts or mental images; compulsions, which are the actions the sufferer performs in order to lessen the anxiety which these thoughts bring. While it is the intrusive and persistent quality of the thoughts, rather than their particular content, which marks them out as obsessions, their content is often of a kind that would distress or embarrass most people, were it to be revealed.

Ian Osborn sums up the usual themes very neatly by calling the relevant chapter of his book *Tormenting Thoughts and Secret Rituals* (1998), 'Filth, Harm, Lust, and Blasphemy'. Common obsessions include fears of contamination and contagious disease; thoughts of the sufferer causing harm to herself or her loved ones, through accident or oversight, or out of some uncontrollable impulse; images of the sufferer engaging in some kind of forbidden sexual activity. Blasphemy may be a less common issue here than it is in the more religious USA, where Osborn has his psychiatric practice, but obsessions relating to religious doubts or fears of damnation have been familiar to clerics for centuries. As this suggests, the content of these obsessions – like stigmatization – is often determined by the sufferer's social and cultural context.

The obsessions are most often shaming because of their content. Sometimes the compulsions are shaming too, because the sufferer can see perfectly well – but without being able to do anything about it – that her behaviour is ridiculous. Some compulsions, like hand washing, list making, or the repeated checking of locks and switches, are widely known about, often written on, and generally laughed at. Others are not so easy to identify. It took a long time for me to recognize it, but my favourite compulsion when hit by an obsessive thought was to seek reassurance – from my husband, from my GP, from my mother – that what I feared couldn't happen. For eighteen months I had to push my small son, in his buggy, across a main road which had no pedestrian crossing, and for most of those eighteen months, at about 4.30 or so, my husband would find himself fielding phone calls about how I had pushed the boy across safely but a car was coming towards us as I did so and it was not that far away, but if I had fallen over it would have had time to break safely, wouldn't it? Or turn aside, do you think? And all the time I knew how wearing it was for my husband to be my human safety blanket, and how ridiculous I was being, but it was still a long while before I managed to prevent myself from picking up the phone and bleating on like an idiot.

I didn't realize that this reassurance seeking could be seen as a compulsion. Neither did I understand how many compulsive activities I was managing to perform inside the privacy of my own mind: I was 'neutralizing' my obsessions with counter-thoughts; I was 'ruminating'. I am one of a large group of OCD sufferers – some think the largest – whose symptoms are mostly in their heads. When I tell people that I've been diagnosed with OCD, their first question, more often than not, is: 'So what do you do then?' My usual answer is: 'Nothing that you can see.'

When your stigma is of this kind, the easiest thing is to take option 3, and keep it zipped.

While we're on the subject of how to manage one's stigma, it's also worth pointing out that OCD sufferers, as a general rule, care more than most about what others think of them. We are known to be 'reward-dependent' (where the reward is someone else's approval) and to have 'tender consciences'. As a group, we are law-abiding, conscientious, exquisitely self-conscious and excruciatingly eager to please. We set ourselves the highest standards, and are disgusted with ourselves when we don't live up to them. We are forever scanning our own faces for flaws and other people's faces for signs of disapproval. We cannot forgive ourselves for ever having acted stupidly; we cannot bear to make a mistake. We can be destroyed by the merest hint of criticism but we criticize ourselves all the time. No wonder that most of us choose to 'pass', if we possibly can.

Neither is it at all surprising that many sufferers don't even know that there's a name for what they're hiding. They would be unlikely to recognize themselves in popular images of the illness. Think of Leonardo di Caprio in *The Aviator*, for example, playing Howard Hughes as a naked, bearded recluse, peeing into empty milk bottles in a darkened room. Or Jack Nicholson in *As Good as It Gets*, playing it for laughs as a tactless, misanthropic neat freak who brings his own plastic cutlery to restaurants. *Dirty Filthy Love*, a play broadcast on ITV in 2004, was written by a sufferer, and managed to convey more of what the condition feels like from the inside, but it was a television play, so it still had to show the afflicted characters doing things: walking strangely up the stairs, wiping seats before they sat on them, that kind of thing. As I remember, every single one of them was bothered by dirt – I'm not. I tend not to notice the dust building up in my house until I can shuffle through it. But I have been diagnosed with OCD.

It is only to be expected that the visual media would concentrate on the more visible aspects of the disease; thoughts do not lend themselves to visual representation, and a film about a life spent feeling anxious while quietly avoiding all possible harm would not make gripping viewing. The anxious, avoidant life doesn't make for a thrilling read either, which may be another reason why – apart from the shame and desire to cover up, or the hiddenness of the disease – even in these self-outing times, there are still relatively few OCD memoirs on the shop shelves. Alcoholism, drug addiction and manic depression make sufferers do all sorts of wild and extreme things that non-sufferers would never do, but find very compelling to read about. A single episode of major depression, suffered and then recovered from, has its own built-in narrative structure, which takes the protagonist and the reader into hell and out again, having learned something on the way, maybe.

When Dante goes into hell in his *Inferno*, what he finds is a place full of damned souls condemned to perform the same painful actions again and again, to go round and round in circles – quite literally, in some cases. Dante is in a privileged position: as the heroic protagonist and narrator of the tale, with Virgil as his guide, he is able to move through the circles in which the damned are condemned to stay. Along the way, various sinners tell him the stories of how they came to be damned, he thanks them, takes his leave of them, and then moves on. As a writer, this journey provides him with a beginning, a middle, and an end. Out of one day in hell, he gets enough material for a third of an epic.

Meanwhile the damned are stuck in their circles. Were Dante to return the next day, all that he could expect from them would be stories he's heard already, told in exactly the same words. So he moves on to Purgatory, and then to Paradise. No sense in boring your readers to death.

At least Dante's experiences are interesting to read about.

Imagine if, instead of witnessing bleeding, weeping trees, lovers blown about by gales, popes stuffed head first down burning holes, and sinners forever eating the brains of other sinners, he'd seen the following:

First Circle: People making lists.

Second Circle: People checking to make sure that they haven't left the oven on.

Third Circle: People washing their kitchen surfaces – again.

Fourth Circle: People touching the back of every chair they pass.

Fifth Circle: People opening envelopes they've just sealed for the third time, to make sure they haven't made any mistakes on their job application forms.

Sixth Circle: People phoning their husbands to ask for reassurance about the roads they've just crossed.

Seventh Circle: People sitting on their sofas trying to anticipate everything bad that might happen if they go out on a planned trip and then deciding it would be easier to stay at home . . .

It's a tormented life for sure, but that doesn't make it an interesting one. In fact, I would say the sheer repetitive tedium of it is a pretty large part of what makes it so tormenting. Then on top of the tedium, there's the anxiety, intense and ever-present; the exhaustion; the frustration, because you know that you are getting in the way of your own life, but it seems beyond you to get out of it; the painful awareness that your behaviour makes you a trial to the people around you; and of course the shame, the shame of not being able to control yourself like a normal, sensible person would, and the shame of knowing that your predicament is ridiculous, *comical* even.

It's not an interesting life, but it is quite an interesting predicament. As I'm a poet, who finds that the admission of this is usually quite enough by itself to interrupt the flow of easy social intercourse, I felt that I probably had less to lose by airing my predicament than most. And I do believe it needs some airing.

Nightmares

27. Sometimes I am not sure I have done things that in fact I know I have done.

The Padua Inventory

—————

Here am I,
Little Jumping Joan;
When nobody's with me
I'm all alone.

Nursery rhyme

Much as it surprises me now, and would probably surprise anyone who knows me, I do know what it is to be fearless – or, at least, I remember how it *was*. One memory in particular shows how different I must have been once. The summer after I was three I ran away at the funfair, and without realizing it, got lost. It's one of those memories that has to be reconstructed from its few surviving fragments. First of all, I see the fair, colourful, noisy and tempting, across the field from the pavement where my family are waiting, and feel my impatience to be there; then I am already halfway across the field and look back to see my family – my parents, my baby brother, uncle, aunt and cousins – standing in a row in the distance; here is the merry-go-round that I had seen from far away and was so desperate to ride on, and across the path I can see a ride I know I am too little for, with chairs on cables that flare out from a revolving disc; next is the view from the back of one of the wooden horses, as the roundabout slows down and my mother and father come into view; now my mother lifts me off the horse – she is wearing a brightly coloured buttoned blouse which is one of my favourites, and, for no reason that I can see, she is crying.

These days I can see the story from the terrified mother's viewpoint, but this doesn't make the memory itself any more frightening. It remains stubbornly sunlit, coloured by a happy child's belief that everything will be taken care of. Some people seem to have retained a version of this belief into adulthood. I see them wobbling down the middle of main roads on their bicycles, helmetless, talking into mobile phones, and I wonder at them. There's no one moment, no one trauma I could identify as the point when I lost that sense of safety, but I know that I still had it a few years later, because I was – in my own head, at least – a tree-climbing legend.

At seven years old, I had managed to climb every flowering cherry with reachable branches that our street had to offer, and decided to move on to the trickier ones. I chose one that stood on the verge at the bottom of our road, a few feet away from the patch of wasteland we called The Green. The fork in its trunk was too high for me to climb into, but halfway up to the fork there was a truncated branch with a few bristly new twigs sticking out of it, and I figured that if I could get a foothold on this stump, I could swing myself up to the fork and climb on from there. I took hold of the trunk and placed one foot on the stump. Then I pulled myself up. For a moment it looked as though I was going to make it, but then I lost my footing, slithered down the trunk and scraped first my knee and then my stomach against the stump I had thought would be my ally. The scratch across my stomach stung like mad so I clutched it, bent double, all the way home. I tried to get my mother and grandmother to understand just how much my stomach was hurting, but they were more preoccupied with my right knee, which had a bleeding chunk taken out of it. I still have both scars, and I'm proud of them.

It was a nasty fall, but it didn't end my climbing career. At nine I was spending my summer days on The Green with the other local children. Halfway across were two tall trees: one was inaccessible to everyone but the biggest boys, but the other was more accommodating. It was an exciting tree, a tree with a view: if you climbed high enough you could see the twin towers of Wembley Stadium. I liked to climb all the way to the top. Branches were pretty evenly spaced all the way, and this dictated my method: as I reached one branch, I would grasp onto the next one above it, then jump so that I was clinging to it upside down with all four limbs like a spit-roast, then haul myself round so that I was sitting astride the branch. Then I would stand up and repeat the process until I came to the top. Nowadays I find it hard to think about this without picturing myself falling onto my spine – which snaps in two. But in those days I liked nothing better than to stand on the highest, slightest fork and make the whole tree sway from side to the side like a metronome. Further down, other children would shout at me to stop it. I only fell out once, off one of the lower branches, and scraped my ankle on a bicycle that was lying on its side at the bottom.

Bicycles were every bit as important as trees. We raced each other up and down our cul-de-sac countless times, and we never wore helmets because excessive risk-aversion just wasn't fashionable then. My small son is a child of a different time, and he does have a bicycle helmet, which he wears as a passenger on the back of his father's bike. My husband always wears his, and just a few weeks ago I finally bought one of my own. As I write this chapter, I am in the middle of another course of cognitive behavioural therapy and as part of this latest drive to modify my behaviour, I have agreed to get back on a bicycle. I don't think I'll ever be ready to join the unhelmeted mobile-phoning section of society, but my dependency on walking, buses and other people's cars is limiting my life and that of my family, so I accept that I should at least try to do something about it. I've started riding around the local side roads; I cast a bigger shadow on the road now, and my left knee complains in a way that it never used to, but I have to admit, it really is still fun.

The cycling exercises are only a small part of the work we're doing. Most of the time, we're trying to address – or redress – a certain negative bias in my thinking behaviour. It did not come easily to me to admit that I'm enjoying the cycling; these few paragraphs, in which I have been describing myself as a happy and adventurous child, have taken far longer than they should, because I felt so unlike myself when I was writing them. I'm never quite sure what to make of those memories which don't support my steadfastly held picture of my life as one long, shameful spell in purgatory. If someone – a new friend, or a new therapist – asked me to tell them about my childhood, and I told the story that automatically came to mind, it would be quite a different one.

You never know what a small child is going to decide to be scared of. My son used to be terrified by a pre-school art show called *SMarteenies*; I think it had something to do with the giant paintbrush that hovers over the presenters' heads during the title sequence. At his age, I was petrified of the Quaker Oats man, and used to imagine his dreadful, grinning face floating outside my bedroom window at night. He sometimes had Wee Willie Winkie with him. My Ladybird nursery rhyme book had a picture of Willie, next to the rhyme:

> Wee Willie Winkie
>> runs through the town,
>
> Upstairs and downstairs
>> in his night-gown,
>
> Knocking on the window,
>> crying through the lock,
>
> Are the children all in bed,
>> for it's past eight o'clock?

The picture showed a wild-eyed boy in a nightshirt, running through some dark, topsy-turvy nightmare of a town, carrying a candle that burned with a ferocious light, like a piece of stolen sun. I was certain that if any child so much as peeped through a curtain after eight o'clock something horrific would happen to them, and that Wee Willie Winkie would be involved in it somehow.

There was another rhyme in the Ladybird books that would cause me even more anxiety than Willie Winkie's evening rounds, and it went like this:

> Hark! Hark!
> The dogs do bark.
> The beggars are coming to town.
> Some in rags
> and some in jags
> and one in a velvet gown.

The accompanying picture showed the beggars parading into a medieval town through its stone gate, watched by supercilious ladies in pointy hats and surrounded by skinny, excitable dogs. At the head of the troop was a brightly dressed boy, walking on his hands.   One night – I think I was four then – I dreamed I was that boy, a little thief sneaking into my parents' room to steal something off my mother's dressing table. I managed to creep up to it without making a sound, but just as I reached out to touch the forbidden things that sat on it, there was a sudden explosion of noise, a blaring and trumpeting, then the floor tilted, throwing me flat on my face. When I tried to get up I found that I was stuck to it, as if I'd been weighted down with stones. The blaring continued, the floor tipped this way and that, and out of my parents' enormous wardrobe burst a huge robot, the size and shape of a fruit machine, covered in flashing lights, sent out to judge and punish me.

I woke up before the machine could get me, but even though I knew that it was only a dream, for years afterwards, every time I went into my parents' bedroom for any legitimate reason, I found I had to sing that reason as I went in, in order to prevent the judge-and-punishment wardrobe robot from springing into action. In retrospect, it's tempting to see this as a taste of what was to come, a little advance warning from the neurosis fairy: the robot thought as my first obsession, the singing as my first compulsion.

Children who develop full-blown OCD before puberty are, more often than not, male. Joe Wells, the teenage author of the autobiography *Touch and Go Joe* (2006), is a good example. He experienced his first symptoms at the age of nine, and, typically for a child with OCD, these were indistinguishable from the symptoms an adult might have: he became obsessed with dirt and contamination, and developed a compulsion to wash his hands. Another child I saw on a recent television documentary was preoccupied with harm. He said that a voice in his head which he called Idiota was telling him to hurt his family, and as a result he was terrified of knives. Idiota also had a habit of reminding him of all the ways in which he might harm himself – by choking, for example. His mother was running out of things he would agree to eat. As I watched, I found I could recognize Idiota for what he was – a wellspring of obsessive thoughts – and fortunately for this child, the people who were treating him also understood the true nature of Idiota. It's not easy for a child to describe the experience of OCD: the capacity to recognize one's own thoughts *as* one's own thoughts is something that takes a whole childhood to develop. The consequence is that the younger and less articulate the child, the harder it is to diagnose them accurately. The same goes for childhood depression, and for a long time the received wisdom was that young children were constitutionally incapable of suffering from it. There just wasn't the evidence.

None generated by mainstream psychology anyway.[4]

Despite the robot in the wardrobe, I don't believe that I met my own Idiota until much later. On the other hand, at six years old I was already well acquainted with my inner Eeyore. I can remember my teacher Mrs Chandler telling me, with some exasperation, to 'Smile, Joanne – you won't crack your jaw!' It must have been around that time that I was standing in the playground one lunchtime looking such a caricature of misery that a few of the nicer girls came up to ask me what the matter was. I said I had a broken heart. This was the only way I could think of to describe the feeling I had, as if I were carrying a bag of wet sand behind my breastbone – it's the same feeling at any age, only as I got older I came to call it 'being depressed'.

I couldn't say what it was that had given me the wet sand feeling on that particular occasion: sometimes it was boredom, sometimes it was loneliness, sometimes it was just that my thoughts had taken me to an intolerable place. Standing in the line for the water fountain one day, it suddenly occurred to me that I was going to die – every one of us standing in that line would die one day; everybody in the world would die, even my parents and my aunts and my cousins. Everybody. In an instant, the playground, the day, the whole planet went tiny and far away. I saw in my mind's eye a map of the British Isles, fading to black like an image from a silent film. A few months later my grandmother died. There had been no time to explain to me and my brother that Grandma was ill, let alone that she was not going to live for much longer. None of my morbid imaginings had prepared me for the real shock of someone I loved suddenly not being there any more, and I struggled to make sense of it. I wanted to know – I *needed* to know – what this being dead actually meant. My mother told me, in answer to my questions, that

4. Ian M. Goodyer (ed.), *The Depressed Child and Adolescent* (Cambridge University Press, Cambridge, 1995, 2001)

Grandma had gone, that the body she had left behind was 'just a shell' and that dead people 'lived on in our heads'. Her answers turned into the strangest pictures: one of my grandmother's empty body as an abandoned brown carapace, resembling a Grandma-shaped woodlouse corpse; another of a cross-section of a head, with a sort of attic space in the top, in which dozens of tiny ancestors ran around like the Numbskulls in *The Beezer*.

The family religion was Judaism, and Jews are not encouraged to meditate upon the next world, whatever that might turn out to be; our proper concern is to live a just and fruitful life in this one, but I wasn't aware of this when I was seven. Neither did I appreciate that God was, in all his divine qualities, beyond the apprehension of any human sense. I had a very clear idea of what He looked like: He was a man of average build, with short ginger hair, a ginger moustache and round, wire-framed spectacles. He wore academic gowns and a mortar board, and stood at all times behind a giant wooden lectern which rested on nothing in the middle of space. From there he gazed out towards the distant stars, with a benign, if rather vague, expression on his face. He looked like one of the Ladybird illustrations, one of the less disturbing ones. Someone must have told me that God knew everything, which would account for the costume and the lectern. I'm unable to offer any explanation for the moustache.

So that was God, but what about heaven? Heaven was keeping me awake at night; I was desperate to figure out exactly where it was. Usually I would start with the assumption that it was at the top of the sky, maybe on the other side of the sky's ceiling. The ceiling would then also be heaven's floor, with God and his staff and all the good dead people walking about on it. But surely heaven had a sky, a ceiling? What was on the other side of that? How could something – the sky, for example – both come to an end and not come to an end? The more I thought about it, the more it made me feel horrible inside, as if somebody were driving me over the same hump-backed bridge again and again and again.

Back at school, I had more immediate concerns. My mother went to speak to Mrs Chandler about my bad dreams. Every night I was doing wrong things by accident and getting myself told off. Here's one typical example: we were all standing in a line outside the Portakabin classroom. I realized that I was facing the wrong way, but before I could set myself right, Mrs Chandler shouted 'Turn round!' and everybody did including me, so I was *still* facing the wrong way. I would wake up with the hump-backed bridge feeling, but this time the sharp tug in my stomach meant I was going to be punished. It was the robot-judge machine all over again, but in its human, teacherly form. I told my mother all about the dreams. I was worried that I wasn't doing very well at school, I described how Mrs Chandler was always telling this other girl that her work was very good; then there was another girl who had been given two gold stars just that week, when I'd only got one silver one for a whole story I wrote that was longer than hers. Obviously I was doing every-thing the wrong way.

My mother told me years later that she and Mrs Chandler had had quite a debate about the best use of stars as rewards. Mrs Chandler explained that gold stars were given out when a child had made an effort and done her best, not because her work was good in itself. My mother argued that a six-year-old could hardly be expected to understand this and that all I saw were other children getting stars. I think they agreed to disagree on the general issue, but Mrs Chandler did speak to me after-wards and reassure me about my performance in the classroom. 'You're one of the top girls,' she said.

I wasn't a popular one. On more than one occasion I over-heard one of my classmates telling another that they didn't like/hated/couldn't stand Joanne Limburg. Often they would go on to talk about some annoying habit of mine. For a little while

I had a compulsion to take my right hand and drag it slowly down my face. Then my hair grew long-ish for the first time, and I discovered that chewing it helped me think. 'Don't chew your hair, Joanne,' said Mrs Chandler. 'It'll go all rats' tails.' But I kept on, and chewed the cuffs of my school jumper for good measure. Sometimes I wiped my nose on the same cuffs. There was an absent-minded quality to all these activities that's never entirely left me: if I'm deep enough in thought I'll just do what I feel like doing and only become aware of it, and any attendant shame, when I become aware of laughter – or disgust. One day I was sent to the welfare officer with a bleeding scab on my face. 'You were *picking*, weren't you?' she said, looking at me as if she could see just what kind of revolting child I was. Maybe I had been picking, but I couldn't remember a thing about it.

When I was quite sure that I was going to write this book, I went to my GP and asked to see my medical notes. I knew that they would come in useful for checking certain details like dates and diagnoses, but I wasn't looking forward to reading what I had always imagined to be page after page of clinically accurate character assassination. In the event, however, they were nothing of the kind. 'You see?' my doctor said. 'You're NOT – THAT – BAD.'

One of the older items in the file is a letter from a speech therapist, addressed to a consultant paediatrician; copies had been sent to my GP and my junior school headmaster. It proved me wrong on one count right away, when I looked at the first paragraph and saw that that I'd first been referred to her in early 1978, when I was still only seven and in my last year of infant school. All this time I'd been assuming that I didn't develop the stammer until junior school, a place I've always found easy to demonize. The letter was written a year after that first referral, part way through what seems to have been a rather spasmodic course of treatment, and describes me on presentation as 'an extremely bright particularly verbally, insightful and shy girl' who 'severely lacked eye contact, and on a number of occasions turned her head to one side'. None of that surprised me, but I was rather taken aback to read that at my initial assessment, I was 'completely fluent', only demonstrating 'hesitancy, initial sound and syllable repetitions, and very occasionally mild initial sound blocks' halfway through the second session.

What emerges most clearly from the letter is that, in the therapist's opinion, it was not my speech as such that was the problem, but rather my anxiety about my speech.

> For a girl of Joanne's age she is extremely aware in a precise way of which people and situations cause her stammer to develop from a very mild dysfluency to what *she considers* [my italics] as a moderately severe dysfluency . . .
>
> The dysfluency is very fluctuating. Neither her class teacher, nor her headmaster, with whom I have spoken at some length have ever detected even the mildest stammer.
>
> Joanne's feelings towards her stammer include embarrassment and anger. Joanne is over-conscious of her speech, in general, and very aware when she makes a 'slip of the tongue'. She responds by stumbling and the form the stammer takes will then depend on the person(s) or situation.
>
> Mrs Limburg is concerned about Joanne's great anxiety about her speech, and is very wary that too much self-pressure regarding academic success (Joanne is a tremendously high achiever) . . . may exacerbate her daughter's stammer.

She discharged me six months later, writing to the consultant of my increased 'confidence' in dealing with my stammer. When I checked the date of this second letter, I saw that it was written during the long summer holiday. That makes sense.

When we moved up from the infants' to the junior school, the classes were shuffled. I found myself with a new group: there was Donna, my bully-to-be. Our teacher, Mrs Bowson, claimed a special interest in those of us she considered particularly bright. 'I'm interested in the professors and prime ministers,' she declared, 'not the road-sweepers and the shop girls.' I was one of the only two girls destined, in her opinion, to avoid the check-out at Tesco's, and we were moved, with a slightly larger handful of boys, to a separate, special table in the middle of the class-room. We were the 'Alpha Group', so named because, while the others did their maths out of the green *Beta* textbook, we had privileged access to the more difficult problems in the red *Alpha Maths* book. It was streaming by another name, and the head-master didn't approve. Towards the end of the year some of the children in the class claimed that they'd heard shouting in his office, and then seen Mrs Bowson come out crying. They might well have been telling the truth.

They may remember it differently, but I think the Alpha males had an easier time with their peers than we did. They could still help to make up the numbers in football and cricket teams, and one or two of them were even very good at games, which helped a lot. To be accepted by other boys, a boy has to do as the others do; to be accepted by other girls, a girl had better *be* as the others *are*, and my all-too-obvious cleverness was something that set me apart. I felt disfigured by it.

The other Alpha girl was Deborah. She had an autumn birthday, so her cleverness had got her put up a year. Being clev-erer and younger would have been enough to have marked her, but these were her least obvious differences. Deborah had spina bifida and hydrocephalus. This was a time when children with far less to contend with were still being shunted off wholesale into 'special' schools, and her mother had fought a hard battle to keep her in mainstream education. At that point in her life she was in the middle of a long series of operations, and her scalp was shaved. She had to stay out of the sun, so at lunch she would go straight into the hall with one of the dinner ladies and then spend the rest of the break in the corridor outside the headmaster's office, playing chess with whichever nice charitable girl had agreed to accompany her. I joined her, but not out of charity: we had interests in common, we were fellow outcasts, and it was the only legitimate way of avoiding my lunch queue problem. When she was in Toronto, having more operations, I was eating behind the prefabs.

Deborah's friendship made school a little more bearable, but whether she was there or not, I would begin most of my weekday mornings by announcing to my mother that I had a headache or a tummy ache or a sore throat and couldn't possibly go. Then one day I sat down on the edge of my parents' bed and sobbed that I didn't want to go ever again. She told me that she was going to take me to see a nice man who could talk to me about it.

The nice, talking man was an educational psychologist recommended by Deborah's mother. I remember being taken to a set of rooms in a town house in some expensive, more central part of London, where I did puzzles and played games. It was fun. The first puzzles came in a booklet and featured things called 'matrices' which each had a piece missing. I had to choose the missing pieces. The puzzles got harder as I turned the pages but I worked quickly, and had managed to finish the last one before the man came back and took the booklet away again. When he had marked it he brought it back to me and pointed out my mistakes. 'You could have got those right,' he said. 'Try not to go through things so quickly – it makes you careless.' I nodded; it wasn't the first time a teacher had said that to me.

After I'd finished the tests I sat by myself outside the man's office while he talked to my parents. The diagnosis was giftedness and the best cure was removal from the state system to some more 'academic' establishment. My mother started phoning around. There were no places available anywhere for my school year, and I wouldn't be able to sit the exams for secondary school for another two. In the meantime, the best she could do was to take the report to the headmaster, Mr Vickery, and see if he could find some extra support for me from somewhere.

Mr Vickery was not sympathetic, either to my mother or to me. He waved the report away and told her that as far as he was concerned, I was 'an average intelligence child with a personality problem'. He complained to Mrs Bowson, who called me up to her desk and berated me about my mother's coming up 'moaning to Mr Vickery'. Then I was called into his office to account for myself. I stood in front of his desk trying not to meet his eye while he spoke to me sternly: I should not pretend to have headaches and stomach aches to try to get out of school; I went through my work 'like a robot' and didn't pay enough attention to it; I was to go and write an extra essay to prove to him and to Mrs Bowson that I was so special and clever. Most of all I was to stop making a fuss about things, put a smile on my face, and join in.

Some ten years or so later Mum told me that Mr Vickery had died. He had suffered a heart attack and fallen down the stairs at his house, where he lived alone. I started to say something conventional like 'oh, how terrible', but found I couldn't stop the huge grin that was spreading itself across my face. It was quite a shock: I don't allow myself to hate people, as a rule.

My father joked that I was 'an intellectual'; he found my vagueness endearing. 'Joanne'll be late for the end of the world,' he'd say, and I would imagine an apocalyptic scene, all red skies and toppling columns. A huge gate stood at the edge of this picture. It was wide open and everybody in the world except me was escaping through it. I was sitting on a broken pedestal with my nose in a book. The gate was about to close and I would be left alone in the burning, toppling, broken world, all alone.

I loved books, and by the time I left primary school I knew that I wanted to write them myself. In my second year I wrote a poem which impressed my teacher. 'You're lucky,' she told me.

'You're *talented.*' Talented. I breathed the word in; it filled me up like helium in a balloon and lifted me clear off the floor. I was talented, and maybe one day I was going to write something as good as *The Once and Future King.* In the meantime, I could live in it. I was Sir Gareth: they thought I was only a smelly kitchen boy but really I could beat them all.

Imagination can comfort, or it can terrorize. My husband recently told me that between the ages of nine and ten he slept with a Lego crucifix under his pillow to protect himself from vampires. He has since grown up into an utterly and infuriatingly rational adult. I sometimes wish I could say the same for myself, but I can't. I was and remain suggestible in the extreme: if I picture someone vomiting I feel sick; if I think about multiple sclerosis the little and ring fingers of my left hand begin to go numb. If I'd been born a hundred years earlier I could have had a promising career as a hysteric.

Over the years, all manner of unpleasant suggestions have wormed their way into my mind and fed there. Some of the most greedy wriggled in during junior school. Many of these involved the soul, that thing which at the time I pictured as a greyish vapour, a twist of smoke behind the breastbone. It's still the image I see when I hear the word 'soul'. I wouldn't claim to believe in it any more, but I've never lost that sense of how precious it is, how easily it can be soiled, lost or destroyed. In my third year at junior school, I sat behind a girl whose big brother had an interest in the paranormal. She told me that he'd told her that if you looked into the mirror, you could see your soul. It was the sort of idea which is perfectly nonsensical during daylight hours, and becomes absolutely true at nightfall. Mirrors at night became dangerous. It would have been frightening enough to have looked in the mirror and seen nothing but the grey smoke, but the image I feared was far worse: a grotesque figure, skeletally thin, with greyish or brownish lizard's skin. It would have hands like talons, horrible teeth and a hunched back, and there would be a dreadful, knowing, ingratiating smile on its face. This was the worst of all possible true Joannes: a creeping thing, of the devil's party, incapable of any good by virtue of being herself. Another girl told me – maybe it was even in the same conversation – that sometimes when girls looked in mirrors, they could see the devil standing behind them. That sounded so horrible that it had to be true. One night I was going to see myself, a crinkly-skinned vessel of evil, standing with my creditor behind me, ready to foreclose on a deal I never realized I'd made. I still can't look in a mirror after dark.

Another threat to my soul came from sleep: where was I when I was asleep, and how could I be sure that I'd always make it back? The girl with the occult brother told me that when you fell asleep your astral body left your physical body and went wandering on the astral plane. At that time, my father was collecting a series of part-works called *The Unexplained*. It was subtitled 'Mysteries of Mind, Space and Time', and it contained a heady mix of physics, psychology and poppycock. I can remember being absolutely gripped by stories about black holes, ESP, spontaneous combustion, lucid dreaming, and that man who walked round a herd of horses and was never seen again, but it was the article about out-of-body experiences that had the most powerful effect on me. One of its illustrations showed a prone, translucent body floating above another body, identical to the first except that it was opaque, and linked to its twin by a greyish-blue cord. The text hurtled breathlessly through history, in and out of different cultural traditions, to show just how widespread and consistent accounts of these experiences were. It quoted Ernest Hemingway describing a moment on the battlefield when he had felt 'my soul or something coming right out of my body, like you'd pull a silk handkerchief out of a pocket by one corner'. Hosts of other less illustrious subjects had reported such experiences, many in situations of obvious trauma such as the scene of a car accident or during major surgery. On the other

27

hand, there were 'numerous cases of people who were asleep or going about everyday tasks, such as shopping or gardening, when the experience occurred'. Clearly it was something that could happen all too easily if you weren't careful.

I relayed this back to my paranormal source at school. None of it was news to her. In fact, she had another detail to add: if the cord snapped, she said, then that was it; your physical self and your soul – for that's what I understood the astral body to be – would be severed from each other for ever, the soul set adrift. This was a terrible risk, and I knew that I could not possibly allow myself to take it. It was far too dangerous to go to sleep, so I did my best to prevent it: as soon I began to feel the familiar falling-away sensation, I would wake myself up again, just in case what I was feeling was my astral body peeling away from my physical body, never to return.

It's just occurred to me how ironic it is that I should once have been so horrified by the idea of my consciousness divorcing itself from my physical self and striking out on its own. Since that time – since the onset of puberty, really – I've become more accustomed to thinking of my body as something that lets me down. Its needs and its pains, its cravings, its illnesses, its blemishes, the bits that are just too obviously female, the bits that don't look female enough, the bits that are starting to age . . . Sometimes I wish I could apply for a better one, and move on. Maybe sit an exam. I'm good at exams: when I was ten they got me my pick of the local girls' schools. That was the first of my getaways.

Body

21. I return home to check doors, windows, drawers, etc., to make sure they are properly shut.

The Padua Inventory

'O wombe! O bely! O stinking cod,
Fulfild of donge and of corrupcioun!'
Chaucer, *The Pardoner's Tale*

In the first flush of a new diagnosis, it's tempting to get carried away, to take every single trait you've never liked about yourself and call it a symptom: you were never wrong-headed or self-absorbed or difficult in your life – it was the Condition all along. You go through your life history, vindicating yourself at every turn; you realize what an extraordinary person you must be, so brave, so long-suffering; you realize that you were a helpless victim twice over, first of the Condition, and then of the Ignorance and Intolerance of those around you, who failed to make allowances, when it should have been obvious to every one of them that whatever you did and said hurt you more than it hurt them.

I had fun like this for a little while, but in the end I had to acknowledge that, whether I was emotionally challenged or not, there was no avoiding at least *some* of the responsibility for my own behaviour, not least if I wanted to be the protagonist of my own life, rather than some pitiful apology for a character who never acted unless she was acted upon. Even so, that still left a satisfying number of odd thoughts or incidents or habits that suddenly, finally, had an explanation. There was the shoe thing, for a start.

Every year, somehow, Jewish girls made up a neat third of my new school's intake, and on Tuesdays, Wednesdays and Thursdays, we were herded into the West Gym for Jewish Assembly. Before we could enter our place of worship we had first to take off our shoes – not for any religious reason, but in order to preserve a gym floor designed for bare feet and plimsolls rather than Clark's lace-ups. You could leave your shoes just outside the gym, if there was room, but more often you had to leave them further away, in the glass-walled corridor that led from the main building to the block that housed the two gyms, a smaller room with a ping-pong table in it, a little office where the lower fourths had to go for their BCG injections and a couple of cupboards full of athletics equipment, gym mats, and nasty folk-dancing skirts that were always either painfully tight or so loose that you had to tuck them into your knickers to stop them falling to the floor. It was probably called the Sports Corridor – it was that sort of school.

After we had removed our shoes, we would go in, accompanied by a few teachers, and sit in our year groups with the juniors at the front. Once we were all inside and the doors shut, whichever teacher was in charge that day would tell us to stand up – or more usually, stand up and be quiet – and then we would recite the Jews' daily prayer, the Shema; some girls did so proudly and accurately, while the less observant among us muttered something that sounded approximately right, shuffling our unshod feet. Then we would sit down for the main part of the assembly. Sometimes a group of girls would enact some religious story, or else someone would sing, or lead us all singing (we used to sing 'Hine ma tov' to the tune of the *The Flintstones*, which was great fun). Quite often a teacher would read from a suitable text, usually from some well-regarded novel for young persons: *I Am David* and *One More River* were particular favourites. On one occasion a sixth former read some passage from a novel about the Spanish Inquisition which described a young Jewish woman's torture in all its bone-cracking detail. We didn't hear anything from that book again.

Once or twice I took an active part in the assembly myself, maybe reading something out, or, more probably, writing something for other girls to perform, but most of the time I just sat quietly on my constipated, brown-clad tochas, thinking about my shoes. There was a lot of work to do: I had to visualize their exact location, then visualize it again to make sure that it stuck in my memory, then I had to imagine what I might do if I couldn't find them, just in case the visualization didn't work, then I had to go through every possible scenario: another girl with shoes just like mine takes my shoes and I have no shoes; I take that other girl's shoes and get into trouble; we take each other's shoes; I find my shoes but take so long putting them on that everyone leaves me behind and I am late back up to the main hall for Notices; I am late for Notices on account of my shoes and everyone sees me come in late through the double doors in the middle and turns round to stare and then the headmistress tells me off in front of *the whole school*; to avoid being made an example of in front of the whole school I decide not to go in for Notices but then have to remain outside the hall alone and find some way to join the others as they come out of the hall, and go back to my classroom through the corridors past the prefects without anyone realizing what I'd done and exposing me as the bad, stupid girl who, shod or shoeless, was always one step behind.

It was unbearable. I couldn't tell anyone about it but I did ask my mother to allow me to go to Main Assembly, arguing that I could get all the Jewishness I required at home, and shouldn't school be the place where I got to discover the Protestant host culture? She said no. Fortunately, after I'd been in the school two or three years, a new octagonal theatre and lecture building – the Octagon – was completed and we had Jewish Assembly there instead, this time with our shoes on.

It was a trivial matter, the shoe thing, and I recognized it as such at the time, but all the thought and attention and worry I expended on it made it grow and grow until, privately at least, I came to see my Jewishness primarily in terms of the potential it provided for shoe loss. It was as if I had been compelled, for no discernible reason, to pick at a tiny cut until it became first an open, infected sore, and then the starting point for systemic septicaemia. Then after the Jewish assemblies were moved, the thought, the anxiety, the dread faded completely, and I could easily have forgotten the whole obsession, because there was no wider context in which I might have placed the memory. I was not in general prone to thinking about the location of my shoes; the school placed no great emphasis on them – or else they would probably have been lined up in the Shoe Corridor; I was not raised in a culture in which shoes symbolized a young woman's honour and modesty and their loss was ruinous; I did not voluntarily subscribe to any ideology which regarded shoes as particularly significant; nor was I swept up in any general current of cultural anxiety about the misplacement of footwear. To put it in psychological terms, what made that particular obsession so straightforward to diagnose, even in retrospect, even by an amateur like me, was that it was so clearly 'ego-dystonic' – that is to say, there was nothing about the shoe anxiety that made any sense to me in terms of the person I understood myself to be. If I did not attempt to explain it to anyone else it was partly because I had no way of explaining it to myself.

When a preoccupation or worry is not ego-dystonic, then it becomes harder to diagnose as a symptom; indeed, if a preoccupation can be adequately accounted for by the culture in which the person lives, then, no matter how bizarre it may sound to those outside the culture, and no matter how painful it may be for the person who holds it, it may well not be a 'symptom' of anything at all. In a community where illnesses are explained in supernatural terms, a belief that one's diarrhoea is caused by evil spirits residing in the intestines may not be delusional; in a culture which associates thinness with high status, a preoccupation with diet, weight and exercise is not necessarily a sign of pathology. On the other hand, when a skeletally thin woman insists that she is too fat, and for this reason refuses all food, even though her beliefs make sense to her – are 'ego-syntonic' – if we label her as 'anorexic' it is partly because her beliefs about her body make no sense to anyone around her. The other reason is that they are causing behaviour which is detrimental to her work and relationships, making her ill and, without intervention, may well lead her to kill herself.

I doubt you needed me to tell you that. I'm assuming that anyone reading this will already know a fair bit about anorexia, bulimia and so on, if only because eating disorders are not an easy subject to avoid in the early twenty-first century; neither are the broader issues of body image and low self-esteem. It's quite possible that you have read articles or watched a documentary about another illness which, like anorexia and bulimia, is seen by some as a member of OCD's extended family, or the 'obsessive-compulsive spectrum' as many psychiatrists would call it. Body dysmorphic disorder is characterized by an excessive preoccupation with an imagined or real but minor defect in one's physical appearance, and by behaviours intended to check, minimize, camouflage or eliminate the perceived defect. These behaviours include excessive mirror-gazing, the use of make-up or clothing to cover up the defect, and constant seeking of reassurance about one's appearance; in extreme cases, the sufferer may resort to endless plastic surgery – which never cures – or avoid company altogether, believing herself too hideous to look upon. Compared with OCD patients, those with a primary diagnosis of BDD have significantly higher rates of co-morbid major depression, substance abuse and suicide. The belief that one is ugly, no matter how unjustified it may seem to others, can cause the most intense distress imaginable. It's also very hard to treat: like the anorexic girl's belief in her own fatness, the BDD patient's belief in the unacceptability of her appearance is, all too often, ego-syntonic. Like the anorexic's calorie-counting and two-hourly trips to the scales, her anxious mirror-gazing and constant foundation touch-ups could be seen as a kind of unintentional burlesque on what most of us think of as normal behaviour. Normal for girls, I mean.

Always more of a tree-climber than a doll-dresser, I had become used to thinking of myself as a boy deep down, so it came as a shock when, somewhere around my tenth birthday, I became aware that my chest was already not quite as flat as it had been. My family became aware too, and sometimes pointed it out; when they did, I would fold my arms or leap behind a chair. The emergence of these tiny bosoms, as far as I could see, was just the first of a whole series of mortifications. Soon I would be strapping myself into elaborate pieces of underwear that looked more like punishments than clothing. I would be expected to begin my days sitting in front of a mirror 'putting my face on', as if the face that I had on the front of my head was not only unacceptable, but actually less than real. Then there would be some kind of extra unpleasantness to do with toilets, which I would have to mop up with special paper. There would be no more tree-climbing, or even much running, because I would be wearing shoes that made me walk in a stupid way with my bottom sticking out and my feet simpering 'click click click' just like the feet of the headmaster's secretary whose bright red pout and wiggly walk made her a legitimate object of ridicule to every child in the middle school.

Even now, the sound of my own feet clicking never fails to make my gorge rise, so I tend to avoid high heels. And then there are other remnants of that ten-year-old's disgust and resentment. Whenever I walk into a kitchen, I become unable to follow verbal instructions and lose the use of my arms. As a girl,

I was no keener to ladle chicken soup into other bodies than I was to adorn my own. I didn't want to be a nice Jewish girl, clothing myself in silk and purple, and giving meat to my household while my husband sat among the elders of the land. There are many women who are perfectly comfortable within traditional Judaism, and they would argue that the home is the spiritual centre of a good Jewish life, and that at the centre of every good Jewish home is a good Jewish woman; there is nothing demeaning, nothing secondary about keeping a kosher home and raising the Jewish children with which God has seen fit to bless you. On the other hand:

> Unto the woman he said, I will greatly multiply thy sorrow and thy conception; in sorrow thou shalt bring forth children; and thy desire shall be to thy husband, and he shall rule over thee.
>
> Genesis 3:16

My mother was not your stereotypical Jewish accountant's wife: she had always worked outside the home and had always assumed that I would too. She also cooked all of our meals, kept the house we lived in clean, stayed home when my brother and I were ill, complained to the headmaster when she felt that the school was failing me, allowed me to bring dozens of Enid Blyton books into the house even though she hated them and, when the time was right, she did her best to prepare me for puberty in a level-headed, secular sort of way. When I was ten or eleven, she bought me a book from Smith's in Temple Fortune called *Have You Started Yet?* Recently, it took me no time at all to find a copy of the 1980 edition on the Internet, and it cost next to nothing, so I bought it and had another look. It's every bit as sensible as I remember: the text explains menstruation in the manner of a kindly biology mistress, and there are plenty of clear, sensible diagrams to show the young reader exactly how her body will change through puberty and across the menstrual cycle. One set of images shows how to insert a tampon for the first time, and it makes it look incredibly easy, which it would be if real vaginas were like the ones in the diagrams: perfect cylindrical spaces, waiting calmly for whatever anyone might push into them.

My dreams were changing along with my body. I would find myself alone in the house, always inadequately dressed, sometimes in lacy underwear. The house itself would be in an unstable, vulnerable state, with a leaking roof and bricks crumbling out of the walls. There was broken glass under my bare feet and loose floorboards to trip me up. The taps would be jammed, flooding the kitchen and bathroom, and worst of all, every time I turned round I would see another *exposed wire*, with orange sparks fizzing malevolently out of its tendrillous ends. The cat had run away. If I was lucky I had a stick or a snooker cue to defend myself, the house and my honour – there were going to be intruders. In some of the dreams I could see them quite clearly, because the front of the house was completely transparent. They could see me too, in my underwear, stuck to the floor – did I mention that I was unable to move? They were big men in little knitted burglars' hats, they were laughing, and they were on their way in.

In my waking life, I wasn't climbing trees any more. I could barely cope with stairs, because I'd realized how easy it would be for me to fall backwards and break my back or smash my skull in. To make sure that this never happened, I began to walk up stairs in a very particular, careful way, holding on tightly to the banisters, leaning forward into each tread. The stairs at school worried me especially, as they were stone, and rose around a stairwell down which one might – in theory – fall through the whole height of the school, from the Science Corridor on the third floor to the cloakrooms on ground level. A scenario of just such a fall played in my head over and over again.

Wherever I was, safety was my first concern. I would make my rounds of the house at night, switching off whatever could be switched off, unplugging whatever could be unplugged. And I liked to be absolutely sure that the front and back doors were locked. But absolutely sure.

One miserable November evening when I was twelve and a half, my parents went out to a dinner party or the cinema or perhaps a supper quiz, leaving me, my little brother, and the teenage boy who was our babysitter for the night. I had been in an uncontrollably foul mood all day, but had put this down to the book I'd been reading – a dreary written-for-teens story about an outbreak of fascism in an American high school – and to the way the seams of my new corduroy catsuit had been digging in all over the place. According to my mother, this foul mood had been going on for months and when she'd raised the issue with my father he'd suggested that perhaps my menarche was on the way. She had pooh-poohed the idea, but as it turned out, he was right. At about eight o'clock that evening I went to the downstairs lavatory, and when I wiped afterwards the paper came up covered in blood. It was very unwelcome but hardly shocking; thanks to my mother and *Have You Started Yet?*, I was prepared, so I crept up to my parents' wardrobe, probably without singing on this occasion, and fetched out the packet of press-on towels that had been waiting for me there, nestling among the collapsed handbags, the old hats and the boot stretchers. They were called Sylphs, as misleading a brand name as has ever been coined. I hated their bulkiness. For my next couple of periods I tried quilted Bodyform towels instead but they looked far too much like surgical dressings for my liking, and the way they chafed my thighs was nothing short of vicious.

There was no way of resisting periods, but I had put off my first bra-fitting for as long as I possibly could, clinging to my white Aertex vests until it was just too uncomfortable to go about so inadequately supported. I had also begun to realize that wobbling about without a bra was even more embarrassing than wearing one to hold it all in place: the girls at school had started to *say things*. When the girls at school *say things*, you know the game is up.

We had sewing lessons in our first year. I did my best not to learn anything during them, but I still had to go. Once a week we would go into a dingy annexe next to the dining hall, where we would sit in front of old Singer sewing machines while the poor, put-upon home economics teacher did her best to make the class of budding lawyers and baby doctors take her and her subject seriously. Now, after years of begging or paying other people to take up my trousers and skirts for me, I wish I had. But at the time, the idea that it might actually be in my interests to learn to alter clothes or make them myself never occurred to me – I liked to boast that my mother had got an A for my wrap-over skirt. Those skirts were supposed to be our introduction to the art of dressmaking. There were three patterns available, but each came in a different size bracket, so each girl was first measured, to see which pattern she should follow. The categories were Girl, for the smallest and least curved, then Teen, and for the really advanced: Miss. Most of the class were still in Girl. Thanks to the small frame my breasts were growing on, and much to my relief, I scraped into Girl too. In the cloakroom at break-time, another girl in my class, who was not a bully, or even particularly bitchy, asked me which pattern I got – Teen or Miss?

'*Girl*,' I said with emphasis.

'No way!' she shrieked. Then she turned to her friend, and pointed at my chest:

'Look at hers!'

That's 'embreasted experience'[5] for you. This is a lovely term

5. Liz Frost, *Young Women and the Body: A Feminist Sociology* (Palgrave, Basingstoke and NY, 2001)

I came across while researching this chapter. It means, as you might expect, 'the experience of having breasts', and it encompasses, among other things: becoming aware of fleshy growths on one's chest; feeling anxiety as a result of their development; wondering if one's breasts are normal; feeling proud of one's breasts; feeling embarrassed by one's breasts; comparing one's breasts to those of others; being aware that one's breasts are being compared with the breasts of others; being aware that other girls are looking at one's breasts for the purposes of comparison; being aware that men are looking at one's breasts for other purposes; hearing men say things like 'Look at the tits on that' and being aware that one is the 'that' in question; suffering tenderness in the breasts during pregnancy and just before periods; wondering if, and when, one is going to get breast cancer –

BREAST CANCER

BIOPSY

CHEMO

DEATH

My apologies. A 'spike' – this is to say, an unwanted, obtrusive thought – just erupted into the text there. Any mention of breast cancer will bring one on, and I'm compelled, first, to follow all the strands of thought which radiate out from the node BREAST CANCER through to their worst possible ends, and then to ruminate for a while to see if I can't think myself back to safety again. That eruption represents the lost three-quarters of an hour I spent sitting in a kind of trance at my desk, ruminating, chewing my cheeks, and picking at my skin.

None of this made me feel any better – it never does. Rumination only ever leads to further rumination, so if I really want to snap out of it I have to make the effort to do something else, go somewhere else, or contact someone else. With half the afternoon gone already, I phoned my mother and asked her why she hated the phrase 'battling with cancer' so much. She thought aloud for a minute or two: 'Because in a battle you can see your enemy – you know who they are, what they are, how many of them there are . . . Because you don't "battle" – you just do what you have to do to make the cancer go away and leave you to get on with your life . . . Because it makes it sound like you have control, and you haven't.' She said she didn't recall doing any battling when she had breast cancer, but she remembered how angry she felt. How had she seemed to me when she was ill? I thought for a moment. 'Distant,' I said. 'Laid out flat.'

I couldn't remember any dates, or even which year it had been. My mother told me that she'd found the lump towards the end of April 1983, not long after my thirteenth birthday; she'd had the mastectomy on 6 May. Before she went in for the biopsy, my brother and I were told as much as we needed to know at that point, which was that our mother was going in 'for a little operation', and nothing more. When I arrived home from school the following day, it was my grandmother who opened the door. She didn't smile when she saw me, which was unusual; she just told me that my mum was upstairs. Mum was lying on the double bed with an unfamiliar, woozy look on her face. She explained what the surgeon had found, that she was going back to hospital in a couple of days, and what they were going to have to do when she got there. She did not sound like herself when she talked.

It never occurred to me that she might die. I must have been enough of a child still to accept things as they happened, and to assume that they would work out. In retrospect, I realize how lucky we were. Breast cancer treatment has advanced a great deal in the last twenty-five years; if Mum had been diagnosed more recently, perhaps she would have got away with less extensive surgery, and lower doses of radiation. Even so, she has never regretted her mastectomy, never felt, as some women have, that in surrendering a breast she was somehow losing part of her identity. Like her daughter, what she fears losing most are her marbles. *Cogito, ergo sum.*

As I could remember so little, I asked my mother to email me the relevant dates, and anything else she felt able to tell me. She sent me a long, detailed message, and at the end she wrote: 'Looking back now I am surprised at how many years it took me to acknowledge that there might issues for you, maybe I was not prepared to face up to that. I focused on surviving and getting the most out of life for myself and my family.' The 'issues' are partly psychological, partly genetic. In recent years my mother's genome has been checked for the breast cancer genes: BRCA1, BRCA2, and a third gene specific to Ashkenazi Jews, which confers the advantage of protection from TB along with the distinct disadvantage of a higher risk of breast cancer. Thankfully, they found none of these, but the geneticist she saw took a family history, saw that two of her maternal aunts had died of the disease and advised her that, just because they hadn't been able to identify a culpable gene, it didn't mean that none was there. I was given the option of going into an early screening programme at thirty-five, which I took. Once a year now I go to the local breast unit for a mammogram, and spend the next two weeks waiting for the results, and wondering if I would cope as well as my mother had if the results turn out to be bad. I hope that I would be able to 'focus on surviving' too.

Back in the spring and summer of 1983, when I was still the child who assumed that my mother would survive, I certainly never caught myself thinking, Oh no, Mum's got breast cancer – that means I have an increased risk, nor did I consciously register the message, 'Female body parts are life-threatening.' On the other hand, I do remember how much my developing breasts disturbed me in those early adolescent years. Sometimes in my bed at night I would take one or other of them in my hand and dig my fingers under it, so that I could feel the lower edge of the gland sitting inside its envelope of skin and fat. It always felt as if I could have lifted it up and away from myself, a separable thing.

If I could have left my body behind and still somehow remained alive, I think I would have done. It was letting me down in so many different ways. Not only was it a female body, which was humiliation enough in itself, but it did not even seem to be developing into one of the better ones. My hair, which had been blonde in early childhood, had turned middling brown, a most uninteresting colour. My early puberty meant that my growth, which had been pretty close to the mean up till then, stopped at twelve or so. I watched as most of my contemporaries overtook me, leaving me behind along with the other 'petite' girls, or 'shortarses' as I prefer to call us. I wasn't going to be elegant; I wasn't going to be willowy; I certainly wasn't going to be boyish; I was going to be entering adult life with short legs, and they were the *wrong kind*.

Increasingly, the sight of my body in the mirror or in photographs became offensive to me. Its proportions were not quite right, and this was irritating to the eye and mind alike. I would fantasize about rubbing my legs out and redrawing them, just that bit longer, or imagine myself having plastic surgery in which my legs would be broken and reset so that they could be artificially extended. Any other set of female legs I encountered would be abstracted from the body and compared with my own abstracted pair. In order that nobody at school should notice my two damning signs of physical inferiority, I took to sitting on the edge of chairs and stretching my legs out so that my feet peeped out from under the desk.

My face was just as displeasing. For a start, one of my front teeth was broken. The accident had happened when I was eight years old, as a consequence of scientific curiosity. We were on a pebble beach on the coast of Scotland. My father picked up a piece of rose quartz, about the size of a fist, that had been worn smooth by the sea. He said he would break the stone open to show me the crystal structure inside, and told me to stand well back. I did, but not far back enough: the stone bounced off the rock he threw it at and straight into my mouth. Screams flew up from the beach like startled birds. I realized with astonishment that they were coming out of me. My mother ran up yelling at my father. I got a trip to the dentist and three *Famous Five* books to cheer me up. But that tooth, a snaggle right at the front of my smile, went on to make a nuisance of itself for nearly twenty years. It could not be built up into the semblance of a full tooth until I was fourteen: it was a young tooth, with its nerve still exposed. A first temporary correction, in which the missing part was replaced by a kind of cement, soon turned yellow. Its replacement was held to the tooth stump by a steel pin, which gave it a dirty, greyish tinge. The tooth wouldn't be mature enough for a proper crown until I was in my mid-twenties. In the meantime, I would have to live with the certain knowledge that people were *saying things*.

Did I ever *say things* myself? Almost certainly, but my most vivid memories are of life on the receiving end. Conventional girlish bitchiness, about weight or breasts or dress sense, was not really my thing. This made sense, of course, because body, whether as an aesthetic object or a vehicle for sporting prowess, was never my thing. I was mind, mind all the way. It was both my treasure and my weapon. While I had been so miserable in primary school, I had been encouraged by some to comfort myself with the idea that my brain was something special, and if people were mean to me, that was just because they were jealous. When I arrived at my secondary school, where the floors strained under the weight of so much feminine brilliance, I risked losing both my claim to uniqueness and my best excuse for being awkward. For the first year I didn't know quite where to put myself, but in the second year I started Latin together with all the other girls who had taken it as an option; everybody in the class was a complete novice, and this gave me the perfect opportunity to make my mark. I took to reading ahead of the rest of the class under my desk, translating with the help of the glossary at the back of the book, so that when it was my turn to be chosen I could turn in an apparently effortless performance. My work paid off, and I became an acclaimed Latin genius. I'd declared my territory, found my perch again at the top of the tallest tree, by myself.

But it wasn't supposed to be like that any more. I had imagined my new school as a non-boarding version of St Clare's or Malory Towers, an ideal polity where clever girls and sporty girls and horsey girls and musical girls and shy girls could all find their social niches, while the spoiled or superficial or flibbertigibbety would come to learn the error of their ways. Unfortunately, the school wasn't fictional and neither was I. Enid Blyton would never have been up to constructing a back-story as convoluted as mine, or working out its consequences for character and plot development. I would have been better prepared had I chucked out the school stories for girls and studied the various overlapping literatures on childhood depression, childhood anxiety, the longer-term effects of peer rejection, loneliness in childhood and the social and emotional problems faced by gifted children. These are rather light on lacrosse matches and midnight feasts but rich in descriptions of the pathology of children who are both unhappy and hard to like.

> Difficulties with social relationships appear to accompany depression in young people. Interestingly, it seems that social problems reflect in part the depressed youth's perception of others as critical and rejecting; which in turn may spark critical and defensive behaviour on their part, which puts peers off, and this leads to isolation. [p. 65][6]

6. Ian M. Goodyer (ed.), *The Depressed Child and Adolescent* (Cambridge University Press, Cambridge, 1995, 2001)

Kovacs et al. described 'dysthymia' as predominantly characterized by gloomy and depressed mood, brooding about feeling unloved and additional manifestations of affective dysregulation, including irritability and anger. The other predominant feature is the 'cognitive' symptom of self-deprecation or negative self-esteem. [p. 121]

It wasn't that I was friendless exactly in my first three years at secondary school – more that my friendships, more often than not, did not quite take. This was partly down to sheer bad luck. Girls who had been friends in the school's junior wing were allowed to stay together, within reason, but as they made up only one third of the senior year, there had to be a different method for sifting the new intake. The school had a huge catchment, extending south as far as the West End and north into Hertfordshire; each new senior cohort was sorted geographically into three separate forms, all the better to help girls pal up with other girls they might like to travel home with. It made no less sense than any other sorting system, and a lot more than most, but it could not take account of girls' differing interests, abilities, personalities, levels of maturity or any of those other qualities by which girls spontaneously sort themselves.

For the first couple of days it was fine: new upper thirds were seated, two by two, in alphabetical order, so for that short time I was able to cling to another girl whose surname began with L. But she soon found someone more to her liking, and two weeks on, when we were allowed to select our new seating partners, I had nobody to choose, and had to be paired with the only other awkward singleton. I managed to make a couple of friends in other classes, girls I had encountered in my French group or at break-times, but this was no help in class before register, in class between lessons, or at lunch when we sat in form groups. The school had extensive grounds, which meant that it was possible to be less conspicuously alone than I had been at the other place, but most of the time I would rather not have been alone at all. Not at school.

There were cliques, usually made up of pairs of best friends, and there were periods when I would hang about hopefully on the outside of some clique or other, pulling on its collective skirt and trying as hard as I could to copy, quip, laugh and flatter myself in. This got me a birthday invite or two, but also led to just accusations that I tried too hard to please people. Whatever the reason, I was unable to follow the rhythms of group interaction; it was all of a piece with being out of step in dance classes and hopeless at netball. Trying to join in one of these conversations was for me the adolescent equivalent of trying to jump over a moving skipping rope while two other girls were twirling it. Almost always I would make the wrong judgement and bring the rope or flow of talk to an awkward standstill.

It came more naturally to me to form one-to-one friendships and spend my lunchtimes with my one friend pacing around the grounds, usually up and down the walkway lined with lime trees which marked the boundary between two large sports fields, having intense discussions. Sometimes we talked about music, about what we'd seen on *Top of the Pops*, or what we'd read in *Smash Hits* or *No. 1* magazine, or about how ridiculous Spandau Ballet's lyrics were but how at least they weren't as irritating as Duran Duran. We talked about *Comic Strip Presents* and *The Young Ones*, *Nighteen Eighty-Four* and *The Catcher in the Rye*. (I still haven't found my way back to George Orwell, despite his celebrated translucent prose; there's something about finding an author incredibly profound when you're fourteen that ruins them for you later.)

Alongside these usual Penguin Modern Classics, I liked to read whatever popular psychology books I could find at the local library or the second-hand bookshop in Edgware. I remember being particularly impressed by 'Sibyl' and her multiple personalities, but what fascinated me most were dreams and their interpretations. I liked to collect my own and those of my friends too, if they could remember any, and if they were willing to share. I also had a way of turning the conversation round to what I thought my own problems might be – was I, for example, a 'manic depressive'? Did you need to be to be a writer? What did they think of my latest story for English? Did they think it was funny? And didn't they agree that I was still quite thin really, not actually that 'developed' yet? I needed my fix of reassurance and fished for it daily.

Camilla arrived in the third term of the first year. She had just been made to leave her specialist performing arts school, which had a cruel policy of winnowing its student body down, term by term. To have been rejected in this way at twelve years old can only have been devastating, and her new school with its staid curriculum and ordinary girls must have seemed like the most dreary comedown ever to be inflicted on anyone. To me, though, she was different and glamorous, a real-life Noel Streatfeild character, a prize of a friend whom no one else had claimed. I spent a term's worth of lunch breaks listening raptly to her stories about the school and what she had done there and how girls with far less talent had mystifyingly been kept on. She would also listen to monologues on my favourite subjects, and on this basis we managed to remain bosom friends for several months. Then in the second year another new girl arrived, and Camilla moved in on her. I liked the new girl too, and continued to spend my break-times with the other two, but I couldn't help noticing that, more and more, Camilla was making fun of me, or cutting across me when I talked, or just ignoring me altogether. One lunchtime, when the other girl was off sick, and for want of anything more sophisticated to do, Camilla and I were playing hide-and-seek in the formal garden next to a Georgian building we called 'the Old School'. When it was my turn to hide, I crouched behind a shrub. Camilla looked for me for a minute or so, then she got bored and called to me to come out.

I stood up and yelled, 'Boo!' We both laughed. Then I stopped laughing, but she carried on.

'You looked so funny!' she explained. 'You just jumped up, and I saw this grin and these two small evil eyes.'

I was stunned. 'I do not have small evil eyes!'

Camilla stopped laughing. 'You do! They're just like—' [Here she made an unflattering reference to the eyes of a third party.]

'They are *not*!'

'They *are*!'

We stared at each other for a moment. It dawned on me that I could only continue as her friend on condition that I threw up my hands and conceded that I was indeed risibly ugly. This was impossible; we both knew that.

'Good*bye*, Camilla.'

'Good*bye*, Joanne.'

That afternoon, during gym, Camilla spent a happy forty minutes sitting next to me on an exercise mat, trashing me to the girls on the neighbouring one: '. . . and she bored me for hours up and down Lime Walk going on and on about how thin she is, and how flat chested – and look at her, the great, ugly brick!'

This was nothing exceptionally wicked. It was common practice, after a nasty 'break-up' like ours, for two former best friends to do each other down to their new mates, preferably within earshot. It was normal, healthy bitching for normal, healthy girls. Looking back, I don't think she can have expected me to sit there and take it, as I did. It seems obvious now that what I was supposed to do was to grab a new friend of my own and retaliate, but I could no more do this than I could catch a flying rounders ball. I sat quietly on the mat, hoping at least that I looked the more dignified, and let her words soak in. I didn't want it all to be true but maybe it was. The notion that I could well be a great, fat brick with small evil eyes stuck with me. It was another breed of thoughtworm, and over the next few years it would be joined by others of its kind. Some to do with my teeth, my dress sense or my resemblance to Neil out of *The Young Ones* came courtesy of other girls, but others, like the ones about the unacceptable shortness of my legs or the hideousness of my nose, were truths I'd discovered myself.

When I was fourteen, my parents bought me a new wardrobe. I chose one without a mirror. I couldn't run the risk of catching an unplanned glimpse of myself any more, not even in daylight.

Habits

52. I sometimes feel something inside me which makes me do things that are really senseless and that I do not want to do.

The Padua Inventory

———

CANINE ACRAL LICK. A compulsive paw-licking disorder seen in dogs that is thought to resemble OCD in humans. Fred Penzel, *Obsessive–Compulsive Disorders*

As I entered my fourth year at the girls' school, I was fourteen, spending most of my time in a room with no mirror, and a firmly shut door. It was during that school year that I painted the Frankie Goes to Hollywood mural on the wall next to my bed. It was in colour in acrylics, on anaglypta backing paper, and showed the band in profile, in full 'Two Tribes' Soviet military regalia, crouching behind an impressive array of weaponry. Just in case anybody had missed the message, I had added the following on the top left-hand corner, in big red capitals: 'ALL UNAUTHORISED ENTRANTS WILL BE SHOT.'

The shelf of Enid Blyton books which had been on that wall was long gone, and it was a different girl who slept in that bed. The few photos I have from that time – for there were few which I allowed to be taken of me – make me wince. In my least favourite one I'm sitting at my brother's bar mitzvah in a baggy-topped mint-coloured dress, white pumps, white tights, a Human League haircut and a face like a slapped arse.

My mother told me that she saw Frankie Goes to Hollywood as bodyguards, there to protect me as I slept. Maybe I thought that they might repel any grinning intruders in burglars' hats. Certainly I was scared and angry most of the time, and I thought that I might die soon. My teeth were causing trouble again, and this time I was going to have to go into surgery.

My adult eye teeth had still not come through, so the dentist took an X-ray. He showed us the plate: there were my baby eye teeth still in place, one with its root almost gone, and sitting above them, at a ninety-degree angle, were their impacted adult counterparts. There were various options, he said, but the only one that was sure to work was surgery, a proper operation under general anaesthetic. The surgeon would pull out my baby eye teeth and 'expose' the adult ones, then I could be turned over to an orthodontist who would find a way to drag them forward and down into the right position. I'd never quite lost my fear of falling asleep in the natural way, so the prospect of a general anaesthetic was beyond horrifying. I begged my mother and the dentist to consider the less drastic options, but he was adamant, and my mother convinced. It wasn't up to me. And so I prepared to die – perhaps.

The tooth people were going to need more detailed pictures of my retarded dentition. My mother took me to the X-ray department at Edgware General Hospital. She had worked there as a medical social worker for most of my childhood, so I had been used to thinking of it as a friendly place, where my brother and I got to roll toy cars down ramps and pretend to buy paper clips and blotting paper from the secretaries. As we walked along the long corridors, women in crisp uniforms smiled at us and came out with amiable grown-up inanities like 'Hello, Ruth! Is this one yours?' I had visited my mother there after her mastectomy and still not seen the truth. But now I understood: a hospital was a place of pain.

We were called into a big room full of nasty-looking machines. The radiographer explained that I would need two different X-rays taken. The first one would be a 360-degree view of my jaw. I had to place my chin in a kind of scold's bridle, and stand still and slightly bow-legged for a minute while an X-ray camera whirred round my head on a circular track. Then I was ushered into a side room where I stood up straight with my head in a vice while the radiographer hid behind a door and took first a shot of the left side, then the right. After a short wait the pictures were ready to see. The all-round ones were especially monstrous with their eye sockets, ghostly wisps of hair and elongated rows of bared teeth. I didn't appreciate the preview of myself as a cadaver.

The orthodontist lived and worked in a tall, ramshackle house near the confluence of the Hendon Way and the Finchley Road, along with his collection of ballet photos, his vast library of classical records and several cats. He had Radio 3 on as he worked and would comment on the music, whether it was a good recording, whether you could hear the wobble in that soprano's voice which was always perceptible when she hit top C: 'Here it comes . . . now, can you?' I would reply, I hoped, as intelligently as anyone could with a mouth full of someone else's fingers.

He needed to take an impression on that first appointment.

'Will it hurt?' I asked.

'Nothing we do here hurts,' he said, as if he'd worn the words out long since.

I watched him as he filled a couple of jaw-shaped impression trays with blue putty. He told me to open wide and then stuck them over my teeth, one set at a time. I thought I would choke while he held the trays in and when he pulled them out it felt for a moment as if he were taking a set of teeth with them. They can't have made a very good impression, because at my second appointment he told my mother that I would have to have a molar removed from each side of my upper set – to make room, he said.

The dentist who removed the molar was kind. She numbed me nicely, and then positioned herself in such a way that all I could see was her face and the back of her hand. Mum could see the enormous pliers she used and told me afterwards what a good thing it was that I couldn't. I don't remember any pain at the time of extraction, but I do remember the pressure and the most tremendous noise filling my head, like a boulder being dragged slowly over another boulder. It hurt later of course. And so did the sight of my smile in the mirror, more than ever. And then a few girls at school, sensing a weak point, would *say things* about my lack of teeth.

By the summer of 1985 my jaw and I were ready for surgery. I was taken to meet the surgeon in his consulting room; it had wooden furniture of crushing heaviness, and overwhelming upholstery. A dental chair sat in the middle of it all, like an instrument in its case. Everything was going to be fine, apparently. Of course it was: he'd taken out the Queen's own wisdoms and she was all right. He shook my father's hand and said he'd see me in a few weeks. On the train home from Harley Street I saw a beautiful man sitting opposite me – an improved Rupert Everett, I told a friend later – and thought about how ugly I was going to be soon, assuming I was still alive, of course.

The surgery took place in the early evening in a small private hospital just round the corner from the consulting room of Mr Queen's Wisdoms. The anaesthetist came up to my room to give me the pre-med, which made me feel so woozily awful that I wanted to be knocked out. A couple of orderlies lifted me onto a trolley and took me downstairs. I noticed – again – that one of them was very attractive, and wondered why there were so many handsome men in the world just when I was about to be definitively uglified. The general anaesthetic knocked me out so thoroughly that when I came round, I asked when the operation was going to be. In retrospect it was terrifying, a perfect hole in time.

After my parents had gone home and the pre-med had worn off, I was left to sleep. It was impossible though – I had never felt more awake in my life. Outside the window, Harley Street was dark and quiet. No nurses came during the night to ask me if I wanted anything, or to tell me to get back into bed, and I didn't summon any either. I had *The Tin Drum* with me – typical reading for me at the time – which I had half finished, and which would remain for ever unread beyond the place where I had given up. This was marked by a postcard depicting the clinic, one of the windows circled with an arrow pointing to it: I was in here. I paced up and down the room, every now and then stopping by the mirror. In the half-light my eyes were bright, and my slightly swollen lips a reddish-purple. I thought that perhaps I could look quite attractive and interesting, provided I didn't attempt to smile ever again.

Now that the dentist and surgeon had made plenty of room in my mouth, it was time for the orthodontist to fill it up with his machinery. First, there were retainers. These were sheets of plastic moulded to my palate, with wires at the front that fitted round my teeth. I wore them at night, and each time they were tightened they hurt like fury for several days. After the retainer had done its work, I had thin wire braces carefully and discreetly cemented to the teeth. These worked with elastic bands. For a while I went around with one end of an elastic band attached to a hook cemented to the more impacted eye tooth, while the other was attached to a wire. Every few weeks he would twist the wire round another notch. My cousins and brother had the same orthodontist and also had their mouths furnished with his interesting contraptions. Saturday lunches at my grandparents' were punctuated by the sound of yelps as another elastic band went pinging into someone's chicken soup.

Whatever the reasoning behind his methods, they were slow. Even as an undergraduate, I still had the odd wire, clear or metallic, cemented to some part of my upper set. They weren't very obvious to anyone else, but were hideous to me. In the end, a new dentist looked at my mouth, was horrified, and instructed me to tell my orthodontist that I was getting married – whether I was or not – and all the material in my mouth would have to go. He exchanged the wire for yet another retainer. I wore it for a while but then I stopped going. My wisdoms have given me no trouble, unusually for a member of my family, but I still have the gaps.

If I seem to be going into too much detail about my teeth, forgive me. For a long time, they were one of my favourite excuses for not bothering with boys and for boys not seeming to bother with me; for staying in my room with my music and my ruminations and my books. I spent a whole year before the operation waiting to see if I might die, and then five years after the operation with a mouth full of intermediate technology and a camouflaged smile. I blamed the fear beforehand, the horror of what was being visited on my body, and my frustration and anger at having no say in what I began to do to myself during that long, shadowy pre-operation year. The stressed-out animal in me began, mutely, to make its presence felt.

It's the first attempt to cover up the damage that sticks in my mind. I was, for one production only, a member of an amateur dramatic society, and I had a part in the chorus of the society's own musical version of *The Prince and the Pauper*. I was being fitted for my guttersnipe costume, a sort of crude grey sack with short sleeves and a deep neckline. 'Not to worry about my arms,' I said to the wardrobe lady, who almost certainly hadn't noticed them. 'It's just the cat scratching.'

My arms were the first bits of me I ever picked, and I've never stopped picking them. Along with my shoulders, they are the first places I go to when I get the urge. At any time, sitting at my computer, or on the sofa, or anywhere else reasonably private, my hand might absently push my sleeve up; then I will rub up and down my upper arm, scanning for any rough bits, any bumps, any scabs or bits of dry skin. If I get a hit, I will grab hold of the flesh and muscle of the affected area and twist it round so that I can have a really good look at it; sometimes I have to screw my head and neck round to get the best possible view. Once I've got a secure enough purchase with my three smaller fingers, I'll pinch the bump between my forefinger and thumb, squeezing out the contents – sebum, keratin, blood, pus, whatever; to me it's usually just 'white stuff' – I have to 'get the white stuff out'. Now I'll have the taste for it, and I'll peer harder, feel around the adjacent area for more spots to pick, more blemishes to burst, then spread my search over the rest of the arm. Then, if I still feel unsatisfied and can't pull myself out of it, to the other arm, then the shoulders, my trunk, my breasts. If I'm still not through when I've covered the top half of my body, I'll start on my legs. If my legs are bare, they're an alternative starting point. Other times I'll find a mirror and have a go at my face instead.

I've been told many times by many people that it doesn't look as bad as I think, but I can see the difference: the general dryness, the scar tissue, the areas of flat hypo- or hyper-pigmentation, so extensive that if I look at myself in the mirror in a certain light, I can see a kind of tidemark running along the tops of my breasts and up to my arms, its boundary marking the area round my collarbone which is impossible to see without a mirror, and where I could never get a purchase.

Now that I'm old enough to be their mother, I look at teenage girls in their pearly skins – so fresh somehow even through spots – and think, 'Aw, aren't they lovely.' I suppose I must have been lovely in at least that statutory minimum way too, although I didn't feel it. There weren't too many scars in those days, only my BCG where I'd picked and picked, my tree-climbing wounds, and the collection of raised right bumps halfway up my ribs on the right where I'd had a patch of shingles as a four-year-old. There was also the blue stain underneath my bottom lip, at the right-hand corner. I thought – and my mother thought – that it was a birthmark, until one winter in my early thirties, where I noticed a fluid-filled swelling on that side of the mouth – the same side where a few days earlier my cousin's baby had stuck her finger in and pulled. I panicked – cancer! – but after consultations with one doctor and two dentists I was told, definitively, that the swelling and the blue stain were both parts of the same 'mucocel', a damaged salivary duct caused when, at some point, I'd bitten my cheek that bit too hard. I think I've been biting my cheeks for as long as I've had teeth – it's an automatic response to any strong emotion. Sometimes there are other blue marks on my face, but only where I've been rubbing it, absent-mindedly, with an ink-covered hand.

Over the years, I've acquired a certain amount of scar tissue, and my skin in the most frequently picked areas is especially dry, but these effects came on gradually. Usually my injuries were of the most minor, superficial kind, and usually these healed easily and quickly. But sometimes I would make a bigger cut, one which somehow I could not allow to heal. There is a crater-shaped scar above my left eyebrow, which I made the summer I was seventeen; that was the summer my great-aunt Ann told me that I was a pretty girl, that I had 'classic features', but I insisted that I could not possibly be described that way – not when I was Marked, when I had Marks on me. That was also the summer when I had a volunteer job in the office of an organization which campaigned for the rights of Soviet Jews. One of the older women there asked me what had happened to my forehead. I said I didn't remember. 'What?!' she said. 'You smashed your face, and you don't remember how?' There is also a flat, white, strawberry-shaped scar a couple of inches above my right knee. At one point, I remember my mother crying out in dismay: 'There's a *hole* in your leg. How on earth did you manage to do that?'

The worst of my picking scars is the hardened purple lump on the back of my right thigh. At some point in my twenty-second year I managed to pick at a spot – real or imaginary – to the point where I made a huge scab. Rather than leaving it to heal I couldn't stop myself from picking it open again and again. It didn't matter what I tried to do with plasters or cream or even bandages: it was there and it was tempting me to pick it. It didn't help that because of the position of the scab I would often slice it off when I sat on one of the high chairs in the library where I worked, and only find out when I went to the toilet and found the back of my thigh striped with blood. It took months to heal. The scar has shrunk and lightened but never disappeared. It's a reminder of a worse, sicker time. But it hasn't ever, as I feared, led to skin cancer. Yet.

From the very start, I was disgusted with my skin habit – 'You were *picking*, weren't you!' – and ashamed in general of the way that I seemed to be wasting my life, pacing round and round my room, listening to the same records again and again, picking and ruminating. My teenage diaries were full of resolutions to stop. I was aware that the picking gratified me in some way and this seemed worse than just little-girl disgusting; it had to be sexually perverse. It didn't hurt while I was doing it, and often I seemed to be in a kind of trance, lost in reverie while my hands continued automatically to search and pick, search and pick. While I did so I would sometimes be distantly aware of a desire to get rid of irritating anomalies, to get what the cosmetic adverts call the 'impurities' out of my skin, so that it could be smooth and even, as it was supposed to be. It's simple housekeeping: if I can just take care of these unsightly bumps, I think, then my skin will be perfect – I'll have tidied up. But skin is a living thing, and you can no more tidy up once and be done with it than you can wipe your worktops clean for ever.

Sometimes I would find enough resolution to wrench myself out of a picking session; sometimes I would simply run out of places to pick and slowly come to, sore, smarting, and ashamed. Now and then I would attempt to make repairs. I would wash the area I had just ravaged with water and cotton wool, and then lather on the antiseptic cream. Once or twice I tried to put a bandage on the whole upper arm, partly to heal it and partly to stop me getting to it again. It never worked. I bought a pair of lacy Madonna 'Like a Virgin' gloves to wear when I was alone as a preventative measure, but I pulled them off and picked away all the same. Before long they were balled up at the back of my desk drawer along with the hair ribbons I'd never worn but couldn't bring myself to throw away.

That pre-operation summer was the last time I wore a swimsuit for many years. Anything short sleeved or too low necked was likewise unwearable. It was vital that I cover the damage. I thought that the appearance of my skin must be as revolting to others as it was to me, both in itself and also because it gave my disgusting habit away, revealing to the whole world that I was in some twisted sadomasochistic relationship with myself. After the picking spread to my face, I started using spot cover, to which I am still nearly addicted. Nowadays I have recourse to concealer which matches my own skin tone; as a teenager and in my early twenties, when I professed to despise anything that actually called itself make-up, all that was available to me was a gungy orange-tinged Clearasil cover-stick, which probably drew far more attention to itself on my fair skin than the picked spots – real and imaginary – ever did.

I didn't know what the marks on my skin meant, but I knew that, like the Mark of Cain, or Job's boils, or a duelling scar, or the psoriasis in *The Singing Detective*, they had to betoken *something*. As one of the many doctors in *Fear of Flying* insists: 'Ze skin is ze mirror of ze soul.' When I studied psychoanalytic theory in my twenties, it only reinforced my writer's sense that a symptom was something to be read. It also seemed thrillingly probable that the meaning, when found, would be a dramatic revelation. When stories about self-harm began to appear in newspapers and magazines, I read them intently, studied the profiles of the sufferers, and almost came to the conclusion that I must be repressing some memory of horrific abuse. Almost – but not quite: I always felt that there was something empty about the behaviour itself, empty and passionless. Only after I'd spent twenty years picking and covering and trying to stop would I come across the concept of 'compulsive skin picking' or 'dermatillomania'. Like trichotillomania (compulsive hair-pulling), or canine acral lick, it is sometimes described as a 'grooming disorder, the result of the inappropriate and repeated triggering of an instinctive fixed-action pattern'[7] which leaves the sufferer stuck in a behavioural loop. There is something very appealing about an explanation like this: viewed from this perspective, it is not 'I' who picks but 'it'. There is no meaning to 'its' behaviour: it is like a pianola following the notes on a punchcard, just because that is what it does. It's a practical sort of view, a good rationale for behavioural or pharmaceutical treatments. And it lets you off that exhausting quest for meaning.

That is, if you're not enjoying the quest too much to accept it. The teenage me would probably have had no truck with such a pragmatic view. I was committed to making a drama out of my picking, and perhaps I could have chosen not to. It became a means of offering intimacy, a terrible and exciting thing to reveal or not as the mood took me. There was my disfigured soul mirrored in my skin, and if anyone could see it and accept it, then they would accept and understand me totally and utterly, something I truly believed, in my adolescent naivety, was both possible and desirable. Now and then I would tell another girl about the picking, for attention, and for sympathy, and to be

7. Susan E. Swedo, 'Rituals and Releasers: An Ethological Model of Obsessive-Compulsive Disorder' in *Obsessive-Compulsive Disorder in Children and Adolescents*, ed. Judith L. Rapoport (American Psychiatric Press Inc., Washington, 1989)

told that I shouldn't do it. I also hoped, I think, that perhaps they would say that nobody as beautiful as I should despoil herself in this way – which of course they never did. But I had to keep trying, to make that comprehensive confession and get my complete absolution. Perhaps I was barely more in control of this than I was of the picking itself.

The picking was also something I could fling at my mother, who had the nerve, the absolute stinking nerve, to think that I was a pretty girl who should be going out and enjoying herself. I remember one particular Saturday morning some time in my late teens. My parents were soon to go on holiday to the South of France with my brother and his friend, leaving me at home, at my own suggestion. They went out shopping with my brother, for holiday things perhaps. Meanwhile I drifted round the house until I found myself standing in the bathroom in front of the mirror, where I started picking my forehead, then carried on picking it. The sound of the car arriving back woke me out of my picking trance. I suddenly saw my face in the mirror – not just the square centimetre of skin I'd been working on but my whole face – and was dismayed, as usual. So I ran straight down the stairs, opened the front door and lifted my fringe to show my mother the torn, lumpy mess I'd made.

'Look what I've done!' I cried.

'We can't go on holiday!' she wailed.

That afternoon, I laughed about this little exchange, and told my mother we'd been playing 'guilt tennis'. We used to play it a lot.

Sometimes my mother would ask me, tentatively, if I would like to 'talk to someone'. I always said NO, as I took great pride in my deep, dark and interesting sufferings and was appalled by the thought of someone ripping them away from me. I believed my fears and my depression: they were there to tell me that I was living in unacceptable social and cultural conditions and that only when these were lifted could I experience any real happiness. I was unhappy because I saw the truth, because they had failed to conceal from me that life was rubbish and that I was oppressed. As Morrissey said, 'To pretend to be happy could only be idiocy (de dah de dah de doo dum day).' Morrissey had some of the answers. Simone de Beauvoir provided a few others in *The Second Sex*.

> The young girl may gash her thigh with a razor-blade, burn herself with a cigarette, peel off skin; to avoid having to attend a tiresome garden-party, a friend of my youth cut her foot with a hatchet severely enough to have to stay in bed six weeks. These sado-masochistic performances are at once an anticipation of the sexual experience and a protest against it; in passing these tests, one becomes hardened for all possible ordeals and reduces their harshness, including the ordeal of the wedding night. When she puts a snail on her breast, swallows a bottle of aspirin tablets, wounds herself, the young girl is hurling defiance at her future lover – 'you will never inflict on me anything more hateful than I inflict on myself'. These are proud and sullen gestures of initiation to the sexual adventure.
>
> Fated as she is to be the passive prey of man, the girl asserts her right to liberty even to the extent of undergoing pain and disgust. When she cuts or burns herself, she is protesting against the impalement of her defloration: she protests by annulling. Masochistic, in that her conduct gives her pain, she is above all sadistic: as independent subject, she lashes, flouts, tortures this dependent flesh, this flesh condemned to the submission she detests – without wishing, however, to dissociate herself from it. For she does not choose, in spite of everything, really to repudiate her destiny. Her sado-masochistic aberrations involve a basic insincerity: if the girl lets herself practise them, it means that she accepts, through her repudiation, the womanly future in store for her;

she would not mutilate her flesh with hatred if she had not first recognized herself as flesh.[8]

It was the 1980s, the decade when Andrea Dworkin published a book in which she argued that sexual intercourse was a form of violence practised by men against women. That made sense to me at the time: sex seemed terrifying – a violation of my physical integrity, of my fragile personhood. Besides that, it was grossly unfair: unfair because losing one's virginity hurt girls and not boys, because women got pregnant and not men, because it was men who bought sex and women who sold it, because there was one standard for boys and one for girls. The asymmetrical nature of sex between men and women was somehow offensive in itself. And if all that wasn't reason enough to be repulsed, this was, as I've said, the 1980s, when television regularly broadcast pictures of tombstones to remind everyone not to have sex if they didn't want to DIE.

Perhaps my picking was then a 'proud and sullen gesture of initiation to the sexual adventure'. I would be defiant. My clothes would be my armour. I identified with the school as a venerable nineteenth-century proto-feminist institution. I even dressed like the proponents of late nineteenth-century 'Dress Reform', in long skirts and boots. When I was in the sixth form, Hobbs came out with a pair of flat-heeled, lace-up boots which were on plenty of other girls' feet as well as mine, so I was even fashionable for a while. A few years earlier, I had asked my mother for DMs, but she wouldn't let me have a pair, because, she said, they'd make me look like Minnie Mouse, and as I didn't have enough money of my own to buy a pair – and I never bothered with a Saturday job – that was that.

My need for heavy-duty footwear was, as you might expect,

8. Simone de Beauvoir, *The Second Sex*, trans. H.M. Parshley (Jonathan Cape, London, 1949). A new translation by Sheila Malorany-Chevallier and Constance Borde has recently appeared from the same publisher.

more symbolic than real. Outside of my family, I hardly saw any men, so I invented my own version of what a man was, made up of paranoia and desire in equal parts. The men I imagined were colossi, with the power, on one hand, to break in and tear me to pieces, and on the other – if they were, say, John Lennon or Morrissey or whoever else I happened to have a distant crush on – to save me and my miserable soul. The Plastic Ono Band album with its primal screaming was a favourite soundtrack for my pacing. *Meat is Murder* was another. My enthusiasm for that particular album led ultimately to my only teenage appearance in the medical notes.

> *Extract from dietician's letter to Dr R, 18 August 1986*
> I have advised her on a generally healthy vegetarian diet including wholegrain breakfast cereals and wholemeal bread. We explored ways of including pulses in the diet without her tasting them too much. I have also given her a list of foods high in iron and suggested she picks on things like fruit and dried fruit which is rich in iron instead of all the crisps.

Somehow it never occurred to me to draw on the men I knew best – my father, my brother, my grandfather and uncles – for evidence about what kind of beings men really were. My father was a gentle soul, and never violent towards me in any way; at a time when smacking was still perfectly uncontroversial, he never smacked me once. There was one occasion though, when I was fourteen, when *I* hit *him*. He was teasing me and I didn't think it was funny, so I smacked him on the arm and told him to *shut up!* We both stopped short, and stared, shocked, at the place on his arm which my open hand had slapped. He held it delicately. I muttered something about being sorry. Then Dad called out to my mum: 'Ruth – Joanne's hit me! What should I do?' That should give you some idea of how oppressed we were by the patriarchy in our house.

I still call myself a feminist, but these days I take a more nuanced view. The books I was reading – most of them – were best understood by grown-up women, who could relate what they read to experiences they'd already had, not by sheltered and frightened little girls who hardly left their bedrooms. Looking back, I don't think I really appreciated the difference between a polemical text and a set of instructions, so I wound up taking the political somewhat personally. I was a teenage fundamentalist.

Reading over the last few pages, I realize I've made it sound as if I never left the house for four years. That would be my negative filter again. If I try to conjure up memories of myself elsewhere I remember that, for example, I went to see *Another Country* with my friend Mina and we were all of a flutter because we'd managed to get into a *15-rated* picture when we were still only *fourteen*. I remember the synagogue youth activities I attended – the discussion group for serious youngsters, the editorial committee that wrote the young persons' page of the newsletter, the local youth branch of the Reform Synagogue Campaign for Soviet Jewry – where I failed to get in with 'a nice crowd' or to hit it off with a pre-approved boy. I remember the Russian course I did one Easter where I met one of my favourite ever people, a bohemian girl from Kentish Town who wore vintage sixties dresses with her big boots and practised Nichiren Shoshu Buddhism alongside her mother. She was into early vocal music but also knew My Bloody Valentine personally. She stayed with me for a week while my parents and brother were in France, and she let some much-needed air into my life.

The difficulty was that all these places and people had to be reached somehow, and teleportation wasn't an option. (It still isn't and I'm still waiting.) I felt safe enough, if increasingly ridiculous, in my parents' cars, so the Saturday visits to my grandparents were no problem. These visits were both comforting and depressing, because they were always the same: we would eat liquefied cauliflower for lunch and then go out hunting in Brent Cross, before returning to eat Tunnock's tea cakes and display our purchases. Their house was so familiar to me that I could treat it as another branch of my own, often slipping upstairs with my Walkman to pace around the spare room for a while.

My extended family took the piss out of my eccentricities, but I could handle that: mockery was the accepted family currency, and I dished out as much as I took. They might find me ridiculous, they might have failed to understand me as completely as I felt I deserved, but I knew they loved me. Similarly when my Kentish Town friend told me that I was 'ignore-ant. You're really intense about some things but then you completely ignore the others,' I took it in good part, because I understood that despite my exasperating ignore-ance she had chosen to be my friend.

In the wider world, I was learning that ignore-ance could be dangerous. Sometimes pacing around my room just wouldn't do it for me and I needed fresh air, so I would go for a walk around a block or two. I must have looked funny when I was doing it; maybe it was my heavy, earnest gait, maybe my facial expressions were all wrong somehow, maybe I just looked like someone who was walking for the sake of walking, and that in itself was weird enough in the suburbs, where there's neither enough scenery or enough activity to justify it. Maybe it would have helped if I had given over and worn my glasses all the time; as it was I either peered at people or looked right through them. It was probably for all of those reasons that I looked mad, and different, and was therefore fair game for ten-year-old boys.

It was the summer after my O levels, and I was following my usual route, down a side street, then along the road past the primary school I'd been so glad to escape, and finally back up the main road towards home. As I rounded the corner between the two, a group of ten-year-old boys came up to me, one of them holding a football.

'Excuse me,' he said, in a sickly sweet voice that reminded me of Donna. 'Could you tell me the time?'

I looked at my watch, told them and then they started. They all clustered round me, laughing, discussing me loudly, as if I weren't there: 'She's ugly, ain't she?' 'She's got big tits, ain't she?' Then in the Donna voice, one asked me, 'Are you mad?' They bumped into me as I tried to walk away, ran up behind me and pulled my bra strap, then threw their football at me – why were people always doing that? After a minute or two I tried to get my own back, wrenching the football out of its bearer's hands and making as if to throw it into the road, growling, 'Get off the streets!' But they just went: 'Ooooh, temper!' and carried on jeering and bumping. When I got home and had finished crying, I decided that the best solution to my problems with the world outside was never to leave the house again, and resolved to develop agoraphobia, which everyone had heard of and would understand. Fortunately my friend Jane phoned to invite me to go and see a film with her in the West End, and I went.

Teleportation was out – so was agoraphobia – how about invisibility? On the day of my humiliation I had been making an effort, wearing a fashionable egg-yellow Top Shop dress with tiny white polka dots and a pair of white pumps. On my more wary days, and especially if I had to walk down the stretch of pavement where I had been subject to sexual ridicule by children, I dressed down as far as I could go, hoping to escape notice. On the last day of my Kentish Town friend's stay, I walked her to Canons Park station and then returned home. I was wearing one of my long, baggy dresses, with my feet peeping out of the bottom in their clumpy lace-up shoes. My hair, now long again, was pulled back into a low, dishevelled ponytail. It was a cool summer day, so I was wearing my baggy shapeless navy jacket buttoned up over the skirt. In this way, I had managed to get as close to formlessness as a solid object could. As I approached the cul-de-sac where I lived, I passed a couple of boys, my age or slightly younger. They looked me up and down with self-righteous disgust and one of them yelled 'Dog!' It felt like a punishment, as if these boys' proper and just purpose in life was to patrol the streets, handing judgements out to any woman who dared to enter their sight looking anything less than primped.

I understood that I was supposed to be ashamed, and I was. When I got home I looked at myself in my parents' full-length mirror, without changing my clothes, and thought that perhaps I ought to have made more of an effort to make the best of myself, to be less of an affront to decent eyes. I had been whistled at plenty of times, and smiled at, and ogled, but surely only by men of peculiar and even perverted taste – that they did not see that I was a dog said nothing good about them, and I would certainly never want to be with a man who was so desperate as to want to see anything in me.

I overheard someone in the sixth form common room telling her friends about a girl she'd met who went to some other private establishment and had alluded to ours as 'that place where all the sixth formers have long flowery skirts and hairy legs and hate men'. As you'll have realized, this was not an entirely inaccurate description of some of us – or of one of us, anyway. Plenty of other girls shaved their legs, wore the right clothes, went out and got themselves boyfriends. To them, girls like me – poorly dressed, boyfriendless and 'innocent' – represented precisely what they did not want to be. We were each other's shadows. A friend once told me how her mother, who counselled teenage girls, had explained that, as she saw it, there were two paths through female adolescence: a girl could either 'climb a tree, or stand around at the bus stop with her tits hanging out'. I stood on the side at the school ball, with my tree-climbing set, all of us in the wrong sort of dresses, watching the bus stop girls strutting their strapless stuff amidst crowds of hair-gelled boys sweating into their rented dinner jackets. It was

68

a strange and discomfiting sight. Later that year, when one of our group managed to get herself down from the tree and find a boyfriend to swoon over and sleep with, the rest of us were horrid about it – I'm rather afraid we *said things*.

In the classroom, on my home turf, I continued to strut my own kind of stuff. My brain stuff. In sixth form, where I took my best subjects, I consolidated my position as the one who had the answers, who got the top marks in the exam, who was despatched by the group to intercede if there was a problem with a teacher. Sometimes I enjoyed it; sometimes I corrected a teacher. Sometimes I wished I could be less conspicuous, as I felt during a session after the English mock A level when I was taking my turn to go over my paper with the teacher; she spent perhaps a little too long telling me how good the work was and another girl broke in with, 'Can you find some time for *me* now – I mean, I know I'm not a *prodigy* but . . .'

Freud says in *The Interpretation of Dreams* that one of the most common dreams he has come across in his practice is one in which the subject risks failing an exam which he or she has long since passed in waking life, panics, and then realizes that they've already succeeded and needn't sit it again. I've lost count of the number of nights I've spent at my old school, at my real advanced age, flapping about because A levels are coming up and I've missed all the classes, before remembering with relief that actually I passed them years ago. In a variant version of the same dream it is the last day of school – for the second time – but I can't leave because I can't find a bag or box big enough to take all my books home in. According to Freud, the purpose of such dreams is to reassure the dreamer that they have already proved their capacity for rising to a difficult challenge, however daunting it may have appeared at the time. I don't feel reassured by them though: I feel trapped.

The school prided itself on its Oxbridge entrance record, and would back no unlikely candidates, so any interested upper sixth formers had to go round and ask their teachers if they would support an application from them, and, if so, in which subjects. The effect of this – in my competitive mind at least – was that it sorted all girls into two categories: Oxbridge material and, less impressively, non-Oxbridge material. Getting a place at Oxbridge would prove, surely, that I was who the teachers thought I could be, and not the useless lump I feared I was. On the other hand, none of the courses offered at either university interested me that much. I wasn't even sure that I wanted to go to university at all – after all, Woody Allen hadn't, so it obviously wasn't necessary for the comic writer I'd decided I was going to be. I sent off for some film school prospectuses; I read them, saw that I was entirely unqualified either for entry or funding, and reluctantly threw them away.

At least at Cambridge they had Footlights; lots of people I admired had come up through Footlights. The teachers were happy to support my application. Feeling that I had somehow to compensate for my privileged and private education, I applied for a place to read social and political sciences at the most left-wing college I could find and got a comfortably low-ish ABB offer.

'Are you happy, now you've got what you want?' asked my Auntie Yetta. 'Because you made your mother *miserable*.'

Perfection

42. When I read I have the impression I have missed something important and must go back and reread the passage at least two or three times.

The Padua Inventry

I am now to review the last year, and find little but dismal vacuity, neither business nor pleasure; much intended, and little done.

Samuel Johnson, *Prayers and Meditations*

Recently, I've noticed that the A level dreams are beginning to give way to undergraduate dreams. These follow a similar pattern, except that I decide to drop out after a few days, as instead of merely being in a panic about exams I am entirely hysterical about everything. In these dreams I am clearly quite unable to look after myself in the most basic ways, let alone undertake degree-level study, and the only thing to do is to pack up and go home.

There's a conversation I had with my father that I really wish I could have again. It took place during the summer holiday between my last term at school and my first at university. I was reading – probably – at the breakfast-room table, when my father came and sat down next to me and asked if he could have a word. He began hesitantly: 'Joanne, you're eighteen now, you're an adult, you're about to leave home, and I just wanted to know – have I been a good father to you?'

His eyes were wet. I didn't know what to say. What I would say now is, 'Of course, you've been a wonderful father.' What I said then was, 'Well . . . it would have been good if you'd been more involved, if you hadn't left so much to Mum, but – for a man of your generation, I think you've been as good as you could have been, yes.'

'I wanted to know because . . . the only thing I've ever done that I've been proud of was visiting refuseniks[9] in Russia . . . and of course I'm proud of you and your brother – apart from that, the past is a dead weight.'

I don't remember what I said then; I think we both sat there sadly contemplating his dead weight, neither of us knowing how to shift it. We didn't have the tools.

Now I would know how to deal with it, in principle at least. I've had several lots of cognitive behavioural therapy; I possess half a shelf full of sensible books packed with fair and balanced statements such as:

> No one is perfect. All of us, at one point or another, have violated our own principles or standards. We feel guilty and ashamed if we believe that what we did means that we are bad. But violations do not necessarily mean that we are bad. Our actions may have been linked to a particular situation or to a specific time in our lives.[10]

No one is perfect, no one ever could be perfect; a certain degree of imperfection is inevitable, forgivable. This is just the kind of thing you are supposed to say to someone when they show you their dead weight. However, it would not be an appropriate observation to make at a job interview, a sales presentation, or the launch of a party manifesto. In these contexts, perfection

9. Soviet Jews who had applied for visas to emigrate to Israel, which had been refused. They then remained in limbo, disgraced and discriminated against, but unable to leave. Jews from the West helped as much as they could, sometimes by paying visits in person. Mum, Dad and I had made one such visit together in 1987.
10. Dennis Greenberger and Christine A. Padesky, *Mind Over Mood* (The Guilford Press, London, 1995, p. 206)

and perfectionism are things to aspire to, part of a shiny, elite little group of concepts along with 'excellence', 'quality', 'the best', 'Britain's leading', and so on. And don't forget 'genius', which Thomas Carlyle (according to *The Concise Oxford Dictionary of Quotations*) defined as a 'transcendent capacity of taking trouble, first of all'. *You're a perfectionist, are you? You accept nothing less than the best? Then I would be a fool not to accept your tender, and I look forward to our working together to compete at the highest level in today's demanding marketplace.*

In the discourse of clinical psychology, on the other hand, perfectionism will get you into all kinds of trouble. A quick search of the Psycinfo citation index produced forty-seven hits, including the following: 'Action monitoring and perfectionism in anorexia nervosa'; 'Parental influences on social anxiety: the sources of perfectionism'; 'Perfectionism and Depressive Symptoms in Early Adolescence'; 'Psychological correlates of fatigue: examining depression, perfectionism, and automatic negative thoughts'; 'Recurrent pain among university students: contributions of self-efficacy and perfectionism to the pain experience'; 'Relation between childhood peer victimization and adult perfectionism: are victims of indirect aggression more perfectionistic?' Here we are looking at a very different cluster of concepts: anorexia nervosa, depression, pain and victimization. We can add OCD as well.

Some psychologists have even spoken of 'clinical perfectionism' as a pathological trait in its own right, suggesting that 'the defining feature of clinically significant perfectionism is the overdependence of self-evaluation on the determined pursuit (and achievement) of self-imposed personally demanding standards of performance in at least one salient domain, despite the occurrence of adverse consequences.'[11] This perfectionism is

11. Roz Shafran, Zaftar Cooper, Christopher G. Fairbairn, 'Clinical Perfectionism: a Cognitive-Behavioural Analysis', *Behaviour Research and Therapy*, July 2002; 40(7): 773–91

'maintained by the biased evaluation of the pursuit and achievement' of these standards. If she does not meet her standards, the perfectionist will not re-evaluate these standards but instead will 'react with self-criticism'; on the other hand, if she does meet her standards, then these standards are 're-evaluated as being insufficiently demanding'.

This is not the gilded perfectionism of marketing language, which promises both efficiency of process and excellence of product. This is a perfectionism which impedes the process and results, as often as not, in no product at all. If you can't finish a piece of work until you believe that it is absolutely perfect – or, worse than that, if you cannot even *start* a task until you can be certain that you are going to perform it perfectly all the way, then you are likely to bring upon yourself a whole sequence of 'adverse consequences'.

Procrastination and avoidance: 'I can't continue with this chapter until I've read through every paper cited in that literature search'; 'My mind is in the wrong state to start working now, it isn't clear and focused enough, I'll just clear a few things up, check my email again, then I'd better call my mother back.'

Paralysis: 'There's too much to read – I can't get on top of it'; 'I've got five possible first paragraphs for this chapter and I can't choose which one – is it three o'clock *already*?'

Hurried, sub-standard work: 'Now I've done nothing all day: I'll just write any old thing down – at least I'll have something to show for it then.'

Or, alternatively, an **Abandoned project**: 'Now I've wasted a whole day – again. No point trying now – I might as well give up.'

And, ultimately, **Depression**: 'In fact, I might as well give up altogether and give my advance back. I always fuck up everything I do. I've let myself and everyone else down. No wonder I'm constipated and tired and have a headache – it's because I deserve it. I won't achieve anything ever in my life and then I'll die young and in pain with nobody at my bedside because by then they'll all have seen me for what I am and I'll disgust them.'

How I managed to leave school with three A levels and an S level history pass I'll never know. I got As in my hard subjects – Russian and modern history – but in English, a combination of a couple of awkward papers and my own boredom with the texts tripped me up, and I earned a mere B. This made no practical difference, because I had more than met my Cambridge offer, but at the time I was as devastated as if I had failed. I couldn't have articulated it to anyone at the time, but that B was an open wound in my brilliant carapace, and now the disgusting mush beneath it would be on display to anyone who cared to look. I was inconsolable. I turned a trip to Scotland with my parents and my Kentish Town friend, which should have been a celebration, into purgatory for all concerned. I whinged at the Edinburgh Festival, then I sulked in the Highlands. I was ungracious, and I was irritable, and when everyone else had gone to bed I picked and picked and picked.[12]

When it comes to clinical perfectionism, work is definitely one of my 'salient domains'. I sabotage myself in this area less consistently than I used to, but it has taken me many years to get to the point where I could even contemplate producing a book-length manuscript, much less sit down and write it. Appearance is another domain for me, which is why I hardly bother with it: I'm never going to be Miss World, so what's the point in trying? Housework, fortunately, is a far from salient domain. Mothering is only salient in some of its aspects, so my son gets to eat sugar, watch TV and even do both at once. What is salient for me in all ways at all times is how I treat other people.

12. I've made my target word count for the day now, but then so could any idiot. I know lots of other people who write twice as much just in a morning.

My default position is to feel entirely responsible for the feelings of everyone I come into contact with, for as long as I come into contact with them. If the cashier who serves me doesn't smile, then it's my fault. If I don't clear out of the way as quickly as possible, so that the next person in the queue can't get served the *very next second*, and they look a bit fed up, then it's my fault. If I phone somebody at the wrong moment, so that by phoning them I cause them thirty seconds of extra stress, then that stress is on my head because I should have realized that it was the wrong moment. If somebody walks past me in the street, and I think something negative about them – say, She shouldn't wear that skirt with those legs, and look at that VPL – then this in itself makes me so much of a bitch that I might just as well have gone up to her and shouted it in her face. Only the people closest to me ever find out when I'm upset with them, because there's always a good reason why someone else might do something upsetting to me, something they can't help, whereas I should always know better. This domain extends a fair way back in time, with its boundary somewhere around the beginning of my adolescence, which makes for a weighty past. Not a dead sort of weight in my case – it's more like a big sack of angry snakes.

That holiday in Scotland is a serpentine memory; my three years at Cambridge are a writhing nest. Arriving with a shameful B on my results slip was just the start of it. Counting down the miles in the back of my parents' car that autumn, I realized too late that I hadn't really wanted to go to Cambridge at all; what I'd really wanted to do was to get in, prove that I could do it, and then walk off to some unspecified, alternative future. But I had failed to come up with a better plan, so here I was, in the back of my parents' car, travelling further and further away from the only places where I'd ever felt safe, and from almost everybody I'd ever known. Some of my friends from school were coming up at the same time, and I had every intention of going to find them in their respective colleges as soon as I could, but apart from them, there was no one there with any good reason to put up with me, listen to me, or give a damn. I had, in the hope of finding a boyfriend, deliberately chosen a mixed-sex college, but I had almost no experience of being taught by men, let alone of socializing with them. I had been to very few parties, hardly ever stayed away from home, never managed more than a sip of alcohol; I had never needed to manage my own time, organize my own work, make a bare institutional room my own, make sure that I ate healthily, launder my own clothes, wash up my own crockery, clean up my own messes or sort out my own problems. I had never bothered getting a Saturday job, and had refused to learn to drive. All in all, I had spent the last five years studiously avoiding responsibility of any kind. I was going to an establishment that worked on the assumption that I was an adult, when I was still in so many ways a child.

At school I had resented the notion that I might be seen as innocent: it implied a backwardness in worldly matters, and I could not bear to be thought backward at anything. I bought new clothes for my new life, and began to wear my hair loose, rather than in a schoolgirlish ponytail. I went straight for the people with the coolest personae, and attached myself to them, in the hope that some of their sophistication would rub off on me. For the first couple of terms, I followed this group around, whining about how miserable I was and asking them why they drank and smoked when it was so bad for them, and trying lamely to get them to laugh at my jokes and tell me I was pretty. I made innumerable faux-pas, usually to do with other people's sex lives, because I had not yet learned to distinguish harmless gossip from damaging scandal. I sat up with them in darkly decorated rooms till two in the morning listening to the right sort of music and waiting for a transformative moment that never came. I even fancied myself in love with one of the cool people.

He was very into his music, he wore a shirt and black jacket at all times, so I thought that he would be perfect for the girl I was trying to be.

Really he was no more sophisticated than I was, and we misread each other disastrously. We flirted for a few days, attempted to kiss with limited success, each of us thinking that the other was the experienced one who would pass their experience on. He soon lost interest, but I had already developed a massive crush, with which I would bore anyone who made the mistake of opening their door to me.

It ended rather messily. Egged on by a new best friend from another college, who liked drama as much as I did, I put some anonymous postcards in his pigeonhole in the postroom. With a good black ink pen I bought especially for the purpose, I decorated them with line drawings and added what I thought were appropriate entries from a pocket dictionary of quotations, also specially bought. The first said: 'Tread softly, for you tread upon my dreams.' The second said, 'Whereof one cannot speak, thereof one must be silent.' It was early spring by then so I added some snowdrops I'd picked from the college beds. Then I posted a bunch of red roses and a somewhat overheated Swinburne quote with more roses in it. Unfortunately, and unknown to me, there were other things going on in that boy's life: another musician had been sending him death threats, and he had hoped that the snowdrops were from a girl in Queen's whom he liked – and whom I was trying to make friends with, as a way of getting closer to him and keeping an eye on the competition. The first I knew of all of this was when he came rushing up to me and my new best friend in Front Court waving my Swinburne note in my face and shouting, 'HEY! HEY!' He shoved the note under my nose. 'Is this your handwriting?' Yes, I said. 'Then FUCK OFF!' I escaped home for the weekend, and ran a temperature. When I returned, there was an apologetic note shoved under my door; later on he explained that he hadn't meant to be so angry – it was just that my friend and I had looked conspiratorial at that moment – but I got the message. We tried to be 'friends' for a bit, but soon gave that up.

Years later, when stalkers were big news, I became preoccupied with the idea that I might be, essentially, a Stalker, and tormented myself over my irreversible creepiness, but the truth was that I was a silly little girl who had no idea how to behave towards men, and who thought that the little notes would make me seem intriguing, sophisticated and mysterious. It's not behaviour I've ever been inclined to repeat. And it was the last time I would so much as kiss a man for six years. I obsessed about them – sometimes I realized they were obsessing about me. I made a fool of myself in front of men I liked and was sometimes offhand to the point of cruelty with men who liked me, because their interest in me made them threatening as well as ineligible. By the time I reached the third year, I was obsessing in my diary about a student in the year below, who had been flirting with me for a couple of terms – and whom I suspected had been put up to it for a joke, because why would he have bothered otherwise?

The main theme of the diary was disappointment, with Cambridge, with other people, and with life in general, but mostly with myself. I was disappointed with my lack of a love life, my stalled career as an undergraduate comedy writer – which I'll come back to later – and disappointed, so bitterly disappointed, with my academic performance. At school, I had, with a bit of luck, a certain amount of forbearance from the teachers and a following wind, managed to get all my essays in, just about. But at Cambridge, with so little structure, so many new ideas to take in, so many choices to make for myself, and with the myth of the place to live up to, I was quite overwhelmed.

It started well. The first essay I wrote was for my sociology

79

supervisor,[13] on Max Weber and bureaucracy. It was handed in on time and was, he said, of First quality. It was the worst thing that could have happened at that stage, because in pouring so much into an early effort I had set myself a ridiculous standard. I found it harder and harder to hand essays in. My supervisors tried to help, but by the end of the second term they were all clearly utterly exasperated. For some reason, I found it especially hard to produce any essays for social anthropology, and became too embarrassed to show up at supervisions; it got to the point where I was looking over my shoulder every time I left my room, in case my supervisor came up and collared me. In the end, I shut myself in my room and worked all out on an essay comparing status symbols in the West and in the Trobriand Islands, where the traditional people used piles of rotting yams much as we use huge muscle cars. I handed it in at the porters' lodge, so I didn't have to meet the head man. It was a good essay – as it should have been, given the time invested. I got it back with the comment, 'It's a shame you don't hand essays in more often – they are very good when you do!' It should have helped but it didn't; I always talked up a good supervision – sometimes hardly allowing my supervision partners a word in edgeways – but when it came to written work there were too many barriers. My social psychology supervisor tried to help: 'You can have all these wonderful ideas in your head, but if you don't write them down you might as well not have them – it's like masturbation.' That didn't help, but one can hardly blame him for trying.

As part of my research for this book, I spoke to Dr David Veale, a leading psychiatrist in the OCD/BDD field, at his office in the Maudsley Hospital. He suggested that what under-

13. That's what they call tutors in Cambridge. An honours examination is a 'tripos'. Students live in numbered rooms not on corridors but on 'staircases'. In June they attend 'May Balls'. It's not just any old place, you know.

lies such crippling perfectionism is the need for that 'just right' feeling that drives all kinds of compulsions from hand washing and oven checking through to counting and word repetition, in which sufferers 'may use emotional criteria that you don't finish something until it *feels* right, rather than taking the objective view'. A healthy student, or writer, can accept that she is unable to judge the quality of her own work for herself, and must hand it over to a supervisor, or editor, to make that final decision as to whether it is, if not 'just right', then at least 'right enough'. For the obsessive student/writer, on the other hand, there is no such thing as 'right enough', 'good enough', 'sound enough' or even just 'enough'.

> While reading, the person may reread the same line or paragraph over and over to make sure it has been perfectly understood and that nothing has been overlooked by mistake. A behaviour that sometimes accompanies rereading is compulsive underlining or highlighting. The sufferer wants to perfectly remember everything that might be important in a book, but due to their inability to discriminate the important from the unimportant, they often end up marking most of or even the entire book.
>
> Fred Penzel, *Obsessive-Compulsive Disorders: A Complete Guide to Getting Well and Staying Well*, pp. 266–7

And so it would be that after forty minutes' study, I would have nothing to show for my labours but a handwritten copy of the first two pages of the introduction, a swollen, aching hand, a splitting headache and stomach cramps so painful that I would have to stop altogether.

So, I found other ways to fill my time. I would spend hours, day or night, shut in my room, picking my skin, listening to the Sugarcubes or Prefab Sprout, and pacing up and down. I was miserable in there, and not only because I had to share it with a growing pile of unread set texts. It had a huge curtainless window which looked across a courtyard into another huge window from which I risked being seen in all my private disgustingness. It had thin-as-my-own-skin walls, through which, my less inhibited neighbour had told me, *she could hear me pee*, and which allowed continual waves and gusts and peals of sociable noise to pass through from her side to mine. Its bile-green door gave out onto strip-lit corridors, which were populated almost entirely by people I sincerely wished to avoid. And I lived in fear of the building's Banshee fire alarm, which could go off at any time and give me a panic attack.

When I couldn't stand my room any more, which was often, I would go and wander about town disconsolately like a virginal nineteenth-century novelist looking for heights to wuther upon. I would knock on doors until I found a friend who was both in and distractable, hoping that we could spend an hour or five drinking coffee and moaning at each other about not getting on with our work. If nobody was in, and it was daytime, I might wander into the shops and spend some of the money I'd saved by failing to drink like a normal student.

Sometimes I went out to eat, to see a film or a student drama production. I wrote comedy sketches and one or two of them were performed in student revues. I even managed to act a little. I made the first of my three appearances in a Dario Fo play. My character was a scared little mouse who spent the play being pushed around by the rest of the cast. It wasn't a stretch. A couple of male cast members clocked how inexperienced and shy I was and teased me mercilessly: 'What pure white skin!' they would cry as I cringed in the unisex dressing room. 'What a Madonna-like midriff!' At the cast party, I sat pinned between them on a bench while they told me that I was grown up now, I was pretty and clever and could do whatever I liked, not just what my mother told me to do.

'Can I tell you to piss off?' I asked.

'Yes,' one of them said, 'but we won't.' He suggested a three-some. Then one of the other girls came over and told them to leave me alone, so they dropped me, the (metaphorical) worry marks still fresh on my nape, and went off to find sport else-where.

I withdrew. I avoided the dining room – dining rooms were still bad places for me – and lived on takeaways. I cried a lot. I phoned my mother most days. I often went home for the weekend. I begged the senior tutor for a quieter room and got moved to the vacant half of an attic in a postgraduate hostel across the road, which meant that I could avoid college almost completely. At the end of the year I changed from social and political sciences to philosophy. Leaving Cambridge was not an option I could countenance, but I had run as far as was permis-sible from that disastrous year.

My main goal for the remaining two years was to stick them out and try to stay out of trouble. The switch to philosophy was part of this damage-limitation programme. I knew that there would be no hope of bluffing my way through supervisions as I had on the first-year courses in SPS, which had been so much *New Statesman* and *Guardian* stuff. Philosophy was new to me and if I didn't do any work this time I would fail the course and be out on my ear. As an extra insurance policy, I planned to go to as many lectures as possible and use my notes as the basis of the revision: the notes from my own reading could on no account be trusted. My brains had broken down and would have to be towed for the time being. Maybe I could get them repaired once I had my degree.

Subject changes are not uncommon in Cambridge, whose system allows for these, and I took a two-week conversion course over the summer. My first essay was called 'Is it Possible to Doubt Everything?' I had to read Descartes' *Meditations* and reflect on the idea that perhaps one's whole experience –

everything that one understood to be reality – was nothing more than a dream conjured up by a 'malevolent demon'. The conceptual equivalent of a perfect vacuum, this is one of philosophy's classic 'thought experiments'. The subjects of such experiments often coincide with those of obsessive ruminations. Take, for example, these questions from my ethics final paper:

> No ethically significant distinction can be drawn between acts and omissions. Discuss.

> Is deciding an action? If so, does that mean that it is something we decide to do? If not, can we be blamed for our decisions?

I took ethics two years running; it was my best subject.

My weakest point was symbolic logic. My first supervisor was a very serious woman who took none of my flaky little-girl nonsense and would send me away if I arrived at a supervision underprepared. She instructed me to take the introductory logic course alongside the first years and to concentrate on catching up. For a few weeks I did as I should, but faced with blackboards and sheets covered with subscripted Ps and Qs stuck inside brackets and on either side of incomprehensible symbols, I took the line of least resistance and gave up. (I still have my logic textbook and the underlinings run out very early on.) Then there were my other responsibilities. Someone was producing *The Importance of Being Earnest* that term and I could not resist auditioning. I went in to read for the part of Gwendolyn and was offered Lady Bracknell. It would probably not have happened had my attempt to mimic Joan Greenwood in the film version not resulted in a passable Edith Evans. It was a dreadful piece of casting: the shortest performer in the company, I had neither the presence to fill the role nor the breath to get to the end of her mile-long sentences. My priority became to do as close to an adequate job as I could, in order not to let the director and the rest of the cast down. Skimping on my work only meant that I was letting myself down, so, from a utilitarian point of view, that mattered less.

In the event, I probably did as well as a tiny, untrained, miscast and only slightly talented nineteen-year-old could, and if the student critics did not single me out for praise, they did not criticize me either, which was a huge relief. After the last performance I had a massive nosebleed and decided that my on-stage career was over.

At that point I should have started concentrating on my work. My performance that first term had been patchy, at best, and my new supervisor had read me several lectures about the commitment that the study of philosophy required. I should have concentrated on my work. Instead I joined the writing team for the Footlights women's review and directed Nikolai Gogol's *The Marriage* with Jane, my old schoolfriend. The sketch I contributed, a dialogue between an insecure fourteen-year-old and her bitchy friend, went down very well, and I had hopes of achieving my dearly held ambition of getting some material into the Footlights' main show, which went to Edinburgh, but it didn't happen. The performers had their own material, which understandably they preferred to use. Perhaps it would have helped if I had been better at what I've since learned to call 'networking', but by the time I realized how important it was to socialize with people with whom one hoped to work, it was too late, and I'd retired disappointed from comedy. This seemed like a shame at the time, because I could see that my writing was probably no worse than most of the others'.

My directing, on the other hand, was dreadful, and the play was a fiasco. It was supposed to be a comedy. For the first four nights, nobody laughed and Jane and I watched the poor actors struggle while we sat in the back row, eavesdropping on a contemptuous and impatient audience. On the last night, when my parents happened to be in attendance, the cast could stand it no more, and in a last, desperate bid for laughs, took over the play, mugging, swearing, stuffing cushions up their costumes, bumping into each other, falling over, and generally clowning as hard as they could. The audience lapped it up, and my humiliation was complete. I sat in silence at the cast party and left early. They presented Jane and me with a bottle of Baileys, which she was happy to take away.

So that was that for me and show business. I wasn't getting on much better with academe. Although I continued to attend lectures faithfully, and take down the thoughts of others, my own remained ungatherable. My essays were late, or superficial – often both – or else non-existent. I was postponing supervisions left, right and centre. Two of my supervisors for my second term were postgraduate students, only a few years older than I was, and they found it all but impossible to teach an undergraduate who never finished any of her essays early enough for them to read them before they saw her. An entry in my third-year diary shows how neatly one of them put her finger on my problem with work: 'T—— always said that I never got round to essays because I worried too much about the doing of it, and forgot about the actual topic in question.'

My director of studies nailed it from a different angle. I had come to him panicking a couple of weeks before the exams, to warn him that I had been 'having a hard time' and that I thought I might fail. He asked, 'Why do you find it so hard to write anything down? Is it because you're afraid of being judged?'

'You must have been very frustrated last year,' he said when we met again after the summer. I had achieved an upper second in the exam – a class up from my disappointing first year in SPS – which had surprised us both. One of my teachers in the sixth form had told me that I was very good at thinking on my feet, and this had served me well in the philosophy exams, where I had found that by thinking the exam questions through from first principles, and performing my own on-the-spot thought experiments, I could to some extent make up for all the reading I'd failed to do. With nobody else's ideas in front of me demanding to be perfectly absorbed before I could write a word, my own thoughts had been free to flow at last. The blessed thing about an exam setting, for me, was that it allowed me no access to my usual procrastination tools, so the only thing left to do was to get on with it.

Outside the exam hall, though, the usual problems remained. My unreliability as a student throughout the previous year had meant that none of my second-year supervisors was willing to take me on again, and my director of studies was reluctant to inflict me on anyone new, so he had decided that he would have to take all my supervisions for the final year himself. It was going to be the two of us, sitting in old chairs at either end of his long, Georgian study, once a week, every week, for the whole of that academic year.

My D of S always sat at his desk by the window, with his back to the light, so that if I left my glasses off, his face was a perfect blur. I had got my first pair of glasses – John Lennon ones of course – when I was fifteen, and had been using them only for blackboards, cinema screens and takeaway menus. Glasses, even John Lennon ones, were neither cute nor cool, so for most of the time I preferred to screw my eyes up and peer at the world, or else let it drift by in a haze. In so many ways the shared external world was less vivid to me than my private internal one, so it didn't make much of a difference. I didn't realize how bad my eyesight was, or the social consequences of this, until I was walking down King's Parade one day and heard, just behind my right ear, 'So what am *I* supposed to have done?'

I had just blanked one of my friends, and not for the first time that term. From that point on, I began to wear my glasses more often.

When I was shut up with my D of S in his long study, I left them off on purpose. I thought that perhaps this would keep my Inappropriate Thoughts out of the room. As I understood it, the two of us were sitting together in a working space, a philosopher's study no less, and the only thoughts I should have in it were of secondary qualities, dialectical reasoning, categorical imperatives, substances, spirit and the like. I should certainly not be entertaining, however unwillingly, mental pictures of myself engaging in acts which I had never witnessed, let alone performed, *especially not* if these pictures included the man in front of me, who was a teacher, a figure of authority, a philosopher to boot. If I made eye contact with him, I thought, he would be sure to read these thoughts in my eyes, these proofs of my psychosexual aberrance, and be disgusted. So I chose not to wear my glasses and to spend three terms addressing a hazy outline. Inside it, I assumed, was a man who paid little attention to what I said because he thought I was stupid. He would be right to think this: I had become stupid because my brain was polluted with sick thoughts. I must not let him see the sick thoughts. So I kept my glasses off. So it wasn't until I forgot to take them off for our final meeting that I realized how much he had been listening, nodding, responding to my arguments, and making encouraging faces. Instead, I assumed he thought I was not worth listening to. Because I was stupid. On account of my thought pollution which I had to hide. By leaving my glasses off.

If only I had put them on, I might have seen a more accurate picture not only of the room, but of myself. So many problems, as Dr Veale explained, can arise from living more inside one's head than out: 'most people, if they are mentally healthy, tend to have about 70–80 per cent of their attention focused *externally* onto specific tasks or the environment or noise or so on, and only perhaps about 10–20 per cent on themselves, whereas it's the opposite way round if you're suffering from a mental disorder – [then] you get all your information, really, from what your *mind* is telling you.' A result of this self-preoccupation – and something which is, perhaps, the defining feature of obsessive-compulsive disorder in particular – is the tendency to seize on certain passing thoughts and mental images, the kind that run through everyone's minds, and to ascribe inordinate significance to them. There was nothing unusual, let alone pathological, about the sexual images popping up in my head: the problem lay only in the excessive attention I paid them.

At the end of that year, another white-knuckle ride of postponed supervisions and tardy, scribbled essays, I managed to scrape a final upper second. My family were delighted; my director of studies was relieved. So was I, writing in my diary that my result 'vindicates my time here, whether I enjoyed it or not'.

That entry was written on 16 June 1991, when I had just received the result. I managed to remain in a positive mood for a couple of pages or so, but later on in the same, long entry, when I asked the question, 'So how do I feel, now that my two-way stretch is coming to an end?' the answer was:

The sight of the slightness of my person-in-the-world, and even to myself, has been frightening. I am not impressive. I am a woman of little grace, almost no achievements, no distinction, a sexual cripple, an awkward social actor. I am clinging most humiliatingly to childhood, refusing to grow up, resenting the very young. I have felt at times this year, less confident in myself, less proud of myself, more frightened of the future, more depressed and despairing than I have ever felt. I have a slight, uneventful, dull outer life, and sometimes it has seemed as if my soul has all but seeped away from me. I am a social cipher, an underwritten character, and an awkward, inadequate one at that.

When I had written my first entry ten months earlier, I had explained that the diary was to be my only extra-curricular activity for the final year. Its purpose was to be that of self-analysis, focusing on the question of whether, after my recent failures, I should really consider myself to be a writer or not, or whether I should give up my childhood dream and settle for life as an ordinary person – like a civil servant or lawyer or something – instead. (The possibility that one might be both a writer *and* something else never seems to have occurred to me.) Reading it today, some entries are as embarrassing as I would expect them to be; some, where I berate myself for not working or for picking my skin or pining over some man, are just sad, but in others I can see the first sardonic glimmerings of grown-up self-awareness.

Sure I've accounted for my social inadequacies, lack of patience and sulkiness as signs of a great artistic temperament, and felt nicely superior to those mediocre, non-creative multitudes.

Sure I've put up with years of depression, lethargy and self-hatred on the understanding that great art must arise from such noble sufferings.

<u>BUT I HAVE HARDLY WRITTEN ANYTHING!</u>

The entry for 13 February 1991 interests me for what it shows about my behaviour towards other people, men particularly. Jane and I had been discussing a mutual friend, a first-year student at her college.

I said to Jane that I couldn't believe X liked me. She said he did but that sometimes I annoyed him. Why? I asked warily. I whinge and I look too much for confirmation, fish too much. This was all the more horrible to hear because I had suspected it. I must watch myself around him, and take care not to do these things. He makes me feel uncomfortable because he just smiles and nods and goes along (or pretends to) with whatever unreasonable behaviour one throws at him. I suppose I fish so much with him because I'm trying to goad an honest adverse reaction from him. Friends let you know, in a nice way, when you're being annoying.

It had to stop, the whingeing and fishing. My neediness, my moods and my dramas had exasperated my friends, sometimes to the point where they could be my friends no longer. I didn't want to lose any more friends. I didn't want to keep putting men off either. From that first 'FUCK OFF!' I had understood that there was something really wrong with me inside, that men could see it, and that I would have to get it fixed.

I had already begun to seek help. In my first year, I saw a university counsellor, who told me that I could choose either to be a victim or to empower myself. In my second year, I saw another counsellor who told me that I had an almost beatific face and suggested that I join the art therapy group. That same year, I went to my doctor who said to try vigorous exercise and hot baths and if that didn't work, to take a year out. My new best friend, who had been seeing the same counsellors, transferred to LSE and began analytic psychotherapy, which sounded like a far more interesting option than the exercise and baths. I found out that there were funds available for psychotherapy for undergraduates and asked my pastoral tutor if I might access them. A biologist by trade, he thought that psychotherapy would be both unnecessary and unhelpful. Instead he had me visit him every two weeks for a sympathetic chat and a discussion of my eating habits, which he clearly believed were the core of the problem. I didn't agree, but he was all I had, so I kept going back to his office for our appointments, where I stared at graphs of fungal growth patterns on his computer screen, and thought about all the miraculous and exciting therapy I was going to have once I got out of there.

Confession

28. I have the impression that I will never be able to explain things clearly, especially when talking about important matters that involve me.

The Padua Inventory

––––––––

Where the epistemophilic instinct is a preponderating feature in the constitution of an obsessional patient, brooding becomes the principal symptom of the neurosis. The thought process itself becomes sexualised, for the sexual pleasure which is normally attached to the content of thought becomes shifted on to the act of thinking itself, and the gratification derived from reaching the conclusion of a line of thought is experienced as a *sexual* gratification.

Sigmund Freud, from Notes upon a Case of
Obsessional Neurosis

For sufferers of what we currently call obsessive-compulsive disorder, the ascent of Freudianism was something of a disaster. This is not because Freud was unable to identify the condition or describe the symptoms: 'Obsessional neurosis [as he called it] is shown in the patient's being occupied with thoughts in which he is in fact not interested, in his being aware of impulses in himself which appear very strange to him and in his being led to actions the performance of which give him no enjoyment, but which it is quite impossible for him to omit.'[14] Writing several

14. Sigmund Freud, 'Introductory Lectures on Psycho-Analysis Part III', 1916–17 (Standard Edition, Volume 16, p. 258)

years earlier, Father Victor Raymond showed that Catholic priests recognized them pretty well too: 'Obsession may be described as an idea that recurs automatically or mechanically and involuntarily, and forces itself irresistibly on the consciousness, in spite of all efforts to banish it. Further, this idea causes pain and provokes various impulses.'[15]

The priest and the analyst differed in their views of what caused the problem, and in how it should be treated. Following the French alienist Pierre Janet, Raymond saw vulnerability to obsessive thoughts as one characteristic of 'psychaesthenia', a deficiency in psychic (that is, mental) energy which also manifested itself in 'enervating' ruminations, feelings of doubt, awkwardness, a sense of inferiority and a tendency to leave tasks uncompleted. Heredity played 'an important part in the genesis of this evil', although 'mistakes in the rearing of children' were also to blame for its development. And as far as treatment was concerned:

> What means, then, are to be employed to remedy the mental weakness of the patients? They are *firm guidance* and a corresponding *obedience* – subjects on which we speak more at length elsewhere. Obedience will be gained in proportion as the director can inspire the patient with confidence. This certainly is no easy matter, especially with those whose malady takes the form of *doubts*. 'What proof have I that I ought to obey you?' one patient used to ask. 'May I not be making a mistake in placing all trust in you?' The director must bring much patience, compassion, and kindness to his task, and impress upon his charge that he has everything to gain by following blindly the advice given to him. It will be well to

15. Revd Fr V. Raymond, O.P., trans. Dom Aloysius Smith, C.R.I., *Spiritual Director and Physician: The Spiritual Treatment of Sufferers from Nerves and Scruples* (R. & T. Washbourne, Ltd, London, 1914)

explain to him that by carrying out this advice he will be enabled to throw off those painful ideas which embitter and cramp both the social and moral side of his life. Then, again, the director must make it clear that he accepts all responsibility for the consequence of the patient's acts, anxieties, and thoughts.

Alongside obedience to the spiritual director, Raymond prescribes full participation in the sacraments of confession and communion. These are particularly important for those patients who suffer from 'scruples', a kind of religious perfectionism in which the patient becomes so preoccupied with the minutiae of dogma and practice that they end up in a state of spiritual paralysis. They are never quite sure that they have confessed correctly, never fully satisfied, as they return to their pews, that there are not still parts of the heavenly host adhering to their teeth. In Raymond's account, only a renewed trust in a loving God and his representatives, the priests, can get them out of this quagmire.

Janet regarded psychaesthenia as a form of degeneracy. Freud disagrees, pointing out that obsessional symptoms 'occur too in distinguished people of particularly high capacity, capacities important for the world at large' [ibid, p. 260]. Like its sister neurosis, hysteria, obsessional neurosis comes about as the result of the repression into unconsciousness of mental contents which cause the individual so much anxiety that he (in psychoanalysis, your quintessential obsessive is male) is unable to acknowledge them in his conscious thought. To explain very roughly and very briefly, these inadmissible contents relate to the patient's sexual and aggressive impulses as they were first experienced in early childhood, and to the parents' reactions to them, as these were perceived by the infant. If the growing child is unable to integrate these impulses into his developing conscious self – his ego – he will only be able to express his 'forbidden' thoughts in symbolic guise: as intrusive, senseless obsessions.

According to Freud, the obsessive patient is not alone in having these primitive, sexualized thoughts – we all have them, along with the drives which give rise to them. An individual who has developed a good, strong ego will be able to cope both with the thoughts and with the anxiety which accompanies them. However, if ego development is compromised too much at any point, or becomes 'fixed' in one of the more primitive stages of development, then that individual will be left highly vulnerable to mental illness. In Freud's model of psychosexual development, the growing individual must pass through four such stages: oral, anal, phallic and finally, genital, which he envisaged as the 'mature' stage. Obsessive symptoms indicate a fixation at the anal stage.

Alongside this developmental model, Freud also came up with a structural model of the psyche, consisting of the familiar triad of the id, from which all impulses arise, the ego, and the superego, which functions as an honorary board to the ego's executive – the judging, valuing part of the self. Viewed from this perspective, the analysis of the obsessive psyche would, typically, reveal a more-than-averagely frenzied id, a weak, frightened ego, and a rather over-zealous, or 'sadistic' superego, which draws its violent power directly from the id. It may not be degeneracy, but it's not much prettier.

Despite this ugly picture, Freud offered real hope that obsessional neurosis might be cured if the patient could be helped to bring the repressed contents to consciousness and to integrate them into a newly strengthened ego. If, in other words, they were analysed.

It was a neat idea. In practice, however, the better-heeled obsessives of the western world would go on to spend the greater part of the twentieth century sitting in chairs or lying on couches and paying people to listen to them while they ruminated – and ruminated again, and then ruminated a bit more just to be on the safe side. As the century progressed, and 'obsessional neurosis' became 'obsessive-compulsive disorder', psychoanalysts had less and less to say about the condition. We had a 'crazy illness' [Freud, ibid.], resistant to treatment, and with a poor prognosis.

The September after I graduated, I wrote in my diary: 'This isn't what I was expecting. Not at all.' I can no longer remember what it was that I had expected. What I had was my old room at my parents' house, and a new job as an assistant in a private library in the West End. It was a one-year post, offered on the under-standing that I would go on to study for a postgraduate qualification in librarianship. As such it met my most urgent need, which was to demonstrate to my sadistic superego that I had a respectable plan. She was a psychic agency of suburban, Jewish, middle-class values, and in her view, getting a job to support oneself was not sufficient: one had to have a *profession*. Time was pressing, she said; I needed to find a career ladder and get on it, or *everybody would think I was a failure*. My ego muttered something about wanting to write. The superego snorted con-temptuously, like a great-aunt taking tea on Rosh Hashanah: So who's stopping you? *I'm* not stopping you. If you were going to do it, you'd do it, and anyway, what would you live on? Where would you live? Some nasty little bedsit in a cheap area full of axe-wielding rapist drug addicts? The ego looked at her feet, and said she supposed so. The id called them a pair of mealy-mouthed, bourgeois shitheads, threw some crockery, and stomped off to her bedroom to masturbate.

It didn't take long for me to realize that I wasn't cut out for a career in librarianship: I loved books, but I couldn't deal with people and it killed me to have to hand the people the books. Most of my working day was spent behind the returns and issue desks, penned in and on display, with no escape either from my co-workers, who were penned in with me and my moods like so many inky-fingered battery chickens, or from the members, who kept coming up and expecting me to issue books, or take returns, or *answer questions* – it was just so unreasonable. My few happy moments were spent in the stacks, shelving or searching for requests out among the books, by myself. I soon learned that if I wanted to write during my lunch break, or cry at any time, I could always flee to some dusty corner or other and be guaranteed a few moments' privacy. The Ecclesiastical History section was particularly good for this.

The job had one major perk, which was a ten-book borrowing allowance for staff. The shelves were groaning with out-of-print riches. I found, for example, the second and third volumes of Noel Streatfeild's memoirs, which she had written for an adult readership. I also found a book I'd read about in *Women's Review* during my more-feminist-than-thou phase: *A Life of One's Own* by Marion Milner. The book came out of a diary she had begun to keep at the age of twenty-six, with the intention of working out what was truly important to her, so that she could live a better, happier, fuller sort of life. I could easily recognize something of myself in her earlier entries, with their lamentations and 'exhortations', their shoulds and their should-nots. She was trying, like me, to think her way logically and rationally through the problem of how to live; was trying, through 'will and strain', to change what she didn't like about herself. I was reading her book as part of my own self-improvement programme, which also included therapy, a correspondence course in creative writing, twenty minutes a day on my father's exercise bike, fifty sit-ups in the morning and fifty at night.

The book is her account of a psychological experiment, a 'seven years' study of living', as Milner puts in her preface.[16] She

16. Joanna Field (Marion Milner), *A Life of One's Own* (Virago Press, London, 1986)

published it in 1934, under the pseudonym Joanna Field. Her reason for publishing, she said, was that 'although what I found is probably peculiar to my own temperament and circumstances, I think the method by which I found it may be useful to others'. Early on in the process, by employing a kind of written free association, she discovered where her thoughts really went when left to themselves. The content of what she found astonished her, so different was it from her conscious beliefs about who she was. She was also fascinated to discover that this very act of paying attention to what had until then been 'blind thinking' enlarged and strengthened her sense of self, giving a sounder basis for her opinions and preferences than the received ideas she had been depending upon. This was the first time I had come across the notion that it was no use trying to be what you ought to be when you could not accept what you were. I knew what she was talking about: your mother tells you your old headmaster has died, and while you're searching for something appropriate to say, your face starts grinning by itself.

Milner went on to train as a psychoanalyst. I wanted to be like her.

The idea that I might one day be a celebrated analyst meant that I could accept the need for therapy *and* save face: it wasn't remedial, it was career development.

7 April 1992

Dear Dr —

re: Joanne Limburg

As I understand you know from Joanne, she came to this centre this past October, seeking help for a number of emotional difficulties. Since that time, I have been seeing her regularly in order to help her sort out her therapeutic needs. She is now starting once weekly psychotherapy with Dr —, a colleague at this centre.

My mother had pointed me in the direction of the centre. It provided a walk-in service for young people in north-west London, and at twenty-one, I still just about qualified as one of those (officially speaking, even a middle-class adolescence is supposed to end promptly at twenty-two). The therapist who helped me sort out my needs told me that I should inform my GP, a man who had helped care for me since I was *in utero*, that I was seeking treatment through the centre. So I went to see him in his surgery and informed him, sadly but calmly, that I was depressed and seeking therapy. As usual, I didn't cry. I never cried in front of doctors and tutors and therapists – only at my mother and to my friends and alone in Ecclesiastical History. Perhaps that was why, like the tutors and doctors in Cambridge, he was less than convinced.

You young girls, he said, you talk yourselves into it, you sit around saying, 'I'm so depressed', having these deep discussions about your feelings, when you should be going out and enjoying yourself. It comes from thinking too much. Look at you there, hiding behind your glasses – you're a very attractive girl – do you have boyfriends? No. You should go out and get one, have some fun. You are very attractive, very desirable. You are *young*, for heaven's sake! Any time you need someone to talk to, I'm here. In the meantime, off you go.

My mother asked me how it had gone. I explained that our idiot doctor thought the best cure for my depression would be for me to go out dancing all night, half naked, with a can of Diet Coke shoved down my bikini bottoms. 'What a shame,' she said. 'He was wonderful with you when you were small.'

Once a week, from October onwards, I would take the Tube after work and head north-west up the Bakerloo line to discuss my difficulties and needs with a Mrs A. There is no reference to these sessions in my diary until late December, but I am quite sure that I mentioned my skin in the first session, because I always did; I think I also said something to the effect that my first Cambridge counsellor had said that I was very insightful, but that I felt I could think my way no further by myself.

My secret hope was that she and the centre could deliver a treatment that would make me as close as possible to the person I thought I ought to be, that I was both entitled and obliged to be, and that it would do it within – say – a year? Then I could get on with life, because I would at last be fit to have one. As I put it in my diary in November: 'I have to get out of here, but I must be reasonably sure of where I'm going to.' So I was just a little horrified to be told that, because of the unusual complexity of my emotional difficulties, my therapeutic need, as calculated by the centre, was to go into full analysis, five days a week, for at least three years.

But – what *were* these complex difficulties?

Developmental problems. I shouldn't view it merely as a negative decision. The recommendation had been made partly because they thought that I had the capability to make the most of an analysis.

But how would I pay?

I would see a trainee at the London Institute – they had a sliding scale.

But *five* days a week?

If it was important enough, I would make the time.

But *three* years?

We were coming to the end of the session. Perhaps I should go away and think about the proposal and she would discuss my misgivings with her colleagues.

The following week, she and her centre made a revised offer: I could see an analyst for psychoanalytic psychotherapy one day a week for three years, on the understanding that this was not my treatment per se, but rather a preparation for the proper treatment to which I felt unable to commit at this point in my life. It was better than their initial proposal; it was much better than nothing. I accepted it. The following April Mrs A and the centre would hand me over to the carefully hand-picked Dr B.

My last few sessions with Mrs A were uncomfortable and fractious. I didn't want to leave. There wasn't much she could do. Come April I would be twenty-two, and no longer eligible for treatment at the centre itself.

I understood that.

. . . and, in any case, obviously she was going to be leaving soon.

Obviously? Why?

She was going to have a baby.

And then I saw it for the first time, the huge bump I'd spent weeks and months failing to notice. Once again, I was shocked at myself. I'd read about 'negative hallucinations', and, as I understood them, only a really really sick person would have one of those – someone halfway to psychotic. Mrs A didn't say anything like this, but I thought it all the same, and assumed she thought so too. No doubt I disgusted her.

My final appointment card is pasted into my diary. It shows that on Thursday 2 April at 12 p.m., one day before my twenty-second birthday, Mrs A introduced me to Dr B. Below it I've written: 'Goodbye Mrs A. Goodbye 21.'

My parents took me out to dinner on my birthday. I wore the high-heeled black suede boots they'd bought me, black leggings, a long, low-necked green satin blouse, and a generous smearing of orange concealer on my décolletage. We were a little late for our booking because after I'd finished applying the concealer, I sat on my parents' bed for half an hour weeping bitterly because I was past it.

All the same, that month I managed to make not just one but three new starts: I began therapy with Dr B; I left the library to get some voluntary work experience because I had seen the light and the light had shown me that it was in the PR departments of charities and not in librarianship that my salvation lay; I bought, as a birthday present to myself, a correspondence course in creative writing with the Open College of the Arts. At this point the diary entries in my A4 notebook begin to peter out and are replaced by writing exercises. The course manual discouraged the kind of angsty, introspective and – I have to say it – pretentious stuff I'd been coming out with. What it did encourage me to do was to throw my attention out into the world, in a way that reminded me of some of Milner's thought experiments from *A Life of One's Own*. The first assignment required me to send in four poems: one about an object, one about the view out of my window, one about an animal, and one about a dream. For the view poem, I took advantage of one of my bouts of insomnia and stood by the window with my notebook and pen, the net curtain hanging over my back, as I tried to get it all down. I can still recall the excitement of it, of trying to keep track of all the changes in the brightening landscape. I remember the satisfaction of realizing that the narrative of the dawn's breaking would give me a shape for the poem; I remember the pleasure I took in knocking the poem into shape, and how thrilled I was to get a positive response from my tutor, and be told what it was I had managed to do: 'You have caught the breaking of dawn with exact precision . . . Each verse works as a metaphor for the daily unfolding of life.'

I'd forgotten how much I enjoyed poetry. A few months after I did those first exercises, I asked my cousin Lisa, who knew about these matters, where I might find a good poetry class, and she pointed me towards Michael Donaghy's workshops at City University. I had no sense of how high-powered these were, which was just as well. I crapped myself every week as it was.

I got a couple of decent poems out of that first term. One of them even made it into my first book:

Skin

She wakes up peeled, absorbing
stale breath. Without her skin,
she will dissolve in the rain,
so she closes all the windows
and locks the doors. Now
nothing can seep in, nothing
out. The day unravels.
She flickers from room to room
like a series of photographs,
appearing unfocused in doorways
and halfway down the stairs,
with no idea of how she got there.
She cannot collect herself,
not remembering what she keeps
inside, or what to leave out.

It's amazing what the third person will allow you to do. Another, rather less successful poem was written as an exercise: it was supposed to be a dramatic monologue in the voice of a minor character who had witnessed some great historic, mythical or fictional event. I chose the story of Ezekiel and the valley of the dry bones.

The Return of the Dry Bones

You won't find him talkative,
but then you must be used to that,
with all your cases. For us,
it's been strange. I did feel it coming:
the day before, I saw chalky
prefigurations in the sky, and then
the wind came up and blew first

the dust, in circles, and then
the papery-skinned men home.
We had to believe it,
but he seems not wholly returned to himself,
a thin, unconvincing copy.
He never speaks, but looks at us
in turn, in disbelief, as if
he wonders what we've done
to the family he left behind.
He's moved the furniture back,
but his old life is blown away –
he spends all day just sitting,
flexing his alien limbs, and
tapping his fingers to worn-out vinyl;
Mum can't face him, my own children hide from him . . .
You know, for years after, every night,
I waited, not accepting that he was
gone. Now I know.

My father had suffered a stroke. I often caught sight of him as I walked past the doors to the lounge, flexing the fingers of his 'alien' left hand. Although I felt very sorry for him, I was no more afraid than I had been when my mother had had cancer – less afraid, if anything: it was only a slight stroke, after all, a warning sign which he was lucky to have had. It hadn't done too much permanent damage, we thought. And he was going to give up smoking for good now, he said.

Dr B's consulting room was in a basement flat in Camden Town. I entered first into a murky corridor with a portrait of Sigmund Freud on the wall, where Dr B would meet me and show me into her consulting room. She would sit down in the chair in the corner furthest from the door while I, the patient, would take my place in a chair in the corner facing hers.

Stretched out along the wall on her right-hand side was the couch, reminding me of the proper, deeper treatment I was expected to have one day. From the first session, I felt as if I were being handled at arm's length, with tongs.

> These have not been a good few days . . . since Wednesday when I first saw Dr B, in a dark basement, where her silence drew me out, and she cut me dead after 50 therapeutic minutes. [Diary, 4/5/92]

When I said to Dr B, some time later, that I knew nothing about her, not even her theoretical orientation, she remarked drily that the portrait was probably quite a big clue. Apart from that, I knew what I could see and hear, which was that she was female, in her forties's probably, and American. I also understood from the centre that she was a senior member of the profession, a training analyst, and that the centre thought us a good match; I didn't know why, but wondered if it might be something to do with her PhD.

Dr B worked through the transference. What the word 'transference' means, precisely, or what it can be said to mean, will vary, depending upon whom you ask. Here's what the standard reference work on psychoanalytic terminology says it means:

> Transference: For psycho-analysis, a process of actualisation of unconscious wishes. Transference uses specific objects and operates in the framework of a specific relationship established with these objects. Its context *par excellence* is the analytic situation.
>
> In the transference, infantile prototypes re-emerge and are experienced with a strong sensation of immediacy.
>
> As a rule what psycho-analysts mean by the unqualified use of the term 'transference' is *transference during treatment*.

Classically, the transference is acknowledged to be the terrain on which all the basic problems of a given analysis play themselves out: the establishment, modalities, interpretation and resolution of the transference are in fact what define the cure.[17]

In order to facilitate the transference, and therefore the treatment, Freud stressed that the analyst should make herself, as far as possible, into a blank screen onto which the patient could 'project' her unconscious fantasies; the blanker the screen, the surer the analyst could be that the material projected onto it came out of the patient's early experiences and was not a product of her relationship with the individual who was treating her. An analyst should not refer to her own experience in the course of the treatment, or to her own feelings.[18] If a patient asks her anything about herself, then she should not give an answer, but rather examine what it means for the patient to be asking that question in those words in that tone of voice accompanied by that body language at that particular moment. The only admissible evidence is that which occurs between the analyst and the patient within the consulting room in the course of a fifty-minute session. Within these strict parameters, anything is admissible.

I can find precious little in my notebooks about the three years I spent with Dr B. What I remember, mostly, are those moments when we seemed to be getting on particularly badly,

17. J. Laplanche and J.B. Pontalis, *The Language of Psychoanalysis* (Karnac Books and the Institute of Psychoanalysis, London, 1988). I did try to explain it myself in an earlier draft, but tied myself up in such knots that I thought it better to leave this one to the experts. Psychoanalysis does that to you.
18. Unless these are understood to be part of the 'counter-transference', i.e. the analyst's unconscious response to the patient's transference; this is allowed to count as analytic material because, as far as the counter-transference is concerned, the patient started it.

along with the dreams I had about us. An early awkward moment just about made it into the diary. I wrote that I had arrived full of irritability, complaining about the heat and my period. She asked me what it was that I hated. I thought about my answer carefully: SQUIDGINESS, I said. Slugs.

So I hated those things where nature had let herself go, where boundaries weren't firm and sure?

Yes.

It seemed that there was some squidginess still in my mind about the arrangements. She wanted to reassure me that there was no hurry with the psychoanalysis.

Thank you.

Also, as my brother kept coming up, was I still feeling pushed away by Mrs A and her baby?

I supposed so.

Later on in the session I was enlarging on one of my favourite themes, my attitude to my body.

> I said at one point that I was not only cruel to my own body, but that I had hypercritical thoughts about other women's although I never voiced them, in compensation for my supposed super-unkindness.
>
> 'So *I* can breath a sigh of relief, then!' she said.

From that moment on, I never entirely trusted her. But I couldn't quite admit this to myself, let alone to her. I just kept turning up and saying only what I thought would be safe for her to hear. One day I spent at least a minute watching in fascinated horror as a huge, hairy spider crept across the floor, between her legs and then under her chair. She didn't ask why I was staring at her feet like that and I didn't tell her.

About nine years later, a practising psychoanalyst called A. H. Esman published a review of the analytic literature on obsessive-compulsive disorder, which he found to be severely wanting.[19] One problem he identified originated from the earliest days of the discipline, with Freud's assumption that 'obsessional neurosis' (OCD) must develop out of 'obsessional character'. This was not so unusual at the time – Janet worked under a similar assumption – but mainstream psychiatry and psychology had since revised their views according to the evidence; psychoanalysis hadn't. Even so, the psychoanalytic literature on the nature and treatment of 'the obsessive patient' is extremely interesting: I found a couple of papers by John Schimel, called 'Dialogic Analysis of the Obsessional' and 'The Power Theme in the Obsessional', which reminded me so much of my own therapy, and my behaviour during it, that I almost squirmed in my seat as I read them. These papers describe a person not unlike the clinical perfectionist who shows up for behavioural therapy, a person for whom being in the wrong is a moral and emotional catastrophe. The psychoanalytic obsessive will do anything to avoid saying, doing or thinking anything not entirely correct, and will do just as much to avoid any possibility of their being corrected.

> The obsessional lives in a world of painstaking efforts to be exactly right. He cannot tolerate being wrong and, for him, there must be a right in every matter and nuance . . . His wife is rather tall, well on the tall side, perhaps 5 feet 6 inches or closer to 5 feet 7 inches, not quite as tall as her sister, but tall compared to the average, although not outstandingly so . . . etc.[20]

*

19. A.H. Esman, 'Obsessive-Compulsive Disorder: Current Views', *Psychoanalytic Inquiry* (2001, 21: 145–56)
20. John L. Schimel, 'Dialogic Analysis of the Obsessional', *Contemporary Psychoanalysis* (1974, 10: 87–100)

While I was working at the library, I tried contact lenses. The optician put them in for the first time and asked me how they felt. How did she mean how did they feel? In terms of what? She smiled slightly. 'How does it feel,' she tried, 'in terms of *adjectives*?'

What analytic therapy requires from the patient is that she freely associates within the session – that is, that she makes available to the analyst anything and everything which comes into her head during the session which she is able to verbalize, without attempting to edit it before it comes out of her mouth. For someone, like me, who was incapable of giving a straight answer to an optician, who could 'not tolerate being wrong', this was never going to be possible. According to Schimel, unless the analyst can keep from getting drawn in, such a patient will be unable to stop herself from turning every session into a fifty-minute power struggle. As the patient's unconscious purpose is to fend off the acquisition of painful self-knowledge at any cost, the treatment is unlikely to go anywhere very fast. A dream I recorded towards the beginning of the treatment suggests that, in some part of my mind, I knew perfectly well what I was doing: 'I was pacing vigorously when I went to see Dr B. I paced the space between my chair and hers, until she suggested that I stop.'

That winter, I saw the light again. PR didn't suit me after all, not even in a charitable setting; it was less about writing, which I could do, than it was about making friends and influencing people, which – well, you know by now. I would go back to university, and this time I would do my best never to come out again. I applied for three MAs: one in applied philosophy at Hull, one in applied ethics at Aberdeen, and a third, in psycho-analytic studies, at Kent. I got three offers, and accepted the Kent option, which had two immediate advantages over the others: I could commute to my therapist from Canterbury for our weekly session, and spend the rest of the week gathering theoretical *materiél* to help me in the battle. I'm trying to remember how conscious I was of the second advantage, but I can't seem to untangle what I knew then from what I know now thoroughly enough for me to say.

MAs cost money, as does therapy, even at the heavily subsidized rates I was paying.[21] I needed to return to paid work to save up enough for my course. Once that was finished, I reasoned, I would find some funding for a PhD, start work on the PhD, and from that moment on I would never have to suffer the indignity of another proper job. To that end, I spent a couple of months crying in the kitchen of a market research company where I worked as a telephone interviewer, after which I managed one week trying to work out how to research advertising leads for a magazine publisher in Kensington before they figured out their mistake and fired me, went back to cry at the market research company for a few weeks, and, finally, got a temporary job researching a directory of euromarket borrowers for a financial publisher in the City.

It was a horrible commute but it paid well. The money I earned there, along with a big overdraft guaranteed by my parents, would cover my first year back in academe. So I phoned, faxed and photocopied my way through the late spring and early summer. I even managed a bit of banter with my temporary colleagues, laughing at pictures of orange Eurotrash in *Hello!* and eating chocolate cake when the afternoons were quiet. In August, the university accommodation office sent me a list of rooms for rent in the Canterbury area, and I made arrangements to view. I picked up another list from the Poetry Library, and looked for writers' groups in the same area. I was planning ahead for the autumn, so I knew I didn't really want to kill myself.

---

21. Many psychodynamic psychotherapists would never see a patient for free on principle, even if they were in a position to give their time for nothing, on the grounds that a patient who pays less than she can afford is less likely to commit herself fully to the therapy.

My best friend was also in a long-term therapeutic relationship. Together we would chew over our more difficult therapy sessions the way other girls might dissect their arguments with their boyfriends. It was a big joke with us that Eliot had got it totally wrong: August, not April, was 'the cruellest month'. August is the month when, in accordance with long tradition, analysts and therapists shut up shop and go off to diagnose each other at conferences. The four-walled, fifty-minute frames in which their patients have grown accustomed to being contained are temporarily withdrawn, leaving the patients and their neuroses to spill all over the place like basketloads of soiled laundry.

So you could say my feeling suicidal that August was just a matter of transferential routine. Perhaps it was. I don't have any diary entries from this time, only a couple of unpublished poems that suggest I wasn't enjoying the London summer very much.

With Ice

No, I don't need a brown beverage
To steam open my pores today,
Not when the air rises in front of me,
And the streets are grinding
corridors of noise, when
Men and women strain towards
Charing Cross, in reeking nylon,
When the river heaves, thick with dirt,
And when the train rasps across the bridge,
Groaning in chains.

I took that poem to Donaghy's workshop in July. 'Well, it's a perfectly good poem about a hot day,' he said. 'That last line seems to hint at something else, but whether it is about anything more, I couldn't say ...' Neither could I. I wrote another poem, which I didn't take to the class.

The Third One This Week

On his way down from the roof, Charles passed,
Behind the sheerness of tinted glass:
Ganglia of writing cable,
Faxes weeping ribbons,
Blinking switchboard,
Quivering screen,
Coffee – the dregs,
Gritty dregs,
Swinging
Receiver
Chiming,
'Please
Hold,
Please
Hold,
Please

I think I was anxious lest, despite the third person, the flippant tone, the formal experimentation, the syllable-counting and the general studenty showing off, I might still have failed not to communicate.

I felt trapped inside myself. I couldn't get hold of my friends on the phone: they were all out, drinking and having sex and going to raves and doing all the things I was too scared to do. I was sick of my family. I was sure that they must be sick of me, no matter what they said; my friends must be sick of me; she wouldn't say but no doubt my therapist was sick of me too. And if the people who were stuck with me already were sick of me, what chance was there of getting anyone else to love me? Surely the rational thing to do would be to call it quits before I sickened us all further. A line from a Practical Criticism paper I'd done in school kept hissing into my mind:

Take her away; for she hath liv'd too long,
To fill the world with vicious qualities.

And wasn't the world quite vicious enough without my making it even worse? The City was vilely hot, the trains groaned, the people reeked, nobody cared about anything except selling and profit, everything and everyone belonged to banks and insurance companies and here I was selling my time and labour to another project meant to make rich people richer. There were earthquakes in Japan, hurricanes over the Gulf of Mexico, and one of my colleagues was driving me mad. She sat behind me. Her efficiency was relentless; she could shriek down the phone in three languages. When she wasn't working offensively hard or forcing us to eavesdrop on her life she was performing it to us: 'I've been up ALL NIGHT with CONSTIPATION,' she'd bellow. 'I've got a FOUR-DAY BLOCKAGE!' One day I happened to be walking past her desk just as she had finished a phone conversation with her friend Françoise – *FRANÇOISE!* – and I saw that she was wiping her eyes and sniffing. I felt guilty suddenly for finding her so annoying, and asked her what the matter was.

'Françoise was on at me about my biological clock again. She said, "You're not getting any younger, you know." I know that, but – most of the time I just sweep things under the carpet, but every now and then, you know . . .'

I thought I knew. She was thirty-four, and her boyfriend hadn't proposed yet. The people closest to her were still her parents. Behind all that desperate play-acting, I imagined she had to be in despair, like me. She was trapped inside herself, like me, and like me, she had never found a safe place to be away from her family and perhaps she never would. She made no secret of the fact that she thought the world a dreadful and dangerous place: people had no manners, people had no morals, they swore, they littered, women went out in short skirts without any tights on. She would start the working day by searching the *Daily Mail* for corroborative evidence, reading the headlines aloud, and cutting the juiciest stories out to put in a sort of horror scrapbook she kept at home. One day she read out a story about the escalating violence of the battle of the sexes among young people in America. Atrocities were piling up on both sides. In one terrible example, a gang of boys had set upon a smaller group of girls, beaten them, raped them, and finally, stamped on their necks just to make sure that they were dead.

Along with my 'vicious qualities', I now had the picture and the sound of cracking neck bones to add to my argument for suicide. How could any young woman with any sensitivity stand to exist in a world where some boy somewhere was crushing some girl's vertebrae under his foot, and laughing – probably – while he did it? It was a clinching argument.

For a few weeks, I really tried, in spirit if not in body, to peel myself away from the world. I suggested to Jane in one of our phone calls that nobody would miss me if I were gone. She begged to differ – well, of course she would: it proved nothing. When I arrived home from work, I would stamp straight up the stairs, without a word to my mother, who noticed a sinister difference in me and phoned her friends about it. Then I borrowed my best friend's copy of Alvarez's cultural history of suicide, *The Savage God*, and, as I read it, I realized I didn't want to die. I was too terrified of death, of non-being, and even though I might pretend to think otherwise, I knew that my suicide would hurt other people. It wasn't for me to decide whether I was fit to be loved or not – my family were going to carry on loving me (idiots) no matter how questionable I found their taste. And it wasn't for me to judge, at twenty-three, that my life was going to amount to nothing – how could such a judgement be rational? So I stopped trying to think my way into suicide and thought my way out of it instead. I chose, quite consciously, not to die, and it's often been a comfort to remember that I did.

To a psychoanalyst, there are no such things as meaningless thoughts or pointless behaviours. Habits, mannerisms, neurotic and psychotic symptoms, dreams, slips of the tongue, accidents – all can be read and interpreted. Take, for example, the mistake I've been making again and again for the last few pages, where I've been running 1992 into 1993, and mixing up my ages of twenty-two and twenty-three. This suggests to me that I don't really want to talk about this part of my life, that at some stage I must have folded these years up very small and then archived them on the Ecclesiastical History shelves of my memory, hoping that I would never have cause to retrieve them again. I want not to have spent those years in that kind of therapy; I want to have chosen one of the other MAs. I'm not sure it's good for anyone – outside of clinical practice or literary theory – to learn as much about psychoanalysis as I did. Especially if you're the sort of person who is perfectly capable of reading too much into things without any help from Freud, Klein, Jung, Lacan and the rest. I studied them all, and I took psychoanalytic theories every bit as personally as I had taken feminist polemic.

For the first two terms, we attended weekly lectures given by a prominent Kleinian analyst. He taught us about the Kleinian psyche, red in tooth and claw. We learned about the 'primitive processes' of splitting, projection and introjection; the paranoid and depressive positions; the internalized good and bad mothers; good breasts and bad breasts; penises; vaginas; shit, blood, spit and tears. Like any natural preacher, he had the gift of using anything and everything to help him communicate his understanding of human nature. One week he read to us from a detailed eyewitness account of the gory exploits of the Spanish Conquistadors, to show us what the world looked like when our innate human capacity for cruelty was given full rein; another week, he encouraged us to see *Alien 3*, which, he said, would give us the most accurate picture of 'life in the anus'. Every week, he brought us numerous examples of neurosis and perversity from his own psyche and those of his patients.

One Friday afternoon in spring he was talking about evil, and how he had encountered it in his consulting room. He had once had a patient, a man of great outward respectability, who had spoken at length of his sexual habits and fantasies. This patient was a sadist, a 'spanker', who could only become fully aroused by spanking his female partners. Hard. The Kleinian told us how he had been sitting in his analyst's chair listening to this man explaining how he had to hit the woman hard enough to *leave a mark*, and became aware of the presence of evil in his consulting room, on the couch, emanating from this man. He went on to talk about another patient. She was quite different from the first, but listening to her had given him that same pungent sense of evil in the room. This patient was a young woman, bright, but something of a drifter. One day, she had told him, calmly, almost cheerfully, that she was wasting her life, and he had seen the evil in her at that very instant. At this point in the story, he paused for a moment or two, just to let his message sink in, and I was sure in that moment that he was looking straight at me. It was as if he had been trying to pinpoint a source of evil right there in the lecture room, and had just that second located it.

This shook me so much that I let myself cry to Dr B about it. It had already been a tough enough session, with my sadistic superego swooping at me from all four corners of the room like a harpy in a synagogue hat. I had gone off on one of my feminist rants, about how I avoided sex and relationships, because I didn't want to spend the rest of my life with my arms in the sink doing the washing-up for some *man*. Dr B interrupted me. That might be so, she said, but in the meantime I seemed happy enough to treat my mother as a servant. She said that stuff I'd been coming out with sounded like a standard piece of seventies polemic – in fact, it sounded like BALONEY!

That winded me completely, but I couldn't let Dr B see that, so I gave her the tale of Kleinian evil, and *then* I cried.

She had moved consulting rooms by then, to a second-floor flat in Primrose Hill, a tower instead of a dungeon. Things were arranged differently here. She still had her chair in the corner, but in a different corner, directly opposite the door as one came in. The room was much larger than the old one, so the patient's chair had no wall at its back, but floated all by itself in the middle of the floor, with the couch lining the wall on its left and a huge window a few feet behind. One week I told Dr B that I felt adrift in that chair, uncontained; when I arrived for my next session, there was a huge pot plant standing right next to it, providing green shelter. We did communicate, in our own way.

Dr B moved in February. Like August, it's a jinxed month for me. By the time August comes, I've already had too much of the heat and the long days. In February, I'm suffering from a surfeit of greyness, cold and rain; my sinuses are blocked and my ears are aching; the world is struggling to wake up from the winter and maybe this time it won't make it – there will come a time when none of us will make it . . . Shit happens in February. February was the month when the male sex made a collective decision and sent their messenger to tell me to FUCK OFF! Five years later, my therapist moved my symbolic container from Camden to Primrose Hill. Some of my demons escaped in transit, burrowed underground and then came up through the floor of a basement flat in Canterbury.

Actually, it was a beautiful flat. The woman who lived in and owned it, herself a graduate of the psychoanalytic MA, needed to keep up with the mortgage payments while she studied for her second Master's, so she was renting out every room but the hall, the kitchen, the two bathrooms and the box room where she slept herself. I had a long room at the back, with its own sink, a desk and chair, a wardrobe and a single bed. It would have made a sizeable living or dining room, and my stereo, my portable TV, my books, tapes and CDs barely filled a tenth of it. I'd never had so much pacing room in my life.

The landlady and I were quick to make friends: we shared a compulsive openness about ourselves and our lives; we both loved art, psychoanalytic theory, and cats. She had a little black-and-white Manx who liked to sit on my desk while I worked. My room was her favourite, and when I lifted her up to move her out of it at night she would hiss, turn her head and make as if to bite me. I loved the cat but I was scared of her too, and spent more and more time dreading the hissing moment. I got in the habit of knocking on my landlady's door, or our flatmate Scott's door, and asking one of them to take her out for me. At school, I'd always asked my science partner to light the Bunsen burner – it was the same kind of manoeuvre.

At Cambridge I had avoided the communal kitchens, mostly because it meant having to light the gas hob with a match, so I had sometimes resorted to heating tinned soup by pouring boiling water into it from the kettle, which I don't recommend. This time round, I had to cook for myself, so I did, if only sporadically, and on two gas rings. I did my own laundry too, as I had done at Cambridge. My usual garb at this time was a pair of leggings with a baggy jumper on top. Some of my baggies were handwash only, and could not be tumble-dried, so I would wash them as best I could in the tiny sink in my bedroom, wring them out and then hang them over the radiators to dry.

One afternoon the landlady knocked on my door. 'Come out here for a moment,' she said.

She pointed to a long, baggy blue jumper hanging on the radiator in the hall, and then to the puddle below it.

'Your jumper has created a flood.' Nobody had told me – and I had never figured out – that after you handwash a garment

118

you need to roll it up in a towel to get rid of the water before you hang it up.

I was trying to be better, I really was. I was cooking – a little – and taking care of my own diet – sort of. I was working more consistently than I had for years, reading what needed to be read, and handing in what had to be handed in, and even if the work wasn't as brilliant as I'd wanted it to be, handing it in at all was enough of a victory for the time being. I was commuting faithfully to London every Monday to play headgames with Dr B. When she moved, and my demons fell out, it was almost too much to bear. It was all I could do to hold myself together. On top of that, I was still smarting from coming back from the Christmas holidays to find that my stereo had been left on for the whole holidays, and had a burned-out sound stage. I had said that anyone still in the flat was welcome to use it, and this was how I was repaid. My landlady swore that no one else had used it, that I must have forgotten to switch it off myself before I left. Perhaps I had, but I wasn't buying it. I didn't like our newest flatmate either, but everyone else loved him, so I kept my mouth shut. And my door. I would try to keep myself and my bad mood in quarantine until it left me and I was fit for human consumption again.

I had been in the habit of sitting and talking with my flat-mates in the kitchen, but the kitchen had become quite unpleasant to be in. There was too much washing-up in the sink. Every time I needed a plate, I had to take one out of the sink and wash it. I remember muttering about that too.

One day the landlady told me that she needed a word. The problem was that I – and only I – had been leaving my washing-up in the sink, and she for one felt shat upon. The new flatmate especially had been getting really upset, and had asked her to speak to me about it. I said it can't have just been me. She said maybe I'd disavowed it, maybe I'd *split* it, but it really had only been me. I felt cornered, so I cried. I cried about how hard I

119

found it just to get up in the morning, how I felt that everyone was judging me. She said nobody else was, but that I judged myself very harshly, and I really shouldn't; I was beautiful and talented and I would come good in the end. In the meantime, she would clean up the mess I'd left in the kitchen, and then we would all start again. I ran into my new flatmate in the kitchen after it had been cleaned and he said, 'I see there is a new deal in the kitchen. Good.' I found him patronizing and a little bit creepy to boot. But I couldn't say so.

I couldn't let go of the washing-up. I bearded my landlady in her clean kitchen and said that I was upset. It couldn't just have been me – anyway, she'd made too much of it, sometimes cigars were just cigars and washing-up was just washing-up, and besides someone had broken my stereo. She blew up: no one but me had broken my stereo, no one but me had left their dirty dishes all over the place; washing-up was not just washing-up – it was my aggression and my shit, and if I didn't realize that it was just me, then that was because I'd split it. 'I hate to say it, but you strike me as someone who's never grown up, and I'm not your mother and neither is anyone else here.'

Scott came into the kitchen with a mug and stood there for a moment, looking from her angry face to my stricken one, and back again. I said, 'OK,' in a very quiet voice, and left.

I've always tied my hair back at night. For the last few years, I've used the same cheap hairbands from Superdrug. They come in black or white, and have a small metal ring at the point where the circle closes. I keep some on my bedside table, some in my handbag, a couple on my dressing table, and a few on the floor under the bed. Sometimes I need to rummage through my handbag in the street. On my street, in the streets round about, outside the local shops, and all over town, I see these ponytail rings lying around. Every time I see one, I wonder if I was the person who dropped it, and spoiled the town for everybody. I'm sure that lots of other women use them and that in all proba-

120

bility the other women dropped some too, but then, who knows what I'm capable of? I certainly don't.

The money ran out after two terms. I moved back in with my parents, and did the London–Canterbury commute in reverse to attend the last few lectures, and discuss my dissertation topic. I had taken a course on Jung and his followers in the spring term. Jung's writings held the kind of appeal for me that Narnia and traditional English hymns had had in primary school: I loved the colour, the myths and the drama. I was especially taken with Jung's model of the alchemical transformation as a metaphor for the creative process. At the same time, I was reading more of Milner's writings on creativity, which she saw as essential not only to art, but also to the theory and practice of psychoanalysis, and to the living of life in general. This is not unusual for a psychoanalyst – one psychoanalytic dictionary defines creativity as 'the capacity to arrive at novel but valid solutions to problems'[22] – but Milner is notable both for the sheer number of pages she devotes to the subject, and to the high valuation she places on creativity as a personal quality. I began to look for secondary literature on Milner. Among other things, I found a paper in one of the Jungian journals called 'Metaphors of the Therapeutic Encounter', which reminded me of a comment of Milner's about how she and a patient had been 'confronting each other in the crucible of the analytic room', and which confirmed a tentative decision I'd made.

My supervisor was staggered: 'Milner and *alchemy*?' Alchemy was a Jungian idea, and Milner was a member of the British Independent Object-Relations School. Not only would it be difficult to square the two bodies of theory – however much Jungians like Milner, and they do – but I would need a

22. Charles Rycroft, *A Critical Dictionary of Psychoanalysis* (Penguin, Harmondsworth, 1972)

second supervisor for the Jungian bits, as this was outside her area. Might it not be more straightforward, she suggested, in the limited time available, to stay within the confines of the British tradition of psychoanalysis, and discuss Milner's work in relation to earlier writings on creativity and symbol formation? I took her advice. I returned the book of alchemical imagery I'd borrowed from the university library, and wrote a dissertation comparing Milner's views to those of her predecessors Ernest Jones and Melanie Klein. The result was workmanlike, but dull. Its title was 'The Free Play of Boundaries'. The irony was unintentional.

The best bits of my dissertation are those where I stop trying to be the good, thorough little student and just stick in a great big, juicy Milner quote, like this one:

> It follows that the aim of healthy living is not the direct elimination of conflict which is possible only by forcible suppression of one or other of its antagonistic components, but the toleration of it – the capacity to bear the tensions of doubt and of unsatisfied need and the willingness to hold judgement in suspense until finer and finer solutions can be discovered which integrate more and more the claims of both sides.[23]

The toleration of doubt – is that the opposite of OCD?

23. Marion Milner, *The Suppressed Madness of Sane Men: Forty-Four Years of Exploring Psychoanalysis* (Tavistock Publications, Inc., London and New York, 1987)

Sin

32. When I start thinking of certain things, I become obsessed with them.

The Padua Inventory

———

The snow was deep and beautiful. When we got to the Newsstand we were cold. Sorrel ordered a *cafelatte* and I had a hot chocolate. We sat at a small table by the window and opened our notebooks. No one else was there but Sorrel and me and the woman behind the counter.

'Okay, let's write about sex for fifteen minutes,' I said boldly.

Natalie Goldberg, Wild Mind

There are depressive ruminations, and then there are obsessive, or anxious ones. Depressive ruminations are typically past-orientated ('If only I hadn't gone to that party and opened my big mouth – then I'd never have made such an idiot of myself') while obsessive ruminations tend to be projections into the future ('What if I go to that party, feel nervous, drink too much, open my big mouth and make an idiot of myself'?) Speaking from personal experience, I find this an unsatisfactory distinction, as it doesn't quite capture the flavour of my own most brain-consuming ruminations. I've tried to parse these, to figure out exactly which tense I'm ruminating in when I'm ruminating at my worst, but they didn't seem to fit in with any tense I could name, so I had a look online.

It turns out that I've been ruminating in the past unreal conditional tense, imagining counterfactual histories, those scenarios that didn't happen, but could have done. Depressive ruminations are in the past unreal conditional tense too, but these can usually be expressed as 'upward' counterfactual statements, such as: 'If I had worked harder at school, I would have done so much better for myself.' The kind of ruminations I'm talking about, on the other hand, are most accurately expressed as 'downward' counterfactual statements, for example: 'If my parents had not been prepared to support me for so long, things would have been so much worse.' My limited reading would suggest that thoughts of this form are supposed to make you feel better, grateful for your blessings and appreciative of your achievements and better qualities.

I haven't found too much so far about the downward counterfactual thoughts that leave you fearful and guilty, so if you don't mind, I'll fill in some of the gaps myself. Here are some examples of the nastier downward counterfactual:

This is the first spike I can remember acquiring. I was thirteen, on a summer holiday in Devon. It was a beautiful blue and green, fuchsia-scented day, and we were taking a walk around the cliff tops of whichever cove or bay we were staying in. I was out in front, and approached a gate with a stile. I was about to step over it and ever so absent-mindedly carry on walking when I realized with a jolt that the grass ran out suddenly just a few feet away on the other side, and ended in a sheer drop. It only took me a split second to notice this, and pull back again, but then it wouldn't have taken much longer, I reasoned, to keep walking and dreaming until I fell over the cliff edge, and ended up dashed to pieces on the jagged rocks, after which the pieces would slide bloodily down the rocks and into the churning sea. It only showed *how easily these things could happen if you were so stupid as to relax your vigilance for a nanosecond.* Once this alternative and fatal scenario had started playing in my head, it repeated and repeated and repeated, like a 1970s public information film on continuous loop. It wasn't on my mind every waking second, but from then onwards, a dozen associations might lead to it, and then a hundred could, and then a thousand more.

Here's another of my top ten downward counterfactuals. Between my second and third years at Cambridge, I went on a cycling holiday round Ireland with two friends. It didn't go well: I found cycling on the roads terrifying, hated roughing it in youth hostels, kept squabbling with one of the other holiday cyclists, got so sunburned and midge-bitten that within two days I had forearms like bright pink novelty candles and suffered all the way through from terrible constipation because I could never relax enough on an unfamiliar toilet. Somehow, though, I kept going west with the others, moving from Dun Laoghaire to Waterford, then to Cahir and Cashel, on to Cork, Tralee and at last to Dingle, as far west as we could go.

I'm guessing, though I don't remember, that we spent a night in a hostel in Dingle. What I do remember is that when we set off again the next morning, I was feeling thoroughly sorry for myself: we were going to have to push our bicycles for five miles up the Connor Pass, we hadn't slept well, we had been quarrelling incessantly and my constipation was all I could think about – my stomach was full of concrete and would never clear and neither would my head.

We were pushing our bicycles up one of the main streets in Dingle. It was quite a slope, my bicycle – which was a totally unsuitable, thick-framed, small-wheeled town shopper – felt as heavy as a juggernaut, my eyelids wanted to close, my lower abdomen was aching, my head was down, I was filled with sorrow and pity and all of it for myself.

Suddenly the bike juddered; my front wheel had hit something. It was the bottom of a ladder. I looked up and there was a red, furious face at the top of it, shouting something I couldn't understand. I muttered sorry and walked on in tears, shocked and thoroughly ashamed of myself.

That was all that happened. But if I had hit the ladder

harder and knocked the man off, then he would have fallen backwards, probably into the road, perhaps to his death – or he might have broken his back at the very least, and never been able to work or walk again. The whole town would converge on me, shouting. I would be taken into police custody and charged with . . . reckless walking with a bicycle? I would become a hated figure in Ireland, the emblem of the selfish English student tourist bringing back bitter memories of colonial oppression by her cavalier maiming of a good, hard-working Irishman. They would all push for the maximum penalty. At the very least, I would never be allowed back into Ireland again.

I have never been back. Anything connected with Ireland has been a spike ever since.

And here's one of slightly more recent vintage. I finished my MA, which I passed without distinction or even merit, worked as a clerical assistant at a trade association in the West End for four miserable months, and then moved up to Edinburgh to live the life of a writer. While I was there, I lost my virginity to, and had a brief affair with, a married man. Supposedly, I was his wife's friend as well, but my behaviour suggested otherwise. Anyway, we slept together a handful of times, they moved away and she hadn't found out. I lost touch with both of them. That was all that happened.

But what if she had burst in and discovered us? Perhaps she would have gone for me physically – I knew she had a violent temper; at any rate she had told me that she had. She might have grabbed a knife and slit my face so that I would always be ugly and no one would ever find me attractive again. I would never have got married if that had happened.

Or perhaps she would have thrown me, butt naked, out of whichever flat she'd found us in and slammed the door. A naked woman in a public place, I would then have been set upon by some hideous characters newly escaped from an Irvine Welsh novel, who would have opportunistically raped, beaten me and left me for dead. At the very least, the neighbours would have heard the fracas and called the police. Once the police had been called, whether I was slit up, naked, or both, the situation would become public. It would reach the papers. The headline would have been something like: 'ANGRY WIFE THROW'S [SIC] HUSBAND'S MISTRESS OUT NAKED' or 'JEALOUS WIFE KNIFES LOVE RIVAL' or maybe there'd just be a picture of me, slit up and/or naked, captioned: 'THE WAGES OF SIN' or 'MAN-SNATCHING "FRIEND" GETS HERS'.

My whole extended family would have to leave the country. Naturally, they would choose to leave me behind.

Now I come to think of it, there is an added imperative element to the past unreal conditional tense in this last scenario: this is what *should* have happened. A crime unpunished or inadequately repented of is an incomplete act, an uncorrected error, an unpicked spot.

I'd kept all other writing in abeyance while I was concentrating on my MA, but I took a break from my dissertation that summer to go on a residential poetry course in the West Country. At my first meeting with the two poet-tutors, I said that what I had come for was help to break my 'writer's block'. They set me an exercise: write a poem, in three stanzas of four tetrameters, about a day in the park. So I did.

Ice-Cream

The gleaming whorls of animal fat
are slithering down cones and arms,
but she prefers to contemplate
the river's mouthwash blue, fresh

127

as an iced drink thrown in the face.
She shudders off the licking sun,
keeping her body a Winter stone
in rivers of chocolate, light, and sweat

for it only takes one button-hole
to leak one drop, and the park and day
will melt into puddles of hot fudge sauce,
slapping round naked, embarrassed knees.

When I read this out to the tutors and the other students on the last evening, they agreed that one of the things that made my poetry so striking was its honesty. They had known me for all of five days.

But I'd had enough of life as a Winter stone. I was fed up with trying to appease my Great-Aunt Superego. Nothing had worked: the library had been a purgatory, the PR had only revealed further weaknesses, and I was obviously not destined for scholarly greatness. I'd had therapy, but I didn't feel much better for it. I was nearly twenty-five, and all my attempts to be a normal person had failed, so perhaps it was time to come out as a writer. My mother had told me repeatedly during my adolescence that writers were people who found that they couldn't do anything else. It seemed I really was one of those weirdos. Writing professionally had the added advantage that people expect writers – poets especially – to be all neurotic and peculiar; in fact, if you appear something like normal, they are disappointed and a bit suspicious.

Counterfactually, I could have simply stayed where I was, worked to earn money, continued attending the workshops at City which I had returned to, and got on with the business of writing. Instead, I decided to escape from my entire life and leave London. I got a place on the MA in creative writing at St Andrews. It was as far away as I could get but it was still a professional qualification, which would placate the great-aunt if she found me and came to visit. The problem with the plan was a practical one: I had only just worked myself out of debt, and there was no funding available for the course, or any guarantee of earning as a result of it.

At one of my cousin's parties, I met a couple of writers from Edinburgh who were into Zen Buddhism and transgressive fiction. I told them about my plans, and Mr Zen said, 'If you want to move to Scotland and write, why don't you just move to Scotland and write?' adding, 'How many more books do you have to read before you start writing?' If I ever found the nerve, they said, I could make use of their spare room.

In April, my three-year term of psychoanalytic psychotherapy (preparatory to entering full analysis) came to an end. I told the therapist that I was moving to Scotland to write: she wasn't dumping me – it was the other way round. So watch my dust.

Now that writing was to be my work, rather than an escape from it, I tried to write every day. This is part of the journal entry I wrote on my way up to Edinburgh:

> . . . that was one hell of a morning. Mum and Dad were set to deliver me to King's Cross. Then Dad lost control of the car round about 11. He first reversed suddenly, ripping a very old flowering bush off its trunk and smashing one of the lights at the front of a parked car, then shot forward, mercifully through the narrow aperture (never noticed before – points on the Tyne do actually <u>dance</u>, jump up and down) between a cherry tree and another parked car, leaving a skid mark across the pavement before knocking the edge off our neighbour's hedge and slamming into the back of his car which was parked in a driveway, forcing it, crunch, through the wooden double garage doors.

So I took a cab to the station and forgot my coat, which my uncle had to send on in a parcel. My father went to the doctor who diagnosed a transient ischaemic attack, a kind of mini stroke. Just another reminder to be careful, to stay on the exercise bike and off the cigarettes we sometimes found in his coat pockets.

Mr Zen had lent me a book called *Wild Mind: Living the Writer's Life* by Natalie Goldberg. Goldberg is a Zen Buddhist and creative writing guru. The fundamental principles she teaches are not dissimilar to those you might read in *The Artist's Way*, or any number of other books in the creative writing section of your local bookshop, but that's because they are good principles: write every day, and when you do your 'writing practice', keep your hand moving and don't judge or edit your writing as it comes out. Just keep your hand moving. 'Give yourself permission,' she says, 'to write badly.' What you see published is just the polished tip of the iceberg: to find your way to a good piece of work, you have to write an awful lot of rubbish first. Thirteen years down the line, I can confirm the truth of this: it can take me as many as twelve or thirteen drafts to get a poem right, and you can barely imagine the great slag heap that's building up on the right-hand side of *this* manuscript.

By 'keeping your hand moving', or 'freewriting' or 'hotpenning' or whatever other term you use for the practice, and writing as if no one will ever read it, you are able to come out with your real feelings, real thoughts – to encounter the real nature of your mind, much as Marion Milner did in her experiments. 'We need to accept our minds,' says Goldberg. 'Believe me, for writing, it is all we have.'[24] What that mind is stocked with, Goldberg and Mr Zen liked to remind me, is first and

24. Natalie Goldberg, *Wild Mind: Living the Writer's Life* (Random House, London, 1991, p. 53)

foremost one's own lived experience. Start with that, then see where you can take it. But in my case, Mr Z added, 'What are you supposed to write about, when you don't have a life?' I took this very much to heart, as I took many things, and I was coming up to Scotland to find one.

It was exhilarating, this getting-a-life business. I remember a song that was playing everywhere that summer, 'Wake Up Boo' by the Boo Radleys. One of the verses began: 'Twenty-five/ don't recall a time I felt this alive.'

I was twenty-five, and I was waking up.

And what is it that wakes Sleeping Beauty? In the earlier versions of the tale, it's more than a kiss. To help procure me a life, Mr and Mrs Zen introduced me to their circle of anti-bourgeois friends. Among them was another married pair, who adopted me in their turn. She would spend the afternoons with me, showing me the best cafes and taking me shopping for bohemian clothing, and he would sit up with me late into the night, talking and listening, and drinking herbal tea. I felt relaxed with him, and opened up: after all, he was married to a friend of mine, which had to be a guarantee of safety. Then one night, after I'd been lamenting my lack of a sexual history, and enumerating all the physical faults I believed were to blame, he came up, as it were, on my blind side, and kissed me. After I had swapped the Zens' spare room for a room in a cheap-but-grubby student flat in Newington, we took it further. I was thoroughly ashamed of my stale virginity and here was a volunteer to help rid me of the stigma. We had sex three or four times. On one occasion, we began to have it unprotected, but quickly thought better of it. That's as much as I'm telling you, and if it hadn't been necessary to the story, I wouldn't have told you anything. I've never understood how people with any relatives still living can bring themselves to write about their sex lives.

Joan Rivers has a definition of a Jewish porn movie: 'Ten

131

minutes – the sex; two hours – the guilt!' My physical relationship with the married man amounted to no more than a handful of encounters, but for a couple of months he was a constant presence in my head, and the notebooks I've kept from that time are full of him. I wrote a couple of poems about my obsession, which, for all our sakes, I won't reproduce here. Any more-than-friendly feelings I might have had for him petered out after those few months, but the guilt is with me right now, thrashing about in the pit of my stomach. What bothered me then, and bothers me still, is not the sex as such, but rather that I had committed an act about which I could never be, at all times and to all people, thoroughly, scrupulously and immaculately honest. Particularly not to his wife, whose friend I claimed to be. That summer, I dreamed about her coming after me with an axe, the latest incarnation of my pitiless superego. But as time went on, I began to feel less afraid about what she might do to me and more sorry about what I'd done to her. My dreams changed accordingly. A couple of years down the line, I wrote this:

Study in Watercolour

Since I became the Other Woman,
my dreams have been as slippery as conscience,
scenes that shift in watercolour

form, unform and run together.
I'm a charcoal mark, ingrained,
the one fixed point in a landscape

that pours like rain through a gutter.
I expect a storm and one appears:
a black cumulus in the shape of a wife.

I brace myself
for a fist like a thunderclap,
but as she grows towards me,

I can see that she is crying
and the tears are washing her face away,
taking the dream with it.

I wake to a voice softer than water:
How could you do this to me?
How could you do it . . .?

A few weeks after I'd had my virginity removed, I met
another writer, a Scottish country lad made good in the urban
literary world, a latter-day Ettrick Shepherd. His writing was
wonderful, he talked wonderfully about it, he was successful
and personable, he was unmarried – he seemed perfect.
Egged on by Mr Zen, I phoned him and arranged to meet up.
Four vodkas, two enchiladas and a chaste cab ride later, I knew
that he *was* perfect, and that I had to be madly in love. He
phoned me at work the next morning, to ask after my head. We
met up again, in a pub. He said he had a few things to sort out,
a few girls, and then perhaps . . . Oh, but he was worth waiting
for, and how sweet of him to put so much thought into how he
was going to let the others down. I kept taking his phone calls
and meeting him in pubs. So did Molly, a new single
friend from the Zen circle. And various other women I didn't
know.

There was always going to be some reason why he couldn't
go out with me properly, why he couldn't do any more than
phone me, meet me in pubs and drop me home at closing time;
the reason, in the end, was that I had gone and lost my virginity,
and so very recently, to someone else – a married someone, a
married someone who lived in that very town. As I did not think

133

it proper to keep any secrets from any man who might be the love of my life, I told him absolutely everything. He was appalled: how could I have had unprotected sex with that man? Didn't I realize that he'd once been a heroin user? Didn't I know how things were in Edinburgh? Now here I was, for all we knew, sitting on a pub bench with a ton of HIV-INFECTED POR-RIDGE running through my veins.

The first popular book on OCD, *The Boy Who Couldn't Stop Washing*, was published in the States in the late eighties. The author is Judith L. Rapoport, an experienced psychiatrist with a special interest in the illness. She gives AIDS its own chapter. It is, she says, 'an illness made to order for OC victims'.[25] An invisible but deadly contaminant, the HIV virus gives 'washers' the perfect reason to keep washing. Even if you're not one to wash, it is still a horribly plausible means by which you might inadvertently harm those closest to you. It is something you could pick up without realizing it and without meaning to. If you are concerned enough, you could go and get yourself tested, but you would need to be tested again three months later to be absolutely sure, and even then, no test is 100 per cent reliable, and even if it were, how could you be sure that, somewhere along the line, some administrator or technician hadn't mixed everyone's results up? And on top of all that, 'AIDS is a judgment, suggesting sexual transgression, and illegal and immoral acts. It causes hideous shame and discrimination. It is so terrifying, so irrational that it could have been the creation of an obsessive-compulsive's worst fantasy' [ibid, p. 164]. And don't bother to point out how much treatments for HIV have improved since Rapoport wrote those lines – you know that's not the point.

*

25. Judith L. Rapoport, *The Boy Who Couldn't Stop Washing* (Penguin, New York, 1989, p. 63)

One of the employment agencies I'd visited had found me a four-month posting at the Scottish and Northern Irish branch of a broadcasting monitoring company, working in sales and customer services. It only paid about £9,500 a year, but I got to call myself a 'Sales Executive', which at least looked better on my CV than 'Clerical Assistant'. My job was to sell tapes and transcripts of radio and TV news items to interested organizations, as soon as possible after they had been broadcast, and before any of the company's competitors could get there first. My hours were from 7.45 in the morning to 4.15 in the afternoon. I would get up at 6.30 every morning and hope that the walk across town would wake me up sufficiently to avoid disgracing myself. After my work finished, I would go home and write, or try to. Then I would have to go to bed several hours earlier than any of my student flatmates, and get up at intervals to ask them to turn their stereos down.

My Scottish spring had turned into a hot, uncomfortable summer, with a turgid, sticky heat at least as bad as anything I'd trudged through in London. Sweating at my office desk one day, I found I had an itchy middle, which I couldn't stop scratching. When I went to the bathroom to inspect the area, I found a large, pinkish plaque in the crease of my waist. It didn't look like heat rash, or hives. Maybe it was an insect bite, but what kind of monstrous fly could inflict something that size? I was none the wiser, and kept scratching. The next day I had a chain of them, all the way round, so I had to keep twisting in my office chair in order to scratch properly.

That evening, in my stew of a rented room, I put the phone down after a long conversation with Molly, and scratched some more: on my stomach, round my collarbone, then under my bra, then my waist again, then my arm . . . I pulled my T-shirt up and started: I looked as if I had been rolling naked in a nettle patch. I spent the hot night, pyjama-less and duvet-less, desperately seeking a cool and dry patch on the sheet. Next day, the rash had spread down my thighs and up my neck. I went to see my latest doctor, and she asked to see my back.

'Oh yes,' she said. 'You've got a Christmas tree there.' Then she pulled a big textbook off a shelf and showed me a picture of someone else with a similar tree on their back. It was a rash which followed the pattern of the nerves, she explained. I had pityriasis rosea, a pretty common skin infection. Students often got it from living in dirty flats and not washing their clothes properly. It would clear up by itself after a while. In the meantime, there was always calamine lotion.

It took weeks to fade. During the day, I wore loose dresses, sweated and scratched. At night, I painted myself calamine-pink all over – this cooled all my tiny fires for a few minutes at least – and lay naked on the bed, stretched out in all directions like a cross on the Saltire. When it faded, my skin was softer than it had been for a long time – I hadn't felt like picking.

A couple of days after I saw the doctor, I met Molly for tea in the Elephant House on George IV Bridge, and told her all about my skin. She was fascinated: 'That's so *weird*! I wonder why your immune system just *went* like that?'

My IMMUNE SYSTEM! The INFECTED POR-RIDGE. It had to be my punishment, it had to be a CONVERSION TRAUMA.

Jane was now a junior doctor. I phoned her in a panic and she told me that I would have to be the unluckiest woman in the world if this were the case. 'And anyway, if I were an HIV virus, I'd choose something a bit more esoteric than that.'

I wasn't reassured. It was the words IMMUNE and INFECTED that kept repeating on me: as I walked to work, as I tried to write, as I tried to sleep, as I showered in the flat's disgustingly filthy bathroom.

'Pityriasis rosea?' asked one of my flatmates. 'Oh, I had that!'

At the end of the summer, the manager came back from her

maternity leave, the sales executive who'd been covering for her went back to his old job, and I negotiated a permanent part-time contract with the company. It suited me, because I had more time to write, and it suited them, because I was cheap, and, in an early-morning business, doing barely less work for them than I had been doing full time. In the autumn, I moved to a cheaper room in another filthy flat, nearer to work and only incidentally nearer to the flat where the Ettrick Shepherd laid his crook. Had I been less insistent on being in love with him, I think I might have enjoyed his company a good deal more: he was very funny, very knowledgeable, full of wonderful stories, enthusiastic about my poetry and a source of invaluable writing advice. At his suggestion, I began to keep a written record of my submissions to poetry magazines. I still have that notebook – a tatty green exercise book with 'SUBMISSIONS' written on the front – and there are still a few blank pages left at the back. Turning to the front, the first five entries are crossed through entirely, but on the fourth page I've listed a submission to an Edinburgh-based journal called *Ibid*. I had sent three poems to the editors at the end of September, and one of them, an eight-line poem entitled 'Hummers', which I had written at the City workshop, has a tick next to it. My first publication.

So I kept writing, kept attending workshops in the Scottish Poetry Library, and kept sending poems out. I became good friends with Catherine, another young poet I met at the library workshops. We met at least once a week to share our poems, helping each other to decide which ones were good enough to send out, cheering each other on when our work was accepted, and commiserating when our poems came back rejected. I got my second acceptance the following January, by which time I had moved again, this time to a tiny back room in a flat which had a magnificent view of Holyrood Park from its living-room window, and a contrasting view over the Edinburgh–London rail route at the back. The Holyrood view was one of the perks of the place; besides that, it was just round the corner from Catherine, and I had the whole flat to myself on weekdays. The owner made a weekly commute to Aberdeen, and spent his weekends in Edinburgh. He was a friendly man, who introduced me to his social circle, liked having company in his flat at weekends, and liked to talk: he would start telling me all about his journey back from Aberdeen as soon as he came in through the door on a Friday night, told me about his plans for Saturday night over breakfast on Saturday morning, and filled me in about how the night had gone over breakfast on Sunday. Once, as an experiment, I sat holding a broadsheet newspaper spread out full in front of my face, to see if it would interrupt the flow of talk in my direction – it made no difference.

That was the weekend. During the week, for the first time in my life, I lived alone. I watched what I wanted to watch on the TV, listened to my own music in any room in the flat, sat up late at the living-room table writing and left my work spread out ready for the next afternoon. Sometimes Catherine came to the flat. More often I went out to meet her, or Molly, or one of my old flatmates, or my newest friend, Maria, whom I'd met through the loquacious landlord. More often than not, I was by myself, and at night, invariably so.

The married man was long gone and the Ettrick Shepherd was spending the winter abroad. Mr and Mrs Zen had left town too. I'd had a boyfriend – a proper, official one – very briefly after we had got together at the Zens' leaving do, but the relationship – if you can call it that – had fizzled out after a couple of weeks. This was only partly because I had finally achieved a drunken fumble with the Shepherd, and then couldn't refrain from a tearful confession to my new man. It was more that we soon realized we had little in common, disagreed about most things and, when it came to it, didn't really like each other. We soon slid out of sync and out of temper, then we broke up, and before I knew it, my newly gained belief that it was physically possible for me to have sex was gone. Over the next year, I answered the odd personal ad – I even placed one – but nothing came of it. Summer was over. The only new people I was meeting were my landlord's friends and – Maria aside – we had little to say to each other. I stopped accepting his invitations to join him on his Saturday nights. Mostly I spent them in the flat with a bag of chips and a video. He shook his head at me: 'If you're not careful, life is going to pass you by.'

Sometimes I did go out – sometimes Maria even managed to drag me into a nightclub, get a drink down me and persuade me to dance. These experiences only confirmed what I'd always suspected, which was that a night spent bumping into drunken, sweaty bodies in an overheated room while trying to hear yourself talk over deafening music just wasn't fun for a person of my type. I could add it to my growing list of things which were not fun, which already included: drinking in basement bars until chucking-out time and getting filthy looks from the staff while you do it; sleeping with people you barely know; sharing a rancid student flat with a drug-dealer whose mates stink up the communal kitchen cooking full breakfasts at peculiar hours, or else propose to you while under the influence of strong hallucinogens; taking a call from an angry, drunken friend at midnight and spending the next half-hour persuading him that beating up a flatmate of yours who had once been a friend of his but had fallen out with him and now didn't want him visiting the flat would be neither an honourable, necessary nor even an acceptable course; turning up for work hungover; reporting to a police incident room to look at photographs of the young woman whose body had been found shoved down a pipe in the building directly across the road from yours; lying to people; reading Irvine Welsh. I had fast-forwarded through my long-delayed adolescence and now I needed to hibernate for a while.

So I sat in and wrote. I sat in with my Walkman, the TV and bags of chips. I attended a beginner's workshop on Buddhist meditation and spent most of the session trying and failing to sit with my legs crossed the right way. I had a consultation with a Jungian analyst; we agreed that I couldn't afford her but she got me in touch with a counselling trainee who was willing to see me, for £10 a session, once a week. Her main job at that time was as director of the Scottish branch of an employees' association, so I would go to see her in her large, pleasant office in their building near the east end of George Street. This was a very different experience from my therapy with the Freudian. The counsellor – let's call her Linda – was not wedded to any particular set of theoretical constructs, and her therapeutic boundaries were considerably less rigid. We remained friends after I left Edinburgh. Recently, I phoned her after a long gap and told her about this book, and the OCD diagnosis. 'That figures,' she said. I asked if it was something she'd diagnosed in me herself, without saying as much to me at the time. She replied that she didn't think or work in those terms, but she did remember my talking one day about how in my poems, every word had to be the right word, and in the right place, and thinking how obsessive that sounded. I said that I remembered her pointing out how often I used words like 'should' and 'ought' when I talked about myself. She always tried to encourage me to be kinder.

My first Scottish winter was, even by local standards, exceptionally tough. The whole country froze. Three Lothian towns with wonderful names – Prestonpans, Cockenzie and Tranent – spent days without power. One morning, I saw a strange rainbow-like ring in the sky as I walked to the bus stop: it was a nacreous cloud, something only seen in the coldest conditions. Another morning – or was it the same morning? – I set off for work with wet hair and arrived at the office sporting a headful of icicles.

Spring came around, but only in the literal sense. The boss's deputy left to pursue a writing career and I returned to full-time work as his successor. The rate of pay was no higher than it had been first time round, but I had been getting more overdrawn each month, so I was grateful for the extra work – until a few weeks in, when I had another of my blinding flashes and realized that I couldn't stand to work in a horrible, pointless job just for the money a minute longer than I had to. I was fed up with Edinburgh altogether: it hadn't delivered a great new me, it already contained too many people I wanted to avoid, and I was still pining over the Shepherd, who was about to get married – and not to me. I did what I usually did when I felt stuck: I began to collect prospectuses. I was going to train – don't laugh – as a careers adviser.

I applied for three courses: two in Nottingham and Edinburgh, which didn't begin until January and so wouldn't interview me until late September; another in Huddersfield, which began in autumn but could interview late candidates in early September. The first day of September was a Sunday, and I was busy preparing my presentation for the Huddersfield interview on the fourth. I phoned my mother to tell her how I was getting on. We chatted for a bit and then she passed the phone to my father. We spoke for maybe five or ten minutes, in our usual bantering way. Then he passed the phone back to Mum. We discussed my application for a little longer, then I said goodbye and put the phone down.

Grief

38. When I hear about a disaster, I think it is somehow my fault.

The Padua Inventory

_____

> Life is hard
> and so am I
> You'd better give me something
> so I don't die
> Novocaine for the soul
> before I splutter out.

'Eels'

The phone rang at 6.30 the next morning, a very bad time for phones to ring. I picked it up; it was my mother, with a shredded voice: 'I'm sorry, there's no nice way to tell you this, darling – Dad died last night.'

That was what she called my grandfather, so I asked, 'Whose dad?'

'Your dad.'

Oh.

Sometime in early adulthood – before or after his national service, I'm not sure – my father spent two years' worth of evenings lying on the sofa in his parents' front room, watching television. Before that he had been a keen gymnast, but had injured his shoulder and given it up. He had stopped playing the piano too, although the reams of unplayed Chopin and Liszt we had lying around years later always suggested to me that he must have once been quite good at it, good enough to have *persevered*. He had wanted to be a research chemist, but his parents had taken him out of the grammar school sixth form where he was failing at A level science, and his Uncle Derek had found him a place as an accountancy trainee. He never bothered studying for the exams, and passed them third time round.

There are bright people with loving families who succeed in sabotaging their lives, but to do a really thorough job you need to be both sicker and more single-minded about it than my father or his daughter ever were. After a while his sister Marian pulled him off the sofa and back into a social life. They went on holidays abroad; he stood in front of cameras and smiled his handsome smile; he bought a red MG and courted my mother in it; he married my mother, sold the MG and fathered two children, of whom he couldn't have been more proud. He read a lot of science fiction and ate a lot of sweets. He smoked and then gave up and then started smoking again. He made some bad professional decisions. He was an excellent auditor but no kind of businessman, lousy at self-promotion, and the sort of man clients found it easy to forget to pay. He hated his work, but he had a family to support, and that's what he did. I realize now what a remarkable achievement that was, and just how much it cost him. He had a family to support, and his growing dead weight.

If I've got my foreshadowing right, this should be less of a shock to you than it was to me. Even leaving aside the fact that he was only sixty-two and I was only twenty-six,[26] he could hardly have chosen a more inconvenient time to die, at least from my point of view. I was just about to move again, this time to a room in a flat just off the Meadows where I would be helping a former flatmate to pay his new mortgage, and my boss

26. At the time I couldn't help wondering if this mirroring of the digits in our respective ages had some sinister hidden significance.

had gone on holiday that very morning, leaving me in charge for the week. But Jews bury their dead quickly, almost as quickly as Muslims, so there was nothing for it but to throw a few clothes in a bag and head straight for the station. When I got to the ticket office, I found that I couldn't think ahead any more, so I asked for a single. The man behind the desk, who was only trying to save me money, kept asking me when I planned to return – in a few days? I said I didn't know. A few weeks? I didn't know. Within a month? I DIDN'T KNOW! So he sold me a single, I left a message on the answerphone at work and then I got on a train. It was a miserable, sweaty journey. I was wearing a black hoodie over my summer dress and the train was packed. Halfway to London I had to shut myself in the loo for a few minutes and wash under my arms. I don't think I read at all. Every now and then, I leaked a few tears.

When I got to King's Cross, I phoned work again and spoke to a person this time, who told me not to worry. Then my cousins picked me up and drove me home. On the way we set about the work that has to be done after a death, that of weaving back into the family narrative the event which has ruptured it. Somewhere between the Finchley Road/Hendon Way junction and Apex Corner, Lisa said that, the way he smoked, that massive heart attack was always going to happen. At least it had been quick – there were so many worse ways to die. But what a nightmare for my mother, crying on the bedside phone at two in the morning, watching the final stages of arrest while the operator at the ambulance station kept her talking. And so sad for our grandparents. And for his sister too. At least you expect to lose your parents – just not so early on in the journey, and you don't expect to be quite so far from home when it happens.

Of course, the house was full of people: my mother in tears, my grandparents looking as though someone had punched them both in the stomach, my aunt worrying over my grandparents, my mother's brother and his wife, who were holding their faces together and sorting things out. The rabbi from my parents' synagogue came and discussed the funeral arrangements. Mum burst into tears and so did I. We were calmed down and then everyone chipped in with stories for the eulogy: what a wonderful sense of humour my father had, what a truly appalling singing voice, what a sweet tooth; how he was first and foremost a family man ... My clearest memory is of my grandfather, who had spent an exciting and improving war in the Eighth Army, telling the rabbi, with affectionate regret, that my father had been the worst soldier in the world. After he'd collected his stories, the rabbi went, leaving his condolences and a special card which would sit on a shelf during the immediate mourning period, expressing the hope that we might be comforted among the mourners for Zion.

My brother was in the States, studying for the PhD in chemistry that his father – and, for that matter, his grandfather – might have dreamed of but could never obtain. It was the Labor Day holiday, the chemistry department was closed and his home number was out of order. In the end my uncle phoned the campus police, who banged on his door and told him to call home. So he called home, swore, and was soon on his way.

That night, when my brother was leaking his own tears somewhere over the Atlantic and everyone else had gone to their own beds to try and get some sleep, my mother and I were alone together in the house for the first time. Around half past eleven, lying in my old room not sleeping, I heard her sobbing in the room next door. I went in, sat down on the half-empty bed and put my hand on her shoulder. And that was the beginning of my adulthood, more or less.

You don't have to be Jewish to experience bereavement, but it helps. Every member of a synagogue is also a member of an allied burial society, which takes care of funeral arrangements on the family's behalf, so they are relieved, at least, of that part of the stress. Besides this, everything about the mourning is prescribed and structured for you. After the burial (cremation being, strictly speaking, a no-no) and funeral, the chief mourners – the spouse, children, siblings and, in some cases, parents of the deceased – will 'sit shiva' at home for five days, while their extended family, friends, neighbours, and interested acquaintances who might have read about the death in the *Jewish Chronicle* and are sorry enough to drop by will come to sit with them, offer condolences, share stories about the lost loved one, feed them, look after them, answer the door, answer the phone, make too many cups of tea and join them in prayer every evening. Traditionally, the chief mourners were expected to rend their garments and sit in ashes; we kept our garments intact but sat in the special, low-slung mourners' chairs the synagogue provided.

From then on, the mourning proceeds in graduated stages. For the first month after the death, the immediate family is considered to be in deep mourning, and must not go out in the evenings, or do anything else that might be considered fun or frivolous. Once that first month is up, they are expected to begin to return to normal life, more or less, and a tombstone will be laid and consecrated in the ceremony I've always known as a 'stone-setting'; the stone is usually set somewhere between a month and a year after the death, and once this has happened the mourning period is over and you are supposed to get on with your life. You are not expected to forget the deceased, for whom you will light a slow-burning memorial candle twice a year, once on Yom Kippur, and once on the anniversary of their death, but all the same, you must get on with it. You don't wear black because God has chosen to take the dead away and you shouldn't criticize him like that. Younger widows, especially, are encouraged to remarry: when my mother's father died suddenly in his thirties, everyone tried to dissuade my grandmother from buying the burial plot next door, but she was stubborn, bought the plot, never looked at another man, secretly took herself off to spiritualist meetings, and was eventually buried next to him at the orthodox cemetery in Edmonton.

Somewhere in Numbers or Leviticus there must be an extra verse especially for London Jews which commands that they shall bury their dead off the M25. The orthodox Jews have another north London cemetery in Bushey; my father's final resting place was in the joint reform synagogues' cemetery at Cheshunt. When you arrive, you come first into a small car park, with trees planted tactfully round three of its sides; the fourth is taken up by the chapel, where the mourners gather to pray and hear the eulogy read before accompanying the body out to its burial. It's only when you walk through the chapel, or round the side, to the burial ground behind, that you get a sense of the enormous scale of the place, with its rows of tombstones marching off to the left, to the right, and in front almost as far as the horizon. They are in numbered rows, mostly upright; the size and shape of tombstones is prescribed, so no Highgate-style flights of fancy here. Some are inscribed in Hebrew only, some in English, most in both. Family members are often grouped together, and here and there you can play Spot the Assimilator – Schneider, Schneider, Schneider . . . Saunders! – as the deceased go down a generation.

They must have started filling up the cemetery from the back, because my father's plot is – or was – one of a new row, far out to the left. My defining memory of the funeral is of walking to that plot behind the coffin on its two-wheeled wagon, then glancing over my shoulder as we were halfway there, and seeing how the procession snaked three or four abreast all the way back down the dirt track and round the corner into the chapel. There must have been more than 200 people there: the family, of course, but also friends, neighbours, committee people, colleagues of both my parents. I remember thinking that surely nobody who had so many people to mourn him could have wasted his life completely.

Then people came back to our house with us, and for the next five days they kept coming. Every day began with a flood of condolence notes through the door and ended with my mother, my brother and I, alone and no longer on show, crying together before bedtime. People told us what a lovely man he had been; such a handsome man, so clever, and so proud of his kids. People told us, again and again, to look after our mother. I went out into the back for some air, saw my late father's discarded cigarette butts littering the lawn and the flower bed, started trying to clear them away, then gave up and went back in. Another time, my grandparents and my grandmother's childless brother, Derek, were sitting out on the patio. My brother sat with them, and then came in, grey-faced: 'I couldn't stay out there,' he said. 'They were talking about changing their wills.' Later, Uncle Derek found my brother and me upstairs; he put one hand on my shoulder, one on my brother's, and told us not to try and get over it – you didn't ever get over it – but you did learn to live with it. Decades before, he had lost his wife, Ivy, to TB, and had never remarried.

The prayers were led by a different rabbi every evening. One or two had known my father for years; others hadn't. One of the less familiar ones had a sonorous, Church of England kind of delivery, which sounded rather out of place in a north-west London through-lounge, and he wound my mother up straight away by launching into the Kaddish, the prayer for the dead, before my mother, brother and grandfather had a chance to join in (my Hebrew was all but non-existent, so I never even tried). Then the eulogy came flowing out of his mouth and nostrils like a largo through a set of organ pipes. It concluded: 'And Maurice will be sadly missed, by his parents Dorothy and Alec, his wife Ruth, sister Marian, his son and daughter, and by his son-in-law Brian . . .' He had just married me off to my uncle. I felt the biggest involuntary giggle of my life surging up from my diaphragm, and tried as hard as I could to choke it down. An old but not very observant friend thought I was sobbing, and put her arm round me, which didn't help. I was irritated at her, ashamed of myself, and furious with the high church rabbi. It wouldn't be long before I'd be unwillingly entertained by him again.

I had been due to take two weeks' holiday anyway, and a week's compassionate leave brought it up to three. After the distant relatives and rabbis had gone, the three of us spent a few days together in Nottinghamshire, where I still had my careers advice interview to go to, and then it was time for my brother to go back to the States, me to go back to Scotland, and my mother to face the house on her own.

At the end of the month, I started writing in my notebook again. The first entry reads, 'New and horrible feelings keep nosing in like strange beasts.' Below it, I've written, 'Like the joke about cutting off your hand to cure a headache.' I know exactly what I meant by that: I'd spent most of life up till then in a fog of mild-to-moderate mental discomfort, but now it had all been blown sideways by a hurricane of grief. And I discovered, like C.S. Lewis, that grief was very much like fear. The world seemed more than usually full of terrible portents: on the way back from London, we stopped at Doncaster, and for the first time, I found I couldn't help noticing what a sinister-looking word 'Doncaster' was, the bleeding stump of a longer word which someone or something had mutilated and then plastered back onto a sign. I was absurdly relieved when the train moved on. I'd never been scared of a word before – not in waking life, anyway.

Another note in the exercise book, marked 'Re – Dad's death' says, 'Suddenly you realize, you/your house are/is open on one side, and the wind's blowing through.' Perhaps I was using the flat I was living in as a metaphor here. My friend and new

149

landlord had warned me that the flat would still need a little work after we'd all moved in, but to me it felt as if I had come in to land at a building site: walls were coming down; there were dirty sheets and plaster dust all over the hall and the bathroom; the washing machine drained through a pipe into the bath. My friend was short of money, so he, his father and his brothers were doing the work themselves as and when they could, and it was going to take a while. The heating was by Calor gas only, and I had a very uncomfortable bed. On my first evening back, I declined an offer of a pub quiz, and phoned Linda the counsellor, sobbing. She turned up the next day with a spare futon, which helped – not only because it was more comfortable, but also because in doing so she had provided a bit of mothering when I needed it most. Therapeutic boundaries are all very well, but there are times when you can stuff them up your arse.

On 20 October, I wrote: 'Grief is not clean after all.' If I had thought about grief at all, I had imagined it as a kind of sacramental, white-robed figure, seated in statuesque dignity, with a single, silent tear running down its marble cheek. As I experienced it, however, grief was more of an irritable, snapping, howling, flailing, red-faced snot-monster. I just didn't know what to do with it, or myself. Linda helped. Molly and Maria, who had both lost fathers in childhood, were wonderful. My friend and landlord – I'll call him Neil – was flummoxed, and got the worst of me and my keening snot-monster. We railed at him about the state of the flat, about the noise his music made – as if mine never did – about how he ate too much junk food and watched too much rubbish TV – as if that were any of my business – and, ironic, this, about the unwashed cups and plates lying around the floor.

In the long run, I would discover that the experience of bigger losses could help to put the smaller ills of life in their proper perspective, but first I had to disentangle myself from the snot-monster, who couldn't tolerate so much as the tiniest smudge on the corner of a lens, and insisted that my flatmate, who was trying to save on bills, switch the combi-boiler back on so that I could wash my glasses in hot running water right *there*, right *then*. One night, we had a party and recorded everyone's height on the wall on the hallway. Next to my name we'd written 'Psycho Hormonal Hellbitch'.

All this time, the bad news kept coming: my mother returned to work after three weeks' compassionate leave and was immediately called into her new superior's office to be told she'd been made redundant. Two weeks after that, Uncle Derek died of a heart attack in Spain, leaving conflicting and half-updated wills in several countries, a partner he'd written out of them every time they'd argued and reinstated every time they'd made up, and enough work to keep half a dozen lawyers with half a dozen Dictaphones happily occupied for half a dozen years. My grandfather had a stroke and went into hospital. Then he came out again, but no one could say how long it would be for. Then Marian, who had sympathized over my stomach cramps on the way to the funeral, was diagnosed with ovarian cancer. My best friend fell unexpectedly pregnant, was frightened, nauseous, and frantically busy with her speeded-up wedding preparations. Up in Edinburgh, my friend Catherine's partner – with whom she now had a child – had been made redundant in the spring and was still looking for work. It was raining knives.

I only lasted a few more weeks at work. I went along to an interview at Napier University for their careers guidance course, where they looked at my chequered CV and asked if I didn't think that it indicated some instability, but offered me a place anyway. I went back to work in my smart blue wool dress that my mother had bought for me to mourn in, sat in the office kitchen, and sobbed. Meanwhile, a young work experience girl, who had lost her mother the previous day, was sitting in the tape room quietly getting on with it. I resented it – how admirable she must seem to everyone next to me and the hideous, attention-seeking snot-monster – and I felt ashamed of myself for being so petty. I don't know what her circumstances were; I don't know what there was at home that made it more comfortable for her to go into work as though nothing had happened. I understand now that she had to do it her way. I couldn't help but do it my way, so I took myself off to the doctor.

My previous encounters with this particular GP had been unsatisfactory and awkward. Somewhere towards the end of my first Scottish summer, I had embarrassed him with my breathless rattling on about why I thought that a summer heat rash on my inner thigh might have been indicative of something sexually transmitted, and he had shoved me into the nurse's room next door, where she'd had a chat to me about safe sex and given me a vast supply of free condoms, which would sit in the bottom of my handbag until they perished. The following spring, he had examined me when I had complained of 'severe abdominal pain', told me that he could feel the hard stools through my skin because I was 'so lovely and slim' and prescribed Fybogel, which tasted disgusting and only made me pee a lot. His colleague, of the Christmas tree rash, had been more sympathetic, diagnosed me with irritable bowel syndrome and referred me to a dietician, who said that she wasn't going to do anything until I'd had some nasty tests done. The nasty tests were never ordered; before long I would move on to Nottingham, a new surgery, new crises, and that would be that.

So, I got my second choice of GP, but this time it was more straightforward for both of us. I was a young woman far from home who had only just lost her father, and I had no energy left for anything but grief. We both knew that there was nothing abnormal in that, that it was only the reflex response to a painful blow, but it was within his power to sign me off work for a couple of weeks, so he did. He made a point of writing 'debility' on my sick note, a term non-specific enough not to stain my medical records, as the word 'depression' might have done. Grief looks a lot like depression, but it is not usually labelled as such unless its symptoms – the 'negative affect', the guilt, the weeping, the sleeplessness and loss of appetite, the preoccupation with what has been lost, the lack of interest in what remains, the intense anxiety – persist longer than our culture deems appropriate. Reading that last sentence over, though, I think I'm running the risk of making this seem too clear cut, so at this point I'm going to throw in a recognized psychiatric term, 'reactive depression', which I would define roughly as 'depressive symptoms triggered by an external event, generally one that would depress anybody', and leave you to see if you can sort out the sick from the well. Thanks to the existence of sick leave and the handy word 'debility', the doctor and I didn't have to.

A fortnight later, I saw him for a follow-up and he agreed to sign me off indefinitely. I spent the remaining few weeks in Edinburgh holed up in my room with the Calor gas heater on and sometimes a throw round my shoulders for good measure, to keep the terrible cold away. I took advantage of the unstructured days, reading a couple of big books, *Anna Karenina* and *The Golden Notebook*.

I accepted a place at Nottingham, applied for a career development loan, and arranged another room to rent. I worked furiously on new poems, and filled page after page in my notebook about my father and how it felt to lose him, trying desperately to catch him between the pages, just in case he should disappear from my memory as suddenly and completely as he had vanished from the world. He was my responsibility now.

In January, I moved to Nottingham and began a new exercise book. I was thinking mostly of my father, his death and my family. On the fourteenth I wrote sadly that he had 'shoved himself into a corner of his life, like a scarf in a glove compartment'. Two days later, I recorded a couple of dreams about him.

16/1
Dreams:
Dad alive, grimacing and shouting behind the wheel, as we drove across the border.

Dad in a nursing home, recovering from heart attack. He flopped. Thought he was pretending to have another. Yelled: 'How could you! How could you! After all we've gone through!' And shook him but he really <u>was</u> dead, grey, floppy, eyes like a dead kitten.

A few pages on, I have recorded another dream, this time in just two words: 'Plastic Sunlight'. I must have seen that doctor already. He was a locum, a retired general practitioner so wonderfully, tweedily decrepit that he looked as if he had been pulled out of some dusty, antique doctor-cabinet. I gave him the sad story: the bereavement, sick leave in Edinburgh, the stress of a new town, a new course, the continued turmoil back in London . . . By this time he was pulling the prescription pad towards him, and clicking his pen into gear.

'Would you say you were depressed?' he asked. The pen hovered.

'Yes.'

'Maybe some medication – something like Prozac?'

'Yes,' I said, and the pen came in to land.

It had only taken a few minutes. He'd got the weeping, blethering girl out of the consulting room and I had my first prescription for mind-altering drugs. I'd lost count of the number of medical appointments I'd had up and down the country in which I'd complained of being miserable for no reason and been sent on my way; only now that my misery might be said to be proportionate to my circumstances did I get the medication. But then, what else could he do – medicate the circumstances?

Sometimes I found myself wishing that I were a nineteenth-century lady of similar temperament but probably greater means, who could, whenever life became intolerable, admit herself to a luxury sanatorium for a 'rest cure', a term which I understood to mean comfortable beds, good food, chaperoned walks in landscaped gardens, sea air and the care of concerned but respectful nurses who would bring tea, toast and smelling salts at the ring of a drawing-room bell; once a week one of them would show a bearded, whiskered doctor into my room, so that he could take my febrile pulse and tell me not to overexert myself. He would be a little patronizing, maybe, but I wouldn't mind, just as long as he allowed me to write in my journal once a day, and once or twice a week to compose exquisitely written letters to my literary friends. A hundred years later these letters would be pulled out of their archives and fought over by research students in women's studies departments. As would the journal.

If I had been that nervous Victorian lady, nothing much would have been expected of me. In the eyes of my whiskered doctor, I would have been constitutionally weak in body, weak in moral fibre and weaker still in intellect. Had I not tried to step out of my proper sphere with my intellectual strivings, I might not have inflicted so much strain on my poor feminine nerves. He would have advised me most strongly to abandon the writing and the reading of fat, heavy books. He might have permitted me to marry an undemanding husband and live quietly somewhere. Depending on his view of my case, he might also have taken the undemanding husband aside and advised him against getting me pregnant more often than he could help. (Meanwhile, my working-class counterpart would sink, gin-soaked, into an unmarked grave.)

And if, a hundred years later, a research student in one of the women's studies departments went to her doctor and complained of symptoms much like those she was reading about in my letters, explaining perhaps how she felt too anxious and too enervated to do what could reasonably be expected of her – work on her thesis, present and defend her work at seminars, travel to conferences, teach undergraduates, take the train to London with her friends for wild nights out, have sex and generally assert herself all over the place – the doctor might agree with her that the depression and anxiety were interfering with what we call her 'functioning', and hand her a prescription. Perhaps he – or she – might suggest that our women's studies student needed to relax now and then and 'make the time' to rest, but there would be no question of giving it all up and spending the rest of her life on a day bed somewhere while other people tiptoed around her. That kind of behaviour is dependent, avoidant and passive-aggressive; worse than that, it's unproductive, so it just won't wash any more. Pick up thy day bed and *function*.

There are people, I know, who can function and grieve at the same time, but I was struggling to do both. The grief work was unavoidable: it could be neither shelved nor postponed. I could have had my place on the course cancelled or deferred, but I was no more able to make such a decision than I had been as a sixth former or an undergraduate. My brother was doing his PhD, my cousins both had their careers, and I had to be seen to be going somewhere too; being bereaved was bad enough, but being a bereaved *failure* would be intolerable. And doing a course, even a vocational one, would be easier than trying to drag myself to work in the morning. I knew how to be a student. It felt safe. Besides, quitting the course would have meant moving back into my parents' – now mother's – house in London, where I had always felt stuck and where my father's unbearable absence would take over my outer world just as it filled my interior one. But I couldn't find the brave face I needed to share a house with other students, to get on the bus to the campus, to join in with class discussion and role play, to socialize at lunchtime, to not start crying for no reason, to not sit around staring morbidly into space, to not get irritable, to not go on about my father and my grieving when it wouldn't be appropriate, to sleep, to feed myself properly, to do what could be reasonably expected of me, to *function*, so I had gone to the doctor, and the doctor had written a prescription for something which might help.

On the one hand, I was thrilled to be given that prescription. There was a kind of Woody Allen heroine glamour about it, and I felt as if I had now achieved promotion to some higher order of neurotic. I would get to partake first-hand in a bona fide cultural phenomenon, and that was exciting too. And, not to forget, it might help. On the other hand, I was terrified. I was very protective of my mind, however much gyp it gave me, and very wary of anything that might alter it. I suppose I had a profoundly held belief in the authenticity, the intrinsic value of myself, my thoughts and my feelings even though I frequently felt nothing but contempt for every one of them. So I made an appointment with my course tutor to discuss my dilemma, then I went to Boots to get my prescription made up, and then I shoved it to the bottom of my backpack and made straight for the nearest bookshop.

I found a book by an American psychiatrist called Ronald R. Fieve. Its title, *PROZAC*, was printed in tall, dynamic green letters on the cover; it claimed to be *A Complete Guide to Today's Most Controversial 'Miracle Cure'*, so I bought it. I do like the word 'complete' in a book title.

The book was arranged as a series of questions and answers. In response to 'What causes depression?' Dr Fieve had written:

The modern theory of depression hypothesizes that mood disorders are caused by imbalance in the number of small amino acid molecules, called neurotransmitters, that travel between nerves across the so-called synapses in the brain. Synapses are the spaces between two successive nerve fibers.

According to this theory, known as the biogenic amine hypothesis, the three major neurotransmitters located in brain synapses are: norepinephrine (NE), serotonin (SE), and dopamine (DA). The regulating mechanism is a complex one. It includes a process called uptake, whereby some of the neurotransmitter molecules in the synapse are absorbed back into the original nerve endings, where they either degenerate or are repackaged and sent back out again. Sometimes, as a result of genetic and environmental factors, this process produces imbalances in the amount of neurotransmitters in the synapses. An excess of one or more of the neurotransmitters is thought to lead to mania. A deficiency is thought to result in depression. [pp. 45–6]

The next question was 'How do Prozac and other antidepressants work?' and his answer began:

Prozac works by specifically inhibiting the uptake of serotonin at the nerve endings in the brain. This results in an increased concentration of serotonin at the synapse, which in turn increases the availability of serotonin at the critically important brain receptor sites, thought to result in normal nervous system transmission.

Prozac and the other SSRIs are highly specific in blocking the uptake only of serotonin, and not other neurotransmitters; this is why they are known as selective serotonin reuptake inhibitors (SSRIs). Because abnormalities in serotonin function have also been reported in obsessive-compulsive disorder, panic disorder, alcoholism, obesity and other conditions, it is not surprising that some of these disorders have been successfully treated with Prozac and other SSRIs. [p. 46]

I liked Dr Fieve's book and still do. One of the reasons I like it is that he does not, in these passages or anywhere else, give the reader any kind of simplistic hard sell. Look at his careful wording: writing for a general reader, he might well have said, 'Depression is caused by . . .' Instead he plumps for the far more cautious: 'The modern theory of depression hypothesizes that . . .' If I was going to be all picky and perfectionist about it, I might point out that this theory is not held by everybody, and so might be more accurately characterized as, say, 'The theory of depression which might be said to have gained currency among the majority of psychiatrists, general practitioners and the public in the western world today [1994] hypothesizes that . . .' but I'll resist the temptation. Certainly, he struck me as far more responsible than the author of the book next to him on the Popular Psychology shelf, who advocated exercise and the regular intake of bananas as the best way to raise one's serotonin levels and thus to become a better and happier human being. Dr Fieve's 'hypothesizes' and 'is thought to' and 'have been reported in' are good examples of the kind of careful, unsensational language typical of the scientific journals where the results of drug trials and studies are first published for their specialist audiences. By the time these reports get to the newspapers and magazines which the laity read, they have lost a good deal of their specificity and refinement, so what gets fed to us is something like:

DEPRESSION CAUSED BY LOW SEROTONIN, SAYS TOP PSYCHIATRIST

Dr Fieve may well be a top psychiatrist, and he seems to have been strongly in favour of the serotonin hypothesis, but that's still not what he said.

As I understand it, what we can say is that there is a *correlation* between low levels of available serotonin in the brain and the presence of some or all of the cluster of feelings, thoughts and observable behaviours which we label 'depression'. To say that there is a 'correlation' between two phenomena is simply to state that they appear at the same time and the same place too often and too consistently for this to be coincidental – probably. A sad person, when tested, might well be found to have low levels of available serotonin trickling about in her brain. Maybe the lack of serotonin made her sad. Maybe her sadness depleted the serotonin. Maybe some other, unknown cause depleted the serotonin *and* made her sad. There was one obvious cause for the sadness I was feeling in January 1997, and that was the death of my father. On page 42 of Dr Fieve's book, his patient asks, 'What are the symptoms of grief or bereavement, and does Prozac help in their treatment?' To which he replies:

> We usually think of grief only in terms of the death of a loved one, but bereavement reactions also occur in response to the loss of a job, a large quantity of money, an important object such as a home, or even an idealistic concept that one has long pursued. Weeping, anxiety, sadness, anger, irritability, guilt, insomnia, and obsessive thinking about the loss are all common reactions, but if these symptoms do not begin to level off after three to four months, psychiatrists usually diagnose major depressive disorder. In such cases, Prozac or another antidepressant, along with therapy, is indicated. Indeed, it may help earlier.[27]

So I decided to give the pills a try.

And they worked, they really did. For a couple of days, I felt drowsy and nauseous, but these symptoms passed quickly, and after a few weeks had elapsed, I realized that it was becoming

27. *Ronald R. Fieve, PROZAC: A Complete Guide to Today's Most Controversial 'Miracle Cure'* (HarperCollins, London, 1995)

easier to get out of bed in the mornings and get on with what could be reasonably expected of me. It hadn't changed my thoughts, it hadn't changed the way I felt about myself, my life or my losses, but it had improved my ability to function. I was no longer wading through treacle.

I say that it hadn't changed me, but a journal entry I wrote in March, in a flat in Bradford, during my first work placement, suggests otherwise: 'Prozac making me very Alpha, pushing Tigger forward & suppressing my Eeyore.'

As the diploma in careers guidance is a vocational course, where students are assessed on their observed behaviour, I have a whole folder of evidence of how I seemed to the people teaching me. The professional development officer at the careers service in Bradford said in her report that I 'came with a positive attitude and willingness to take part and learn. Negotiated her programme with staff and made full use of the access.' 'Generally', I was 'willing to get involved, help out, answer phones, etc.' She noticed no difficulties in my punctuality, dress, attendance or self-presentation, and said that I was able to 'relate and interact . . . satisfactorily' with 'a range of clients'. My 'approach and manner' were apparently 'a refreshing change'. It makes me wonder what the others had been like.

Other documents from my DipCG Part I file tell a similar story. For a start, my written work – essays and project reports – was completed and handed in on time. I got very good marks for it too, but as I'd always been strong academically, this was not really a surprise. What took me aback at the time was the discovery that I wasn't, after all, especially lousy with people. My 'skills work' was pretty good too. The most important part of the careers adviser's role is, obviously, the careers interview, for which the overwhelming majority of interviewees are likely to be kids in their mid- to late teens, probably still in compulsory education. The CA is supposed to engage the kid – sorry, *Young Person* – with the whole process, establish a working relationship with them, assess and if necessary enhance their decision-making skills, find out what they believe they can offer the world of work, find out what they think the world of work might offer them, and enable them to look at ways in which they might employ their decision-making skills to bring themselves and the world of work together in the most satisfactory way. Our practice interviewees came from local schools and colleges; the interviews were videoed if they came to us, and audiotaped if we went out to them. You never knew, beforehand, who you were going to get, or even if they were going to turn up. Some of them talked too much and threatened to run away with the interview; some of them hardly talked at all, and needed lots of encouragement to stop the interview spluttering to a stop; some were utterly charming; others were obviously bored. They all knew that I was only a student. Still, I was the only adult in the room, and I was supposed to be in charge. I couldn't control them, but, all the same, I was solely responsible for, as they call it, 'managing the interaction'. I must have managed the interactions reasonably well, because I got good marks on my assessed interviews all the way through, but I was every bit as scared before my last interview as I had been before my first – more scared, even. There were just too many ways to fail.

I enjoyed the 'group leading' more, and discovered a talent for off-the-cuff speaking that I'd never known I had, but the termly group-leading assignments involved teaching the other students, and they were not only adults, but also known quantities. Besides, the group leading always took place in the safety of the university premises, and didn't entail walking into secondary schools, smelling the adolescent pheromones, serving as an object of transient curiosity to the wary, secretive half-child/half-adult beasts who roamed the corridors, watching the teachers compete in front of you in the staffroom to see who could come across as the most tired and cynical, feeling sick, or wanting to run away.

I know I could have made it easier for myself: I could have volunteered for fewer unpopular things, or not have thrown myself into class discussion with quite so much gusto; I could have asked for nice cushy placements instead of opting for Bradford in the first term and Birkenhead in the third; I could have stopped chasing the highest marks for everything and allowed myself to cruise a bit – there were no firsts or distinctions up for grabs, only passes – but as far as my inner perfectionist was concerned, any assessed course was a salient area, so cruising was out of the question. On good or reasonable days, I went in and hurled myself at the day's business; on bad days, I phoned in sick and hid at home. There was little in between. At one point my tutor said to me that she was concerned that I was putting more into the course than I was getting out of it. The medication might have lent me just enough energy to continue overdoing it, but the habit of overdoing it was, and had always been, all mine.

In the spring holiday, I made my first transatlantic flight, with my mother, to visit my brother in New England. We landed at JFK in the dark. All I could see from my window as the plane banked were lights on water and I remember a few panicked moments when I thought that we were about to plunge straight into Long Island Sound. This I know from reading the notes I made on 28 March. They were all about the flight, what the clouds and ice floes over Greenland and Newfoundland looked like from above, what it had been like to land so close to water. I also recorded a dream, the weird, intensely detailed kind that I have on SSRIs.

. . . found myself after some events or either [sic], in some place or other – which maybe I was on the run from? – through a gap in a rock onto the strangest shore.

A rust beach under a dark sky. For far around black cliffs –

163

not easy to see how you get out. The sea was up in dark blue peaks with white flecks, like Sydney Opera House domes, or irons, or shark fins. I realized the waves were still, dead – all was still & dead & motionless here, nothing could grow and there was no time, it just kept looping back on itself – they were made of cardboard or plaster, arranged in painted serrated rows, as in a toy theatre – I pulled at one & a corner came away crumbly, in my hands – like stale . . . ?

A storm was brewing over the black cliffs up in the brown-orange sky. The odd fork of lightning & thunder. It was dangerous to be there – with the sun/moon so low and heavy in the sky – but I couldn't remember where to go or how to get there.

Mum and I went shopping at a local mall, where we bought far too much. The three of us went on a day trip to New York, where we visited MoMA and the Guggenheim, and an elderly lady in a delicatessen on Lexington Avenue exclaimed at my brother's hair, which his housemate had sprayed to look like a Mondrian painting, and asked what his mother thought of it. 'Your *sister* doesn't have hair like that,' she said, in case her disapproval wasn't clear. We returned to the small town where my brother lived, and ate some very good breakfasts; I spent much of my time during the day watching the household's enormous TV set and discovering that, for the most part, America was as bad for television as it was good for breakfasts. Mum and I moved on to Boston. We went to the Science Museum and shopped for bargains in Filenes's Basement. Mum took photographs of me walking through the Boston Holocaust Memorial, hair and trench coat flaring out behind me as steam rose up through vents in the flagstones. In our hotel lounge, I interviewed my mother about her career as a social worker so that I could write an occupational profile, another assignment for the course. I read *Don Juan* and empathized with Byron's bowel trouble. Wherever we were in the northern hemisphere, we could see Comet Hale-Bopp, setting a burning seal on the strangeness of it all.

Late in April, my mother called to tell me that Grandad was in the Royal Free Hospital again. He'd had another stroke and couldn't speak. She told me that if I wanted to visit him, I'd better do it soon. I remember the harrowing look – half sharp, half terrified – coming over his face as I approached his bed, as he took in what an unscheduled visit from me must mean. No offers of tea, no bad jokes, no war stories, none of the pet names he used for me and I loathed – just that penetrating, utterly truthful look. It wasn't just because he couldn't speak; once people know they're dying, and soon, they tend to drop their usual spiel.

He died a few days later, on the day of the general election. I was still on the register in Edinburgh then, and had already voted by post. Blair's face was all over the covers of the newspapers for sale at the station. I was a member of the Labour Party, and this was going to be our glorious day. The day after the previous election, in 1992, I had been stuffing envelopes at the offices of a left-wing magazine, and the mood had been dismal. The others commiserated with me when I told them how jubilant my father had been. A few months later my grandfather had talked enthusiastically of the Major government, how they had cut taxes which put, he said, 'more money in your pocket!' I had probably said something sanctimonious about how I'd rather the money was back in the Treasury where it belonged. We joked later that the date of his death was no coincidence: he just couldn't bear the thought of a Labour government.

That reminds me of my only really vivid memory of that day, which is of my going to answer a knock on the door at my grandparents' house early that evening. I opened it to a neat young man sporting a shiny blue rosette, who asked if Mr

Limburg were there, and if he needed any help to get to the polling booth. I had to tell him that Mr Limburg had died that morning, and as I watched him try to find an appropriate face, I found myself, for the first time, feeling sorry for a Tory. It was the weirdest year.

I believe that I write better when medicated. It would be fair to say that I choose to continue to take fluoxetine (the generic name for 'Prozac') almost as much for performance enhancement purposes as I do for treatment, although my GP, quite properly, prescribes it only for the second reason. While I was working on this chapter, I found a copy of Peter D. Kramer's book *Listening to Prozac* in an Oxfam bookshop, and took it home to read. He wrote about certain patients of his, typically women, who were often, like me, awkward, conscientious, 'uptight' and highly sensitive to rejection or perceived slights, but who blossomed once they were given this new drug. Like many of them, I found that year, and continue to find, that when I am taking fluoxetine or a similar drug, I am more socially confident, more assertive and less inhibited. I also share the sense many of his patients had that when I am taking the drug my thoughts seem to move faster. Most crucially for my writing, it makes me better able to stop worrying about whether my work will be any good or not, and what people might think of it, and how difficult it will feel to do it, and to just get on and try instead. I once asked my husband, who has known me both with and without any pharmaceutical assistance, whether he thought I seemed 'better', happier, when I was on SSRIs, and he replied that he couldn't say for sure, but one thing he was certain about was that I was happier when my writing was going well, whether I was popping pills or not.

Of course, it's impossible to know precisely what can and can't be attributed to the drugs, but the mess my office is in at the moment attests to how much I got done that year. Every time I start a new chapter, I first retrieve whatever writing I've kept from the relevant period: not just the notebooks already mentioned, but all the drafts of all my poems, whether these have been published or just abandoned. In strict chronological terms, this chapter should be relatively short: it only covers a year of my life. But in terms of inches of paper covered that year, it could almost make a book in itself. Between the month of my father's death and the last month of my year in Nottingham, I completed twenty-five poems, seventeen of which were finished enough to be included in my first book, where they made up about a third of the whole collection. I also have four paper exercise books and one larger hardback book which cover the same period, and include the beginnings of many later poems. And that's all on top of the coursework I was doing.

At this point, a Prozac-sceptic would point out – and they'd be right – that what was happening to my family and to me gave me a lot to write *about*. They might add that it was hardly surprising that, in my grief and confusion, I would turn to writing as a way of containing and expressing these intense feelings, that in making these poems I was seeking to remake my broken world. It makes perfect sense to me that my grief would be the source of the extraordinary *drive* to write that I had that year: I needed to write my ideas down, I needed to give shape to them, and I needed to finish the poems as best I could in order to get the feeling of resolution that only a completed piece of work can provide. I was already addicted to that feeling. I had bereavement counselling that year, and it helped, but the poems were vital. They were helping me figure out what I could preserve of my father and my family and my old self, and what I could only let go. They were helping me to take stock of my inheritance from him.

The Return

Dad,
I come home
and find you sitting
in every room in the house,
its smell your smell,
as if it were a jacket
you'd only just thrown off,
still warm.

As the house recalls you,
so do I,
resurrecting you
fifty times a day,
in the way you clench my teeth
when something fails to work,
as we prowl in step together
round my room,
hours into the night,
as you fret me into being ready
an hour early for every journey.
As I bite into something undercooked,
I feel you pull
that comical, disappointed face.

You prefer to hide
in better foods:
strong cheese, strong coffee,
anything sweet.
I find myself eating
a whole quarter of wine gums
just to give you
twenty more minutes
of borrowed life.

A first round of chemo had had only limited success for my aunt. By the time I went down to London for the long summer holiday that year, her cancer was back and she was in and out of hospital again. Her mother, my mother, my uncle, and my cousins were spending much of their time travelling back and forth to the hospital. Marian had always hated being alone. My memories of my own visits are very hazy, but I'm sure she was doing her best, when she could, to be as she always had been, trying to extract every detail of everything I had been doing or planned to do. It was a private hospital with pleasant rooms and a nice view; it had less of a fearful smell than NHS hospitals, where the blood and antiseptic is left to hang around in the air undisguised. Yes, she was ill, but they were treating her. They were trying some other drug first but they were keeping Taxol in reserve.

One day, the phone rang. It was for me, someone called Malcolm. I didn't know who the hell he was or why he was calling. I was polite but that much was clear from my tone.

He said he was Sarah's son. Sarah's son?

'Your aunt didn't say anything to you, did she?' he said, as he realized the awful truth.

'No?'

'Oh ... well ... I'm the son of a friend of your aunt, and she thought, and my mother thought, that we might get along, and that I should – er – phone you.'

Now I understood. It was excruciating for both of us. He was also interested in writing so we attempted to have a chat about that, for the sake of my aunt, his mother, and the saving of our red faces, but it was clear very soon that the conversation was never going to take off with such a heavy freight of embarrassment, so we said our goodbyes and hung up as soon as it was decently possible. It turned out my aunt and his mother had got their wires crossed: he was not supposed to have phoned until my aunt had spoken to me and prepared the ground. She was mortified. Malcolm and I never met. Never mind, it was sweet of her to have tried. She hated to see other people on their own too.

Early in July, I went on another one-week residential writing course. It was an advanced course, tutored by Miroslav Holub and George Szirtes, and I had only managed to get a place because someone else had dropped out. It was a tremendous privilege: George was (is) as fine a teacher as he is a poet, and Holub was a truly great man, a writer who had stood up to the communist government in Czechoslovakia and had his poems and essays banned from publication, a long-standing contender for the Nobel Prize for Literature – and possibly for medicine too, for his work as an immunologist. He approached poetry with a scientist's eye. The directness and clarity of his language, the way he used poems to explore ideas, his characteristic mixture of humour and seriousness had drawn me to his work from my first encounter with it in the school library. It later acted as a powerful influence on my own (a reviewer once described my work as 'second-hand Miroslav Holub', which I chose to take as a compliment – thanks). When I said in one of his tutorials that the process of grieving was 'interesting', and he commented that the two of us used the word 'interesting' in the same way, it was, in context, the most wonderful thing anyone had ever said to me. OCD, by the way, is 'interesting' like that.

At the time of the course, Miroslav was preoccupied with the story of Sisyphus, and suggested that we all write our own Sisyphus poems. This fitted in well with some notes I'd been making: 'walking among the shades'; 'Orpheus in the Underworld'. And I kept thinking of a line from the Eels song 'Novocaine for the Soul': 'Guess who's living here / With the Great Undead'. So I wrote this poem, about my father and me and our twin dead weights.

Sisyphus' Daughter

A mourner's work is never done.
There was no way to compensate my Dad
for all the small betrayals
of every day I lived
when he did not,
for the indifference of my washing, dressing,
walking, working, talking,
as life on the surface ground on and on
and he was stuck beneath the mud
without so much as a phone
to hear what I was up to.

I couldn't be remembering him all day –
I had enough to think about,
so I resolved to rescue him instead,
packed sandwiches, a handful of change
and my karaoke machine,
and set off for the Underworld,
imagining that when I sang
the dead would flutter to my shoulders
like birds charmed from trees
and I would bring them home.

But when I reached the bank,
I saw my father on the other side,
washing, dressing, walking,
working, talking.
He didn't seem to hear a note –
he had enough to think about.
The afterlife ground on and on.
The work of the dead is never done.

Sometime during that week, I went to look round the local church with a few other students. Next to a stone pillar I found a small table, with candles; there was a wooden board with little prayers pinned to it. I wrote one for my aunt – OK, it was the wrong religion, but I figured we needed all the help we could get.

Later that month, my brother flew home for my father's stone-setting, and we went to Cheshunt again. My aunt was in terrible pain, and couldn't go. A few days passed, and Mum, my brother and I decided to go out for a meal in a nice restaurant – the three of us together, why not? The hors d'oeuvres had only just reached the table when my mother's mobile went. My aunt had a developed a blood clot, and there was nothing they could do. We paid for the hors d'oeuvres and drove straight to the hospital.

You could hear my aunt's laboured breathing all the way down the corridor. My uncle showed us into the room. She was lying on her back on the bed, her head to one side, her eyes closed.

I said something lame like, 'We've come to see you.' She acknowledged us with a flicker of her eyelids, and a very uncharacteristic remark, then fell back into her painful sleep.

Back outside, Mum asked my uncle if he wanted my grandmother – my aunt's mother – called. For the last couple of months, she had held on alone in the house in Cricklewood, surviving on visits from the family, home helps and meals on wheels. He thought it best not to disturb her. We went home, and in the early hours of the morning got another phone call. Mum said that she would drive over to my grandmother's in a few hours and tell her about her daughter.

My brother and I went with her. Mum had a key and opened the door, calling out, 'Mum? It's us.'

My grandmother appeared at the top of the stairs and asked, eagerly, 'What news?'

Mum told her.

She took it as a blow to her body, bending double, and letting out a wail so terrible I thought it must crack the sky.

The prayers were at my uncle's house, and it was the high church rabbi again. At my grandfather's funeral, he had alluded to the deaths of my father and great-uncle, and expanded a little on how we were, all of us, caught 'in the Cycle of Life and Death'. That was all very understandable, but we felt that we could all do with a different approach this time, so my cousins and I went up to him beforehand and asked if, for the sake of our grandmother and their father, he might focus on what a loving and positive person my aunt had been, rather than on all the *deaths*. He nodded and said he understood.

When the time came for him to speak, my cousin Lisa was sitting next to our grandmother with her arm round her and I was kneeling on the floor in front of her, holding her hand. The rabbi took a deep breath, and began: 'It was only last September . . .' Lisa and I looked each other in the eye, and then at the ground. He'd done it again.

In the space of ten months, my grandmother – Nanny – had buried her son, her youngest brother, her husband and now her daughter. Still, she held on in her house. She had end-stage lung disease. When I went to visit, I tried to help her with her meals on wheels and she tried to persuade me to eat them for her. For the twenty-seven years that I'd known her, she'd been in and out of her kitchen in one of her nylon check overalls, the pink and white or the brown and white, stuffing food into us while evading it on her own account. Every now and then my grandfather would go into the kitchen to try and help, and she would tell him to go away. She was by definition the subject, not the object, of the transitive verb 'to feed'. Dependency did not suit her.

She knew that she did not have much time left, and she

wanted very much to die in the house where she'd lived for sixty-odd years. In the event, though, she spent her last two weeks, as her husband had, in the Royal Free. I don't have the exact date of her death in front of me, but I'm quite sure that it must have been at least two weeks, because I remember her saying how awful it was that the Princess of Wales had been killed, and that she said this from a hospital bed. The televisions were showing, I thought, far too much footage of people weeping by banks of flowers. At the time, I felt almost proprietorial about grief, and resented the weeping Diana-mourners, muscling in on a bereavement that had, I thought, so very little to do with them. I'd lost real relatives, while all they'd lost was the chance to look at more pictures of a tall blonde in *Hello!* It could have been that they were just taking advantage of one of the few short periods in our history when the populace were encouraged to express sadness and discouraged from telling each other to cheer up. Shame it didn't last long.

Nanny's last few weeks fill the last few pages of one exercise book and overflow into the next. 'Hard to find veins in her thin arms – how they hurt her – huge bruises on her inside elbows,' it says on one page, and on the next: 'Disorientation from lack of oxygen and moves between wards of confused and rattly-breathing people. Thought twice when they moved her at night that she'd been moved into a room with dead people.' They could hardly have blamed her for being so preoccupied with the end, with *her* end. On one visit, she leaned over to me conspiratorially and said in a low voice that someone had come to ask her if she would like any help to – 'you know, *pop off*' and that she had said yes to the offer. It turned out that a psychology student had been going round the medical wards researching elderly people's attitudes to euthanasia. He was horrified, and went straight to her bed to explain the misunderstanding. I think she was disappointed.

Matriarch to the very end, she tried to sort us out. She tried to get my mother to post £50 to her brother Louis, because she thought he needed something. She told Lisa, the eldest of her grandchildren, that she would be in charge now and that her advice to us all was: 'Don't worry about money – money comes and goes. Always stick together and enjoy yourselves.'

Her last words to me, hacked out painfully through the plastic muzzle of her nebulizer, were, 'I don't know why you worry, dear – a lot of men go for short women.'

I was with her when she died, and it was a privilege.

Avoidance

31. I invent doubts and problems about most of the things I do.

The Padua Inventory

When it gets bad, the patients hide.

Judith L. Rapoport

When people ask me how I am, I usually do the correct thing and say, 'Fine, thanks.' I'm never sure if I mean it though. Right now, it is about half past eleven on an overcast August morning, I am sitting at my desk writing, and I might, for all I know, be ill. One thing I do know is that I'm terribly anxious. My skin is clammy. My chest feels corseted on the inside. My legs are tightly crossed and my bottom is on the edge of my seat. A tiny cloud of a headache is beginning to gather behind my left eye. Most of all, though, I can feel it in the pit of my stomach; if depression is a bag of wet sand in the chest, then anxiety, as befits its more primitive nature, lives further down, in the viscera. It isn't a feeling of weight, like the depression, though it has its weighty aspects; it isn't just a sinking feeling, either, or a knotted feeling, or a butterfly feeling – it's all three of them, and more than the sum of them. It's the mother of bad feelings: I think of it as the Unbearable Feeling. I would crawl out of my skin to escape it.

There's nothing more natural, or easier to understand, than the desire to avoid pain. It helps us to prevent harm to ourselves, and, when empathy widens its scope, to others. If, for example, you happen to touch the handle of a hot metal saucepan, then you'll pull your hand away before you've even thought about it. If you anticipate that when you touch the saucepan you will feel pain, then you avoid touching it in the first place. Even if you've never seen a saucepan full of boiling water in your life before – let alone touched one – then an inference from your general experience of hot things, or something your mother told you about hot saucepans, or the memory of reading an article or watching a documentary in which hot saucepans featured, will lead you to anticipate that pain, and you won't touch the saucepan. And this whole process will take only a fraction of a second: SAUCEPAN – HOT – OUCH! will flicker up in your head somewhere, accompanied probably by a just-perceptible flash of anxiety. You'll pull your hand away, and by the time another fraction of a second has elapsed, you'll be finishing the sentence you were uttering, or deciding to switch on the radio or heading for the fridge. SAUCEPAN – HOT – OUCH! will then turn itself off, and won't make another appearance until the next time you need it, when, again, it will appear for a sliver of a moment and immediately vanish.

Unfortunately, for some people, SAUCEPAN – HOT – OUCH! won't turn itself off when it's ceased to be useful; it may even get in the habit of switching itself on out of its proper context. In these cases, SAUCEPAN – HOT – OUCH! has become an obsessive thought. Every time it intrudes, it will bring with it a flash of anxiety. Anxiety is uncomfortable. It needs to be: it's there to signal danger and to prompt us to take evasive action. Every time that thought appears, the hot saucepan obsessive will do what the anxiety prompts her to do, which is to take whatever action she can to make it go away: she might engage in compulsive behaviour, making frequent trips to the kitchen to check that she hasn't left any water boiling in it; just to make sure, she might unplug the kettle and put all the saucepans in the cupboard; then five minutes later she will return to the kitchen to check that the saucepans are indeed safely in the cupboard, and the kettle unplugged. This may reassure her briefly, but five minutes later she will get the overwhelming urge to check again.

Alternatively, she might try to neutralize the anxiety by ruminating about hot saucepans and kettles (it has spread to kettles now), working through every possible convection-heated kitchen-receptacle accident scenario that might have happened in the past or could be happening in the present or that might conceivably happen in the future, and looking for ways of convincing herself that every single one of them has been, is being and will be prevented.

Then again, she could decide to avoid going into kitchens altogether, thus eliminating all possibility of her being responsible for any overheated metal vessel at any time, which will reduce the anxiety she feels to bearable levels. Avoidance is a popular strategy, not only for obsessive-compulsive patients, but also for those suffering from social anxiety disorder (I won't go to the party because I'll make an idiot of myself and then I'll feel terrible), panic disorder (I won't go the party because I'll have to travel on the underground, and the last four times I did that I got that feeling that I couldn't breathe and I was going to die, and nothing could be worse than that), body dysmorphic disorder (I won't go to the party because if I do then all the people there will look at me and all they'll see is my ugly nose, and knowing that all the people are thinking and talking and laughing about my ugly nose will make me feel so sad and worthless that I'll want to die), and a whole range of other conditions. They all convince themselves that they don't want to go to the party, that the party or the journey to it is the thing to be feared, but really, deep down, they would *love* to go. What they are ultimately afraid of are their own unpleasant feelings. Their Unbearable Feelings.

I've always been very good at avoidance. When I was in junior school, I avoided going into the dining room most days, and on some days I could persuade myself that I felt ill, and avoid the school altogether. As an adolescent, I increased my repertoire considerably, avoiding, among other things, Bunsen burners, Van de Graaf generators, the active centres of lacrosse games, the deep end of the swimming pool and, as time went on, the mirror. Then I started picking and began to avoid showing my arms or shoulders. Then I got picked on by ten-year-old boys and started to avoid a certain street corner. All the while I was avoiding dressing in any way that might make me look sexually available. By the time I got to university, I had also got into the habit of avoiding work until the last minute, so as to stop myself experiencing the unpleasant tension I feel when I'm in the middle of a piece of work and I don't know if I'm going to make a good job of it or not. I avoided the college dining room and, for one term, the whole college. After I graduated, I avoided leaving home and going out. I think I rose to the status of a Master Avoider at this stage, managing to avoid the very process of maturation for three whole years by sitting in an analyst's consulting room and discussing it instead. At the end of the three years I avoided going into full analysis, which had been the ostensible purpose of the discussion. I moved to Edinburgh to try to stop avoiding in my own way and, for a while, it looked as if I had succeeded pretty well. Then I had a few discouraging experiences. I went back to staying in. Then my father died, I left Edinburgh and tried to try again, to train for a proper professional job, a responsible job, acting not thinking, out there in the Real World. But then, when the time came to take up the job, I avoided it.

5/10/97
Dream last night – my hair turned white – every comb stroke pulled down a new streak till no brown was left.

A year of hospitals, cemeteries and lawyers' offices had left the whole family punch-drunk. It was surely no coincidence that, about this time, three out of four of the newly ex-grandchildren were suffering from physical illnesses that needed hospital treatment, while the fourth dreamed that she combed her hair white. I was back in Nottingham where, following the usual protocol for the treatment of reactive depression, my doctor and I began to reduce my Prozac doses, preparatory to taking me off the drug. In my notebook, I mentioned 'the flat feeling, the game-playing feeling' and then 'the stage-set feeling. Rusty bolts and peeling paint,' and, then, a few pages later, I add that, 'Life tastes thin and flat at the moment, like gruel.' I couldn't bring myself to care what career step sixteen-year-olds took next. They were all going to die anyway, some of them of accountancy. My anxiety over my interviews was as hard to bear as it had always been, and I could no longer see any point in trying to master it. So I would avoid it instead, and the money I was inheriting from my dead relatives would help me make a clean escape.

I finished the taught part of the course, though, so that I could gain my half-qualification. The last term was difficult, and I was difficult through it: the snot-monster returned, throwing herself about the classroom, and trying the patience of the other students. My second work placement, in Birkenhead, ended prematurely when I caught a stomach bug off the friend I was staying with, and couldn't bring myself to go back to the office when I recovered. I couldn't face any of it: the dark streets, the sad-looking shop windows hung with cheap clothes, the confused, drugged-up boys who occasionally wandered into reception, the fifteen-year-old girls arriving at drop-in sessions, 'because I'm going to have a baby and me mum told me to come and see what benefits I was entitled to'. The staff meanwhile were bright, determined and cheerful. They were up to the challenge: they were strong, they were useful, they were practical, they had resources to give to the world. I obviously didn't; I was a person who cried in toilets.

My superego had changed personae. The great-aunt had gone along with the rest of her generation, and had been replaced by a contemporary of mine, a young urban professional I called The Person at the Party. She had been to university at the same time as me, but she hadn't been messing about since. She had gone straight into law school, or postgraduate medical school, or the civil service 'fast-track' programme, or perhaps into an accountancy firm, as a graduate trainee. She earned enough money to share a flat in a decent area, perhaps even with her boyfriend. Perhaps, along with the right clothes, the right shoes and the perfectly applied make-up, she was sporting a tasteful little engagement ring presented to her by this same boyfriend. Perhaps he was standing next to her as we talked, and, as we talked, the two of them would exchange the odd glance. In their shared vocabulary were killing words, like 'waster' and 'loser' and 'sad'.

She would ask me what I did.

'Erm . . . I've just finished a course in careers guidance.'

So I was a careers officer now?

'No . . . I – I did an MA in psychoanalytic studies before . . . and I realized this year that I really didn't want to practise, that . . . actually . . . the theory interested me more. The model of decision-making we were supposed to follow, I thought it was – from the perspective of my background – that it privileged the rational too much, and I wanted to see if I could combine the two – the psychoanalytic stuff and the careers theory – and come up with something that incorporated the role of the unconscious . . . so I'm going to do a PhD.'

And where would that be?

'Oh, I haven't got a place yet . . .'

Oh.

'. . . But I do other things, I write as well.'

Was I published?

'Yes – in magazines – poetry magazines.'

Oh.

Then we would move on to where we lived, and I would feel compelled to tell her the whole truth, that I was living back with my mother. She would say that must be awkward, mustn't it, bringing my boyfriend home? I would have to tell her that I didn't have a boyfriend.

But I could save some face, at least. I had a rationale for avoiding a career in careers guidance. I was going to do a PhD. People would ask me what I was doing, and I would be able to tell them that what I was doing was a PhD. People at parties understand that whatever obscure nonsense a PhD might be about, it is, at least, a qualification – career-progression, of a kind. If all you can tell them is that you are living off a small inheritance while you write poetry – *poetry!* – they'll only think you're a complete sadloserwaster, as opposed to just a partial one.

Most people are, at best, indifferent to contemporary poetry. Some commentators think that this is the fault of most people, while others blame the poetry. Some people, in what, for the sake of a coherent paragraph, I'll call 'the poetry world', try to elbow poetry into mainstream culture, through National Poetry Days, and work in schools, and accessible events, and placements of poets in unpoetic places. Others make a virtue of its marginal status, seeing the writing and non-commercial distribution of a poem as an act of resistance against the commercialization and commodification of just about everything else. Meanwhile, most people remain indifferent, with the consequence that the market for poetry is negligible. If you manage to get a collection published, you are a success. If you sell more than a handful of copies, you are a great success. If you manage to sell in the thousands, and do a few radio broadcasts, get your work taught in schools, then you are, in poetry terms, a superstar. But most people still won't have heard of you, and unless you get some steady job, a chair in creative writing, say, or a regular radio slot of some kind, you will still struggle to make a living.

If you rank among the merely successful, your relative poverty will bewilder and embarrass people – if you're as talented and hard-working, so widely published and well respected, as you seem, indirectly, to be claiming to be, then how come you earn so little money? If you're not bullshitting them, then you must be deluding yourself. When your mother tells the people *she* meets at parties that you've got a poetry book out, they ask her, in all sincerity, how much you had to pay to get it published.

Poetry rewards in other ways. I'd had a difficult few months with it, as with everything else, but once I arrived back in London, I found a new momentum. In 1998 I completed twenty-one poems, thirteen of which would make it into my first collection. I wrote of course about my family, my father and grandparents, their deaths, the grief we all felt, and always in the process of writing, the technical and emotional difficulties would get all tangled up together – as they must do – and I would think that whichever piece I was writing was never going to work. But then, more often than not, suddenly, it would. And every time I began work on another poem, it was a whole new start, always with the distant but irresistible possibility that this time – *this* time – I might manage to do something, well, perfect? Please?

Travelling Light

Never underestimate
the ecstasy of chucking out:

the clean desktop, the orderly wardrobe,
the black bags stacked by the shut front door,

the softness of a shaven calf,
the bracing soreness of the friction glove –

a text that could edit itself would know it,
linen being boiled must know it,

the godly joy of cleanliness,
the pleasure of being stripped bare

and blameless, a born-again,
with just one suitcase, on the right road.

In March, I got some excellent news: the previous autumn, I had made my second submission to the panel of the Eric Gregory Awards for the encouragement of young poets, a self-explanatory fund administered by the Society of Authors. Now I learned that I had been shortlisted and was to attend an interview, at the society's offices in Kensington. When the day came, I wore a black, sack-like dress, with a grey knitted jacket over it, and I'm sure I looked every bit as eccentric and badly dressed as people expect poets to look. I may have had some idea that my financial situation might be taken into account, so I didn't want to look too well finished.

I arrived early, and was shown into a waiting area where I could relax for a bit, or, alternatively, finish working myself up. So I worked myself up for ten minutes or so, and then someone ushered me into a committee room. Sitting round the table were lots of poets I'd heard of. And they were very nice to me, asking lots of encouraging, not-too-difficult questions about my work, mostly presaged by 'What I particularly liked . . .' I wondered, because of the whole tone of it, if the interview might be a formality, but didn't dare to hope. A few weeks later, an envelope stuck in the letterbox told me that I was one of that year's six winners, and would be presented with a cheque at the society's award ceremony in the summer. It was the first really nice thing to happen to anyone in my family for a good while, so it's a shame, really, that I so quickly got into the habit of forgetting about it. I find it so much easier to recall the things I *didn't* win.

Back in what many people like to call the Real World, I was still struggling to escape a life sentence of sadloserwasterdom. I sent a rough draft of a research proposal to a concrete-built campus university within commuting distance of London, and got a reply from one of the professors of psychoanalytic studies there, who was interested in my project. He helped me come up with a finished research proposal, and I was formally accepted as a full-time, self-funding student, to begin the following autumn.

In the meantime, I found a decent poetry workshop to attend, and a new therapist to visit. I asked Linda to ask her Jungian analyst if she knew of any good and affordable Jungians in the north-west London area. I was shy of Freudians now, but the poet in me remained drawn to the Jungian approach, with its narratives and its pictures. She came back with the name of a woman in Finchley, a therapist who was training to be an analyst, and who could see me at the lower trainee rates. I liked her: she was thoughtful and funny. She was Jewish, so nothing about my background needed to be explained. And she took me seriously as a poet – it wasn't a symptom to her. On the debit side, she lived on the wrong branch of the Northern Line, but if I was having a bad avoidance day, I could always take a taxi.

Summer 1998 arrived, and now I had the poetry award, the PhD place and the therapist. Money was coming in in fits and starts from my great-uncle's estate. 'But,' said my party-girl superego, 'you're still in your old back bedroom, aren't you? And an adult should really have a job. That money's going to run out, especially if you spend it all on' – she smirked – '*therapy*. What if you want to get a mortgage? You need a back-up.'

So we compromised: I got a very part-time job as secretary to a helpline adviser at the National Autistic Society, a particularly nice post for me as it enabled me to spend my breaks in the library, trying to discover if there were any grounds for my long-held suspicion that I had Asperger's Syndrome. The pay was minimal, but if I added it to my dead relative income stream and my poetry award cheque, it would be more than enough to pay the rent on a room somewhere. I had no financial excuse for living at home any more, and I wanted to live closer to my London friends. I bought a copy of *Exchange and Mart* and circled some ads.

One of my circled ads had been placed by a rental agency in Camden. When I phoned up, they offered to pair me up with another young woman who was looking for a flat, so that they could show us some two-bedroom places together. I met Sally at their offices the next day. She was friendly and seemed easy enough to get on with. So did I. We took the agency up on their offer. Then they showed us a couple of places which turned our stomachs, so we decided to look together on our own behalf. I suggested we look further out – East Finchley maybe? – but that was further than Sally wanted to go, so we kept looking in Hampstead, Camden, Kentish Town, where the prices were high and pickings thin. We took ourselves to another Camden rental agency, a bigger one with shinier offices, and they showed us round a flat in a newly refurbished concrete block in Chalk Farm. The surroundings were rather squalid, and the block itself looked like a Brutalist lift shaft in a multi-storey car park, but the flat itself seemed pleasant enough, and the block well-secured, so we took it.

Sally moved in first, and within hours I had the first phone call: 'Well, it's just turning into a *nightmare* . . .' Plumbing was blocked, circuits had fused, the man at the rental place was shirty with her when she tried to complain . . . Worst of all, the paved-over flat roof outside our living room backed straight onto another roof, which was easily accessible from another flat, which was occupied by a riotous group of Italian squatters. There had been squatters in our new flat before the property managers had thrown them out, and whether these were the same people, or their friends, they apparently hated us already. Sally was convinced that when they played their games of roof football, they were kicking the ball against our French windows on purpose.

It did sound like a nightmare; in fact it sounded like one of my adolescent nightmares, where I was living unprotected in a house with dodgy wiring and even dodgier men banging on the windows, but I'd already paid my deposit in cleared funds, I was committed, and I couldn't leave Sally by herself, so I moved in. I had the smaller of the two bedrooms: Sally had told me that as she was a 'clothes and shoes person', she would take the bigger bedroom, if that was OK. I said OK. As long as I could keep some of my books in the living room.

'You do have a *lot* of books,' she said, dismayed, as I lined up crate after crate against the wall. The Nigerian student who guarded the front door at night, always with one of his business textbooks or the Koran in his hand, was more approving: 'You are a *clever* girl!' he cried.

I did try to stick it out. For all of two weeks, I tried. I walked to Camden station on workday mornings, slapping the pavements with my thin shoes (at that time I was wearing boys' slip-on plimsolls, size 5 from Woolworth's, the cheapest summer shoes you could get); I had a couple of friends back to the flat, and they admired its good proportions; Sally, who had been a hairdresser before she moved into tourism, gave me the best haircut I'd ever had, plus some excellent advice about hair-care, which I've followed ever since; I wrote some decent poems on my Powerbook, sitting at the dining table with one nervous eye on the windows; when I wasn't writing, I spent most of my time pacing my tiny bedroom, listening to *Hello Nasty* by the Beastie Boys over and over again on my Walkman.

The nights were harder than the days. It was a hot summer, and I slept uneasily, while noises from the streets outside seeped through the open window and into my dreams. At least there were no more football games after dark. Sometimes we would venture outside ourselves, and if the boys from the squat saw us on the patio or through the windows, they'd shout, 'Eh, *brutana!*' Sally had lived in Italy and told me '*brutana*' meant 'bitches' or 'dogs' – I'm not sure which is worse.

'Italian men never grow up,' she said. 'If their mums were here, they wouldn't dare.'

Not long after I arrived, I developed a painful sore throat that wouldn't shift, so I took a couple of days off work, and registered as a temporary patient at a surgery in Kentish Town. It was huge, with a waiting room like a bus station, filled to bursting with the slumping dispossessed. I was told to wait, and slumped in my turn along with all the others. We avoided one another's eyes, and kept them on the long electronic strip sign that showed us who was to go and see whom next and in which room they were to see them. Years later, when I was watching Ian Puleston-Davies' drama about OCD, *Dirty Filthy Love*, I'm pretty sure I recognized the waiting room in one of the scenes: it suited the bleak tone perfectly. After a short wait, I was summoned by the strip. An unfriendly young doctor took a quick look at my throat and said she would write me a prescription for antibiotics. She obviously begrudged me them.

While I was off work, I opened the *Guardian* one day and saw that Miroslav Holub had died. Since the poetry course, I'd sent him a postcard and he'd sent one back. I cried because he wouldn't now send any more to me, or to anybody. No more essays, no more poems, no more anecdotes about laboratory mice or domestic cats. It was too sad.

My previous experience with GPs had taught me that they would rather trust their own observations than take the patient's word for it, so instead of waiting till the crying fit had subsided, I phoned the surgery *during* the crying fit.

'I can't stop crying,' I sobbed, when the receptionist asked how she could help me.

'Do you think you might be depressed?' she asked.

I said that seemed probable.

She got me an appointment straight away. I saw one of the Unfriendly Doctor's kindlier colleagues. I told her that I was depressed, my father had been depressed and that I was scared that I was going to fail and succumb and die young just like he had. She said there was no need for that to happen: there was a new treatment out there called cognitive behavioural therapy, and this, she said, could help me get out of my depressive thinking patterns. In the meantime, of course I could have some more Prozac. I clutched the prescription gratefully. I was someone's pill-popping patient again, and the role felt familiar and comforting.

Back at the flat, I lay on the sofa reading *Prozac Nation*. Elizabeth Wurtzel made bad mental health seem like a romantic destiny, a vocation. At the same time, she gave a wincingly accurate account of what a self-absorbed pain in the arse a depressed young woman can be.

When I told Sally that I couldn't hack it any more, that I was heading back to my mother's, she was very sweet about it. She even said that, London rental prices being what they were, she would commute from her parents' herself, if she could. I promised that I would pay my half of the rent until she found another flatmate, and she found someone else almost straight away, but there was no denying that I'd done her a shabby turn, leaving her alone in that concrete block to deal with the football-playing squatter pests.

'Can you accept that you let her down?' my therapist asked.

'Yes,' I said, trying my best not to choke on it.

The move meant changing doctors, again. I had got it into my head that the next doctor might disbelieve me and take my lovely Prozac away, so I asked the kindly Kentish Town doctor to write a letter that I could take in with me, to explain the need for the prescription. There was no way that I was going back to my old GP to be patronized, so that left me with the big medical centre round the corner, down the hill, round the roundabout, up another hill and next to the car park by the disused railway line. Its waiting room reminded me of Kentish Town, only with much less slumping room. The receptionists spoke sharply. When I showed the letter to the doctor, it was obvious that I had done the wrong thing by bringing it.

'What are you giving me *this* for?' she snapped. Never mind: she renewed my prescription. Then she said I'd be better off seeing one of her colleagues next time, as he had been a psychiatrist, so he knew much more about mental illness. I got out as quickly as I could, which was what we both wanted.

When my next renewal came around, I saw the mental illness expert. He smiled broadly at me, and delivered a little lecture about how negative thinking activated the 'depression centres' – not a concept I've come across anywhere else – and what I needed to do was to stop dwelling on these depressing ideas and focus on the positive side. 'We can't always get what we want,' he said, grinning from ear to ear.

'I certainly can't get my father back,' I might have replied.

On the positive side, he renewed my prescription.

Leaving the flat had been a retrograde step but, again on the positive side, it had been twelve years since my humiliation by ten-year-old boys, and I'd managed to claim my local territory back from avoidance. These days, I was able to travel home late on the underground, and not always in the guard's carriage (not that I'd used them much anyway since a guard had hit on me a few years earlier, an incident which seemed to me to negate the whole point of his carriage, and of him). And when I got into Canons Park station on the late train, I would walk home. In the dark. All by myself.

I wanted to be able to go out at night and I didn't want to avoid meeting men. Observing the mourning rituals for my father had given me a new set of unexpected warm feelings towards my Jewish background, and, as I said to my mother, I was starting to think that settling down with a nice Jewish boy might not be such a bad thing after all. I had a look at the personal ads in the *Jewish Chronicle*, and left a message in a promising-sounding box. The man called me back, we had a pleasant enough chat, even laughed a few times, and arranged to meet in a bar in Covent Garden.

We found each other fairly quickly, and he suggested that we move on straight away to another, swankier bar, where we could sit at a quieter table and order a better sort of drink. As I sipped my whatever-it-was, he told me how he had just completed his MBA in London, and was now working for some type of management consultancy, which specialized in 'rationalization' – or was it 'downsizing'? He boasted about the vast numbers of people he was going to help make redundant, and did a little sub-machine gun mime with a twelve-year-old schoolboy's glee. He waved a platinum American Express card around when it was time to pay. Later, over dinner in an Indonesian restaurant, he told me that he'd been on about ten blind dates now, and on some of them – not this one, *of course* – he'd wished he *had* been blind, ha! ha! For all his platinum gallantry, I don't think he was that taken with me either. We said our polite goodbyes at the station, and boarded our separate trains.

It was about eleven o'clock when I arrived back at Canons Park tube station, and began without a second's thought to walk home. I was about halfway there, when I heard the voice say: 'This is a bit late for you, isn't it?'

I jumped and turned round. I recognized him, this man in the beige raincoat with his too-bright smile. I had often passed him on this street in the daytime, and as he had always said hello to me as if he knew me, I had always thought that perhaps he did know me and, not wanting to be rude, had got into the habit of saying hello back. Now that he was blocking my way at eleven o'clock at night, I realized that I had never known him, except as the Strange-Looking Man Who Always Says Hello.

He said again that this was late for me to be out; he thought I must be on my way home, as I lived – and he pointed in the right direction – up there, didn't I? Yes, he thought so. And round the corner there, *that* was the street where *he* lived. He'd been meaning to talk to me for ages – he'd seen me around and wondered, who *was* that beautiful girl? He'd never seen me so late before, but as it happened he was often walking about at this sort of time – you know how it is, you get bored at home alone in the evenings, you spend too much time and money in Internet chat rooms, or you just go and walk about for a bit, save on the phone bill . . . So, anyway, what about me? How come I was out so late?

After a few minutes, I said I'd see him around and went home.

I stopped walking down that particular street after dark, but he'd introduced himself now, so he felt bold enough to strike up a few one-sided conversations in daylight. A couple of days later, he stepped out in front of me in the same place, and gave me some pens from his work as a gift – he knew he should give me flowers really, but take the pens. No, he meant it, don't be silly, *take the pens*.

I stopped walking down that street at all. I took the bus. He sat down next to me and asked me where I was going. I pretended that I was off to see my boyfriend. Then I opened my book and read it. He marched to the front of the bus and shouted at the bus driver. He didn't bother me again, but then I made damn sure he wouldn't, by avoiding all the places where I'd encountered him.

MAN – ENCROACHING – AAAGH!

Dependence

A few weeks back, my husband asked me how far I'd got with the book. I told him I hadn't quite got to the part where we meet, but it was coming up shortly.

'I presume I'm the light at the end of the tunnel?' he asked.

Up to that point, the history of my relationships with men had been exactly what you might predict for a neurotic, obsessive, rather self-absorbed, dermotillomanic young she-poet: slight, shallow and unsatisfactory. I met Chris in the late autumn of 1998, when I had just begun work on my PhD. I had decided to drop my NAS job by then, and was beginning to think about looking for a flat near my latest university; property prices were cheaper there, so I would be able buy a small place, find a part-time job to help pay a small mortgage, and share my shrunken life with my ever-growing book collection. If I was going to be on my own for ever because the only men who found me attractive were quietly desperate characters in tan macs who forced pens into my hands, well, then so be it. I was beginning to be aware that I was giving off some whiff of desperation myself –

various men I had met at the university had thrown their *girl-friends* or *partners* into the conversation with a certain pointed casualness, and I read this as a very bad sign.

So I worked hard. The task for my first PhD year was to take in as much as I could of the voluminous psychoanalytic literature on creativity, review it and then refine my research question in terms of whatever I'd managed to make of what I'd just spent the year reviewing. A literature review breaks down, roughly, into three stages: 1) Gather the material, read it, scribble all over it (if owned or photocopied) and take far too many notes. 2) Sit down at your desk, make a few notes on the notes, panic, eat, cry, pick your skin, pace the room, go for some real walks, avoid your desk until you lose patience with yourself. 3) Finally write a summary of what you've read, comparing the different schools and authors and offering the odd thought of your own if you happen to be feeling clever that day.

I began by returning to my favourite, Milner, then went back to Freud, revisited Klein and Winnicott from my MA, then moved on to Anna Freud, her followers, the Annafreudians, then Klein's followers, the Kleinians, the followers of Klein's followers, the neo-Kleinians, and so on until I came to something like a contemporary position.

It was very interesting to see how much of what was written – though by no means all of it – tallied with what I'd learned from my own experience, as a student and as a poet. To accomplish any creative task, the analysts said, the individual needed to be able to tolerate a certain amount of internal discomfort: anxiety, doubt, uncertainty, conflict, confusion – in a word, *mess*. This is harder to manage if that individual is faced with difficult internal conditions, such as, for example, the presence of a superego with a loud and carrying voice who keeps asking you how far you've got, belittling whatever you've managed to do, and telling you to tidy up all the time. In Kleinian terms, such a figure is a 'persecutory internal object', an unintegrated, impacted part of the self powered up with nasty feelings and dead set on its mission of thwarting other, healthier parts of the self that are trying to get on with their work. It represents one kind of creative block. Here's an extract from a paper about an artist who was suffering from one:

> When the analysis proceeded to deeper levels it became clear that her depressions were related to a system of phantasies in which she felt herself possessed and inhabited by devils. These devils – at the beginning of the analysis they were innumerable – persecuted her constantly and in ever-varying ways. They roamed about inside her, caused her physical pain and illnesses, inhibited her in all her activities, especially in painting, and compelled her to do things she did not want to do. When she wanted to get up in the morning they moved about violently in her stomach and made her vomit. When she wanted to paint they interfered. They would roar with laughter when she tried to achieve something. They would force her to go to the lavatory constantly, and during a certain period she had to urinate so frequently that it disturbed her work seriously. They had forks with which they prodded and attacked her in the most cruel ways. They would eat her up from inside and force her to take food for them. But she felt she could not eat because they would poison her with their excrement and thus turn food into poison. Owing to these persecutions she was in agony, especially when painting.[28]

I knew exactly what she meant: anxiety can be hell on the digestion, and it makes you wee a lot too.

Early that summer, at the Society of Authors awards ceremony,

28. Paula Heimann, 'A contribution to the problem of sublimation and its relation to processes of internalization (1939/42)' in *About Children and Children-No-Longer: Collected Papers 1942–80* (Routledge, London, 1989)

I had made friends with one of the other Eric Gregory recipients, a computer science student who lived with her fiancé in Cambridge. In November, we travelled to the Aldeburgh Poetry Festival together, and in December she invited me round for dinner. Although I had said many times, and meant it, that I would never go back to That Town, I accepted the invitation: I wanted to see more of my new poetry friend, and there would be single men there, but no pressure. Chris was sitting opposite me, but the only thing I remember him saying to me over dinner was: 'That's the best Cartman impersonation I've ever heard.' I wasn't aware that he was particularly taken with anything else about me, so it was quite a surprise when he sent an email to my mother's address the following January, and asked me out.

We met at Belsize Park station, realized that neither of us really wanted to see *Life is Beautiful*, and went to a restaurant in Hampstead. I already knew a little about him: he worked at the Computer Laboratory, and he liked to paint in oils; he knew that I was a poet, who could do good Cartman impressions. During a long evening in the Hampstead restaurant, we learned more. Chris liked photography as well as painting; while painting, he preferred to listen to Underworld, or Orbital, although he still carried a torch for the Cocteau Twins. He didn't share my desire to live by the sea, because he had grown up on the Solent, near Portsmouth, and to him the seaside meant floating detritus, drunken sailors, noisy shipping, and boys sitting in sullen rows on the harbour wall smoking during lunchtime. But he did like cats, and had two of his own. He had two siblings as well, but they were much older, and living in New Zealand.

Next weekend we met at the Tate for lunch, looked round an exhibition of Francis Bacon sketches together, and carried on talking. Chris, like me, had lost his father. Like my father, his had smoked, but in his case it had been narrative irony that had killed him, as he had died in a car accident on his way to get the all-clear from his oncologist. It had been a different kind of bereavement in other ways, too: Chris's father had moved to New Zealand some years before to join his older children, and it had been impossible for Chris to get to the funeral. In any case, he had not lived with his father since he was six years old, when his parents had divorced. His father had remained behind on the RAF base in Malta where he worked, while Chris and his mother had moved home, to England, to the south coast. The years that followed had not been easy for either of them: his mother had suffered frequent bouts of ill health, and had spent some time in hospital. When Chris had not been in foster care, he had been the man of the house. Sometimes it would seem to me that, while I had taken for ever to grow up, Chris had been grown up for ever.

The following weekend, I went to visit him at his house in Cambridge. I learned that his paintings were wonderful and his cats were very endearing; he had fully stocked bookshelves and he knew how to cook. I stayed the night. The next weekend he came to stay with me. We carried on alternating weekends, and on the weekdays, we emailed. I introduced Chris to my family; we met each other's friends.

How could it possibly be going so well? For the first few weeks I was deeply sceptical, but I really couldn't find what the catch might be, so, with the help of my analyst, I gave up trying. Tunnel, light . . . OK, yes.

Meeting Chris was a watershed in my life, but I couldn't find too much about it in my notebooks: then, as now, I used them mostly to record the kinds of feelings – fears, embarrassments, misgivings, griefs, vague sensations of dread – that I could most reliably turn into poems. Success and happiness just don't do it for me or my muse: we both suspect that those whom the Gods wish to destroy, they first allow to be happy, because then the happiness adds a certain extra piquancy to the destruction part, and that makes the whole thing so much more fun.

So I can't find too many references to the other momentous good thing which happened to me that spring, which was that Bloodaxe Books accepted my first poetry collection. I had sent fifty poems to them in March, bound together under the title *Sisyphus' Daughter*, and in May I received a fat envelope in the post, with a catalogue, a couple of contracts to sign, and a letter offering publication on condition that I agreed to certain changes, including, for a start, a different title. On 19 May, I was trying a few out in my notebook:

The Gulping Hourglass
The Frequent Flyer's Book of the Dead
Scaling the North Face of Hopkins
The War on all Dolls
The Accident Book
Left Luggage
Not Yet Human
Death of an Accountant
Plastic Sunlight
A Book of Accidents
A Feminine Itch
Seven Shades of Guilt
Leave God Out of It

In the end, I settled for *Femenismo*, one of the poem titles the editor had suggested and which I liked well enough to use. The book was scheduled to come out in early autumn 2000. In the meantime, I took out the weaker poems, added a few newer, stronger ones, and worried myself sick about how my work might be received. My worries became my own devils, and they would possess me every time I tried to write. I didn't understand then that, certainly in my case, creativity comes in cycles; I didn't realize that I was simply entering a natural fallow period, so I panicked, and kept on pushing myself. My work became stiffer and more stilted as the year progressed, then slowed almost to a standstill. By the time November came around, all I could manage was:

Laundry

So my life has come to this:
all I ever make is laundry.

Awake or asleep, I'm always
shuffling round some shopping mall,

raking through knitwear carousels
that whirl into infinity,

searching, with the fever of teething gums,
for the ultimate cardigan.

Is it any wonder the wardrobe's bursting,
the linen basket overflowing

like an archive of disproved hypotheses?
The grey bras, the shrinking T-shirts,

that embarrassed puddle of lycra,
my favourite dress – now ruined dress –

my lost, remembered, perfect dress:
all laundry, in the end. More laundry.

Strictly speaking, it was Chris's laundry basket. I had moved in by then.

We made the decision in the summer; I was to move in sometime in the autumn, after Chris had returned from a long-planned trip to see family in New Zealand. He was away for three weeks. At the same time, my mother was in the States, visiting my brother. I was alone in the house. I wasn't used to being alone any more, and I soon realized that at some point, or maybe gradually, I'd shed the me-alone carapace I'd grown around myself when I lived in Edinburgh. I wrote that I was becoming 'uneasy about knives', that I was having 'train anxiety dreams', that I was finding it harder and harder to cross the road when there was no one to cross it with me.

One particular little non-incident left me with an instant and very uncomfortable spike. I've sometimes thought of it as that moment when my adult OCD fully revealed itself – or would have done, if I'd been able to recognize it as such. At the time, I described it in my notebook as being 'one of those could've-happened-but-didn't shock/panic experiences'. I was standing at a pelican crossing on Station Road in Stanmore, waiting to cross the road. The green light turned red, the green man started bleeping. As I prepared to take my first step into the road, I turned my head to the right, as I always did and always will, to check that the oncoming traffic had done the proper thing and stopped, and . . . a van, a white van with a wire cage full of evergreen shrubs trailing behind it, sailed through the red light and all the way across the crossing. That was all that happened.

But, I wrote in my notebook, 'what if I had had a moment of absent-mindedness and just stepped across when I saw the green man? That would have been the end of me. What if I'd been in hospital, unable to speak – and both Mum & Chris out of the country?'

VAN – CROSSING – SQUELCH!

When I was alone, I ruminated about the crossing, about the van, about vans and crossings in general, about the kind of injuries one might sustain if thrown into the air by a van at a crossing, about the chances of surviving these injuries, but, strangely, this activity only seemed to make me more anxious. If my mother or Chris were available, I could ask for reassurance, about that crossing or the risks of road-crossing, or anything else that was making me anxious at any given moment, and just as long as they gave it, the anxiety would stay away for as long as I was talking to them. If either of them was with me when I had to cross a road, I would take the nearest available arm, usually without thinking about it. Inevitably, as Chris and I grew closer, and after I moved in with him, he emerged as the new chief guarantor of my safety. And the safer I came to feel with Chris, the less safe I would come to feel in his absence.

We expect grown men and women to take responsibility for their own safety and well-being: it's probably the minimum requirement for adulthood. It is ridiculous for a woman of twenty-nine to feel unable to cross a main road by herself, or take a plane by herself, or walk round the track side of a group of people on a Tube platform, or ride a bicycle on the road in a town where half the population does just that every day, but I did feel unable to do any of these things, and I would struggle to do most of them now. I still have to force myself to take out-of-town journeys, as I can never quite be certain that I'm going to return home alive. It would probably help if I could manage to stop visualizing the gap between my starting point and my destination as a wide and depthless black abyss, but old habits die hard. Every time I think of a journey I'm going to have to make, up it flashes, the thought: ABYSS. I can't see my way to the other side, I can't see the bottom, and there's no way of crossing except for one tatty rope bridge; it has a guide rope on one side only, and half the slats are missing.

If I have someone travelling with me, ABYSS is still there, but it shrinks to something like:

ABYSS

The anxiety it represents shrinks proportionately, and I have a far more comfortable journey. It's not that I'm incompetent: I can do all the practical things – booking tickets, getting to the station on time, finding my way to the right platform, giving directions to a cab driver, everything – but I just can't shrink my ABYSS. If I'm on my own, I can't stop ruminating about all the ways in which the journey could go wrong, because taking responsibility for one's own safety, in my book, means anticipating every conceivable problem, and planning evasive action for every case. So if I'm travelling to London, for example, I need be aware that the train might derail, that one of the other passengers might be a psychopath, that a terrorist plot might be due to reach its climax at King's Cross at the very moment of my arrival, that I might trip up on the escalator at the underground, that I might jostle someone on the underground and provoke a fit of Tube rage which will result in a fatal stabbing, that I might step out in front of a car, bus, taxi, lorry, or white van with a trailer full of shrubbery on any one of London's unreasonably busy roads. These are just the scenarios I can conjure up sitting at my desk at home; if I were actually making this journey at the present moment, I could do much better than that. Travelling with somebody for whom taking responsibility for one's safety means behaving sensibly and not thinking about problems until they actually come up is so much less draining for me, so much less challenging, so much *easier*.

As taking responsibility for safety is so much more straightforward for the non-ruminator, it also makes sense to hand certain other tasks over to them too: handling knives, lighting gas flames, using power tools, climbing ladders, wiring plugs, opening the front door at night, giving medication to cats, deciding when it is safe to cross the road, administering eye drops to babies, carrying babies over hard surfaces – but I'm getting ahead of myself now. I'm sure you've got the main point here, which is that the OCD sufferer becomes more and more dependent on her safety guarantor, and as time goes on, everyday life for that guarantor becomes so much more draining, so much more challenging, so much *harder*.

It would be hard enough for these partners, parents and children of sufferers if all they had to do was to take care of whatever tasks the sufferer was avoiding, but most of them end up carrying further responsibilities. What these are will depend on the nature of the sufferer's obsessions. My husband, for example, was my reassurer in chief – until he got wise to it, at least. Compared to some, he has it easy: he's never had to keep a complete change of clothing in the front porch so that he can take off his contaminated work clothes and then walk through a bleach-infused foot bath before entering the house every evening; he's never had to spend an evening going round the house checking that everything is unplugged, and then checking again, because the words he used in his first checking report weren't quite convincing enough; he's never arrived late to work because he's had to spend an hour going through bin bags to make sure, but absolutely sure, that nothing essential has been thrown away by mistake; he's never had to take extra care to move about his own home in such a way as not to disarrange a single ornament, cup, footstool, coffee table, coaster, book, newspaper, handset or tissue box; he's never had to give up his job to become the full-time carer of a woman so petrified of germs that she can no longer touch anything or anybody; he has never been the parent of an adult so paralysed by her obsessions that she can no longer leave her bedroom and will only speak to her own family from the other side of a firmly closed door.

It's not just the sufferer who suffers.

I didn't think for a moment that someone like me deserved someone like Chris, I couldn't quite see how I'd managed to wind up with him and I didn't understand why he chose to stay with me rather than choosing one of those sane women you see walking around all over the place. Our relationship was simply implausible.

Even if I could be certain that Chris would never leave me voluntarily, there was still the possibility of early death. As I saw it, the women in my bloodline didn't have much luck with their husbands in this respect. My mother's husband had succumbed to a heart attack and left her widowed at fifty-nine. Then there was that dreadful day back in 1941 when my grandfather, in a moment of spectacular carelessness which cost his family dearly, tried to run for a moving bus and wound up crushed under it instead (you see what a lack of vigilance can do?). Whenever Chris left the house, especially after dark, I would extract a promise from him that he would be careful, not get knocked off his bike by a car, or beaten up, or knifed or anything like that. When I was having trouble sleeping at night, and his breathing was too quiet for me to hear, it was all I could do to stop myself poking him.

Loving makes us so vulnerable. Every day we face the risk of losing the people we love, of disappointing or hurting or inadvertently betraying them, of dragging them into our pains and problems, of getting dragged into theirs, or being disappointed or hurt or betrayed in our turn. The partner you share your life with can cheat on you, the parents whose acceptance you have always craved can use every visit and phone call as a new opportunity to undermine you, the child you brought up, fed, educated and loved can grow up to write a memoir; she might not even have the decency to wait until you're both dead. I'm painfully aware, as a I write this, that someone or other said that any family which produces a writer is finished,[29] and I really don't have the slightest desire to finish mine, or wound it, or annoy it, or embarrass it ever so slightly. So I'm being as careful as I possibly can.

29. I've just put 'Quotation Family Writer Finished' into Google: apparently it was Czesław Miłosz, and what he said was: 'When a writer is born into a family, that family is finished.'

During the pause between the last paragraph and this one, I phoned my mother and asked her if it was fair to say, in writing, that her early loss had left her with a legacy of anxiety? Yes, she said, it had, and it was fair to say so; she added that she had always got herself terribly wound up if my father was a bit late coming home. Then would it also be fair to say that that kind of anxiety gets handed down in a family? Yes, it was perfectly fair. So, I've said it, I've written it, and my mummy said I could.

Like my mother, my husband encountered more than his fair share of adversity early on in life, but in his case the legacy has been made up, mostly, of preternatural toughness and eerie calm. So when I asked him what I should call him in a book which couldn't help but be revealing of both of us, he said to call him Chris, because that was his name. And when I kept him awake in the wee small hours of the first day of the new millennium, 'talking', as I put in my notebook, 'about my angst', he said one has to shrug and accept that life *is* horrific and unbearable, but live it anyway.

That's what he does.

I wrote very little poetry in 2000, and most of what I wrote was dismal. Hence the line: 'all I ever make is laundry'. I probably did make quite a lot of laundry that year, and laundry, along with pacing, picking and procrastination, is what I chiefly remember, but when I looked back at the written evidence, I found quite a few other activities.

That was the year in which I founded a local fundraising group for the Medical Foundation, volunteered as the group's secretary, taught my first evening classes in creative writing, got engaged to Chris, planned our wedding, travelled to London once or twice a week to see my Jungian analyst, then made the decision to terminate the analysis, decided that for the qualitative research part of my PhD I would interview undergraduates about their essay-writing, drafted a semi-structured interview to use for this, carried out pilot interviews, then the main group of interviews, got married, went on honeymoon to Venice, came back, held the first copies of my book in my hand, had my book shortlisted for a prize for debut poetry collections, attended the ceremony, didn't get the prize, read my first reviews – which were good, by and large – made my first tentative attempts to analyse the data I had collected, wrote and presented a paper on my methodology to the department's PhD forum. In December of that year, I took on a new paid project, helping a prolific but untutored poet to organize her work into a book. Of that last, I wrote, 'Not at all sure I haven't bitten off more than I can chew, there.' But I wanted to take the job, just on the off chance that it might make me feel other than useless, for once in my life.

My analyst said that her one worry about terminating the analysis that summer was that my guilt seemed to have lost little or none of its claws-into-me ferocity. Leaving analysis at that point seemed justifiable to me because I was soon to be married and published, and these two facts together would mean that I could never again be a sadloserwaster in the eyes of Party Girl; everyone knows that only a sadloserwaster would need to spend so much time and money on therapy. Or should that be, *waste* so much time and money?

Thanks to my great-uncle's legacy – that which should have been my father's – and Chris's willingness to work and pay the bills while I wrote and studied, I had ample supplies of both, and I felt just terrible about it. The bereavements which had yielded the money had also inspired my best poems, which had led to my award and my publishing contract, and I felt, if anything, even worse about that. I was both parasite and patriphage. If I was becoming more and more fearful, it had to be because I knew, deep down, that I had it coming.

My journey to and from the university, which I made as little as possible, became suddenly more abyss-like around the end of the summer term, when I travelled down for my last supervision of the academic year. I got on the train at the end of the line at Cambridge, as usual, and had the carriage to myself for five minutes before a tall, lean man hopped on. He leaned out of the doorway smoking for a few minutes, then he threw the butt onto the platform, smiled at me with pointy Bond-villain teeth and sat down in the seat opposite. Unlike me, he obviously enjoyed talking to strangers on trains, and entertained me all the way to Harlow Town with vignettes from his life: somebody had spread rumours around the estate that he was a kiddy-fiddler, all because he had opened the door to a child in his underpants – I don't remember all the details but I think the whole thing ended up with him in court because he'd bitten a bit of someone's ear off, which was a perfectly reasonable thing to do, because he hadn't started it, but all the same *he* was the one who got charged with GBH, and where was the justice in that? I agreed that there was none, and shook a little. All the time, I kept my finger on the page I'd been reading: it seemed more than my ear was worth to ask if I might get back to it. He got off at Harlow Town, with a 'God Bless You', because I was obviously a good girl, and now we had established that that stretch of the Liverpool Street line would ever after belong to him, and all the other pointy-toothed bogeymen.

It was a pity, because up until that day the Cambridge–Liverpool Street leg had been the easiest of the trip for me. The worst time had always been the beginning of the return journey, when I had to wait, helplessly, in an underground concrete car park, often after dark, for the taxi I had ordered to pick me up and drive me back through thunderous and unwalkable streets to the local station. The wait never failed to set off my Unbearable Feeling, which would only abate – a little – when I had sat myself safely down in the cab and it had begun to move away. God alone knew who or what skulked about on the campus at night, and I didn't want to find out. That evening, after my encounter with the ear-biter, I found myself waiting with a worse-than-usual case of Unbearable Feeling, so it was another pity that this turned out to be the one occasion when the cab driver who'd been sent to pick me up decided to pick up somebody else instead. I phoned for another driver, who arrived five minutes later, outraged on my behalf and very apologetic. It didn't help much.

They were the most trivial incidents, I know that: someone talked to me when I didn't want him to, and later that day I had to wait longer than usual for a cab. I'm at a loss to explain why they were such terrible experiences at the time, and why they left me so shaken for so long afterwards. I can't, in the end, find an explanation that would satisfy a rational reader – I suppose that's why they call it a disorder.

Chris married me and my disorder at the end of August, and then the three of us went off on honeymoon to Venice, the perfect venue for generating both romantic memories and imaginary near-drowning incidents. In the week that we were there, Chris took an album's worth of photographs and I took copious notes: what we saw, what we did, what we bought, what we ate, what I feared, which bits of me hurt and when, and what we saw on Italian television: 'Bath in rose milk. Cut armpit. *Ally McBeal* in Italian.'

My entry for 2 September begins: '3 a.m. woke up thinking 2 September, it's significant – why? Then realized why "Papa was a Rolling Stone" had been going round my head for a couple of days: Dad's death.'

I know it's 3 September in the song, but the unconscious recalls feelings more precisely than it does numbers.

The 3 September was our last day in Venice. We went up to the restaurant on the hotel's roof for our last Venetian meal; we had eaten breakfast there every morning, and I had once peered over the edge of the parapet, a mistake I didn't make twice: 'once had seen over the edge, cld't get the thought of plunging over ought [sic] of my mind – what is it with me and fear at the moment?' We had beautiful food and 'an added light show – courtesy of an electrical storm on the Adriatic horizon – pink & orange sheet lightning – Chris thought the strange colours might be the result of pollution.' I recorded that a huge Cunard liner drifted past, slowly, like a 'lit-up glacier', and that there was a 'cute cherubic two-year-old' sitting at the next table. Finally I noted my 'slight alarm when realized had a great lamb bone in my mouth, but got rid of it after a second – worry quite out of proportion, as was my unease over the high location of the restaurant, and the storm – as I said, why is my fear so disproportionate, so out of control?'

One possible explanation was that I had come off the Prozac again; another was that I had declared myself officially normal and terminated the analysis. Maybe I was overdoing it with the laundry. What's clear from my increasingly whiney and repetitive journal is how much I was struggling with my PhD. The wedding and honeymoon had given me a useful excuse to ignore it for a couple of months, but then the new autumn term came around and I needed to come up with something to show my supervisor. I had reached the crucial stage, the data analysis stage, where I had to take my interviews and relate them to the themes in my literature review in some meaningful and reasonably novel way, knit the separate parts together into a plausible thesis, identify whatever my point was and then get to it, in an appropriate number of words. My supervisor thought that I had some promising ideas. I didn't. I was painfully aware that I had never received any training in qualitative research, and to me my methods, both for gathering and for analysing data, looked pathetically patched together. The whole thesis looked patched together to me. I told my supervisor that I needed to go back and transcribe all my interviews in full, just to make sure that I didn't miss anything. This would take a nice long time, it was a huge task, and while I was doing it nobody could reasonably expect me to produce any conclusions and in doing so risk saying something, in a public forum, that might be uninteresting, irrelevant, stupid or wrong. I was supposed to be writing a thesis about the anxieties which arise in academic work and I couldn't get over my anxiety about it. It was a *mise en abyme*; an oroboros; a slow, reflexive disappearance up an arse.

I obsessed about all kinds of things. I ruminated, and asked my husband for reassurance about my ruminations – a habit we called my 'what-iffing': What if we had fallen over while crossing the road and the car hadn't stopped? What if that swelling on my lower lip (which turned out to be the mucocel) was cancerous? What if that mobile phone company that kept sending me bills for a phone I wasn't using sent in bailiffs and big black dogs while I was in the house by myself? What if the clear discharge from my vagina was a symptom of *cancer of the womb*? What if nobody wanted to buy our house? What if somebody wanted to buy our house but the house we wanted to buy got taken off the market? What if I had fallen into the Venetian lagoon while wearing a heavy backpack? What if the only reviews people took notice of were the two bad ones I kept wailing on about? What if the two bad reviews were the only really incisive ones and I owed it to the world to give up and stop pestering it with my God-awful poetry? What if I finished my PhD, handed it in and it failed? What if everyone else went on to have babies and I never did? What if I had a baby but fucked it up because I was too neurotic? What if I NEVER WROTE ANOTHER DECENT POEM AGAIN? In April, I finally went to the doctor, and took Chris with me – which made sense to both of us, as he was undoubtedly suffering too.

Now the medical notes can pick up the story again, beginning with a letter from my latest GP to the head of psychological treatment services at the local hospital, saying that he would be 'much obliged if this lady[30] could be assessed for treatment within your service'.

> She has recently come onto my list and presented on 26 April saying that she was in a crisis on that day. She was tearful, overstretched, had taken on too much, was moving house and was not getting to sleep easily. She had been in therapy in London with —, and was requesting that she could re-start therapy here. I prescribed Fluoxetine 20 mg daily for her . . .

He made his request for an assessment for me, and concluded with: 'I should say that she is married, and says that she is very happy in this relationship, and the house that she is moving to in Cambridge is very much to her liking.'

Of course, there was a waiting list. There always is on the NHS, but I can tell that this one wasn't too bad, as the referral letter was dated 11 May and my appointment for assessment was sent out on 18 July. That's really not bad at all, and in the meantime, I saw the kind GP again. We discussed what he called my 'depression/anxiety thing'. He didn't tell me to go out and have fun, nor did he read me a lecture about not getting all put out because I couldn't get everything I wanted. I might well have been luckier with this GP – and I think I was – but our better working relationship might also have reflected a more mature attitude on my part, or perhaps health professionals always take a married thirty-something woman more seriously than they would a twenty-something girl. I think perhaps we all do, and it's not entirely fair of us.

So he listened, and I told him how I felt as if I could die at any time; it wasn't that I wanted to, but all the same it seemed

30. In letters to and from GPs, as I've discovered, one is always 'a lady', sometimes even 'a pleasant lady'.

212

so implausible that I should keep surviving, day after day, when everywhere I went there were a hundred stupid little senseless deaths lying about, waiting for me to trip over them. Every time I crossed the road, I said, I wondered how I'd made it to the other side intact. Often when I stood at a pelican crossing, I said, I was aware of how easy it would be, in a moment of absent-mindedness, say, to step out at the wrong time and get fatally squelched by a juggernaut.

'Do you think there might be some suicidal ideation behind that thought?' he asked me.

'It would make sense,' I said, 'though I'm not aware of any conscious intent.'

I didn't want to die, but I feared for my life. Many times a day I would feel some mute, destructive urge, in me but not of me, which it took all my energy to resist. I didn't want death, but it – something, the death instinct, whatever it was – kept propelling me towards it. In June I noted these '[a]larming mental events – or in the brain? – urge to swallow glass penguin'. The glass penguin-swallowing obsession was quite possibly the most bizarre I've ever had, even more absurd than what if I can't find my shoes? It started while I was wrapping up our ornaments in newspaper, ready to move to the house that was so much to my liking. The penguin was a tiny thing, only about an inch and a half long, if that, and rather less than an inch round. As I wrapped it, I found myself thinking about how small it was, that it was about the same size, maybe, as a liquorice torpedo. Then I had a mental image of the penguin in my mouth, followed by another of my giving in to an urge to swallow it, failing, and choking to death. Almost simultaneously, I had an impulse to put the penguin in my mouth right then, right there, and try to swallow it, just to prove to myself, because I needed to, that this wouldn't necessarily kill me . . . Terrified, I smothered the innocent little penguin in newspaper, as quickly as I could, and shoved it down into the very bottom of the box I was packing.

Even though I'd buried the penguin, the thought of it kept bobbing to the surface of my mind, again and again and again. When we unpacked at the new house, I made sure that Chris, not I, unpacked the penguin, and then insisted that he put it on the highest shelf he could find. I laughed about it at the time, but all the same that penguin scared me shitless. I almost named this book after it.

Early in September, one of the clinical psychologists in the department of cognitive and behavioural psychotherapies wrote to my GP to thank him for referring me. She mentioned that I was currently taking a break for a few months from my PhD, and commented that:

> She obviously has very high standards, which she is well aware of. A lot of her thoughts centre around 'should' statements, in that she always feels that she should be doing more than she is. She also tends to compare herself to others a lot, although she tries not to. At times, when she is down she spends a lot of time crying. She is able to recognise the pattern of her thoughts and that they tend to centre around a fear of failure. Although she can look at these rationally at times, she told me that she has more belief in her negative thoughts.

It's a very long letter, reminding me of how comprehensively I'd jabbered my heart out in the session. We were both very tired at the end of it.

Going back to the letter, the psychologist agrees that 'she certainly does seem to have had episodes of depression in the past and that she is a generally anxious person, with a lot of her anxieties centred around a fear of death'. She describes me as 'somewhat hypervigilant of dangers in her life' and recommends cognitive behavioural therapy as a treatment which would provide 'some strategies to help her break the cycle of rumination that she engages in'. She mentions that, although I have had 'numerous treatments' in the past, I have not yet had CBT, and that she believes this would provide 'a very different treatment approach than she has previously experienced', as it would focus on the 'here and now', rather than on my childhood and family history. Straight away, she offered me a different perspective on my mental health: it seemed to her, she said, that my primary problem was not depression as such, but anxiety.

That really threw me. I had so long thought of myself as 'a depressive': I'd read the books, written the poetry, listened to The Cure and bought the black T-shirt. I'd identified willingly with Sylvia Plath and Spike Milligan and Franz Kafka and all those other clever, gifted people whose depression had somehow seemed an integral part of their giftedness. As the doctor had said in his referral letter, I believed that 'some of [my] talent might come from adversity'. You could make depression sound like a valid philosophical position if you chose – hadn't Camus written of *The Logic of Suicide*? Depression even had that beautiful and noble-sounding synonym, *melancholy*. No, I'm not a bit down, I'm *melancholy*; I *languish*; alone in my brown study, I *palely loiter*. Coleridge, Shelley and Keats wrote odes to it. Every word on the 'Meat is Murder' lyric sheet justified it.

I understood depression to be an affliction, or at least as a state which lay outside the norm, but I had trouble seeing anxiety in those terms. From both my psychoanalytic and common-sense perspectives, anxiety was a normal, everyday human feeling; looked at from the perspective of common sense alone, it was trivial, and to be so bothered by such a trivial thing that I asked for treatment meant that I must be making a fuss about nothing. That I took the diagnosis as a put-down was partly the result of a certain intellectual – or maybe diagnostic – snobbery on my part, but I think it also had something to do with the poverty of our language when it comes to mental states, which means that we use the same word for both the mild, temporary tension you feel when you need to get back to work in ten minutes and you're trying to get to the front of a checkout queue, and for that other kind of tension which, if not always with you, is never far away and makes you wonder if a person's chest muscles really could squeeze her ribs so hard that they cave in and squelch her lungs into fishpaste. There's something in the very phonology of the word 'anxiety' that's too quiet, too *polite* to describe what that other kind of tension feels like: it's a third-person word, a clinician's word. The Unbearable Feeling is a much better term. That, or 'terror'.

Let's say I was suffering from a 'melancholy/terror thing': it's so much more aesthetically appealing. Or feel free to stick with 'depression' and 'anxiety', if that's what you prefer. Whatever you choose to call them, you'll usually find them together.

The psychologist placed me on the waiting list for CBT. It was over a year long. She encouraged me to complain about it if I wanted to, and gave me a list of local private practitioners I might see in the meantime. I couldn't face a year's wait, and I had a little inheritance money left, so I phoned one of the people on the list, and by early September I was in his office, ready to start.

You'll have heard of cognitive behavioural therapy: it's very popular with the department of health, because it is, as Wikipedia puts it, 'cost-effective' and seen by many as 'evidence and empiricism based'. It is often recommended, with or without medication, as a treatment for mild-to-moderate depression as well as for a variety of anxiety disorders, including OCD. If you are offered therapy on the NHS, it will most likely be some form of CBT, and most probably a short course of it – somewhere between six and ten sessions. The fact that it is administered, like antibiotics, in a set course means that health authorities can budget for it: we have x number of qualified therapists working y hours per week, and therefore we can provide z courses of therapy in any given financial year. That gives it a certain practical advantage over psychoanalysis and its sister psychodynamic therapies, which by their very nature are open-ended. Another advantage it has, at least from an administrative point of view, is that its effects can be measured with instruments that are regarded as valid and reliable tools for the job. Of the two concepts, validity is the harder to pin down: in this context, it would be reasonable to say that a valid instrument can be shown to have measured what it set out to measure. For example, if excessive lethargy plus tearfulness equals depression, then an instrument that measures the degree of a patient's lethargy, and of her tearfulness, is a valid tool for the diagnosis of depressive illness. To say that an instrument for psychological assessment is reliable is to state, among other things, that it would produce the same results with the same patient no matter who administered it.

This is in clear contrast to the knowledge a psychoanalyst has – or claims to have – of her patient's condition, as this knowledge will be grounded in her relationship with her patient, in her experience of that relationship, and in her application of psychoanalytic theory to the insights gained from that experience. This theory, along with the body of recorded clinical knowledge which the analyst may use to inform the treatment, is, in itself, drawn from a hundred years' experience of these private, unobserved, clinical encounters. I don't think, myself, that this means that psychoanalytic theory has no explanatory value, or that psychoanalytic psychotherapies have no clinical use, but it does have the consequence that conventionally reliable evidence for psychoanalysis is in rather short supply. It is also worth remembering that the existence of the unconscious – in the psychoanalytic sense of the word – is hypothesized rather than proved. Neither the unconscious nor its workings can be directly observed. That doesn't help either.

The aim of psychoanalysis, in its classical form, is nothing less than a fundamental rearrangement of the patient's psyche, which is a tall order. On the other hand, the aim of behavioural therapy, in *its* classical form, is the modification of particular behaviours. Unlike the primitive processes of the unconscious, behaviour can be directly observed and precisely recorded: you can measure, for example, the number of minutes per hour a patient spends washing her hands, and if the aim of the treatment is to cut this down, you can measure her improvement in terms of minutes cut. Therefore, it's evidence based, it's empirically sound, and it's cost-effective.

It doesn't stop there, though. CBT is designed to improve mood as well as behaviour. This mood is measured using the valid and reliable instruments I mentioned earlier. The instruments which mainstream psychologists and psychiatrists use for both research and clinical purposes are structured clinical interviews, and self-administered questionnaires, or inventories. These inventories are identical in form to quantitative market research surveys: the patient is handed a list of statements, and is asked to mark the boxes next to them to show whether or not she agrees with them. Some inventories, like some market research surveys, also have a five-point scale next to each statement, so that the patient can indicate to a more precise extent how much she does or doesn't agree. Each inventory is designed to measure that patient's condition against a particular scale; when the completed inventory is handed back to the clinician or researcher who is making the assessment, he or she can then follow a set of precise instructions to convert the patient's answers into a numerical score, check this score against the scale, and thereby get at least an initial sense of whether this patient's OCD, for example, is absent, mild, moderate or severe.[31] The scores are no substitute for clinical intuition and

31. You can find an example of a statement from the Padua Inventory, which is used to diagnose OCD, at the beginning of each chapter.

judgement, and most psychologists would not use them as such, but they are useful in so far as they can be measured at the beginning and end of a course of treatment, and the difference noted as a precise number. That's a demonstrable result.

At my initial consultation with Ben, the CB therapist, I filled in three questionnaires, designed to measure, respectively, anxiety, depression and hopelessness. I came out as moderately anxious, moderately depressed, and moderately hopeless. The letter which Ben sent to my GP following the consultation, like the letter from the hospital psychologists, covers an immense amount of ground, and this time in smaller type. It takes in my hypochondria, my concerns about knives, my physical anxiety symptoms, my worry that I talked too much and said the wrong things when I 'encountered people situationally'. Behaviourally, he mentions my skin picking, my reassurance seeking, my rumination and my avoidance, terms which are very familiar to me – and boring to you – by now, but which meant very little to me at the time. His impression was that the woman in front of him was 'showing different symptoms of anxiety, focusing perhaps on mild hypochondriasis with possibly some obsessive compulsive symptoms where she ruminates'. I remember him asking me if I didn't agree that I was a little bit obsessive. I did agree, but assumed he meant it in the general sense.

In the closing paragraphs, he outlines his plan of treatment.

My plan is to help her to understand the link between thinking, affect and behaviour with a view to helping her challenge automatic thinking, as well as using behavioural experiments to explore the risk issues. The more general issues around guilt may be explored through schema focus, which may be done later using Beck's Early Model. Usual questionnaires will monitor progress.

As the methods of CBT – unlike those of psychoanalysis – are intended to be transparent to the patient, I have a copy of a diagram which, very handily, sets out that cognitive-affective-behaviour link.

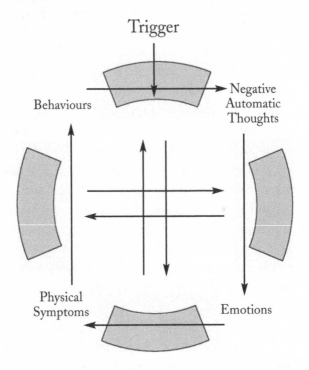

Trigger

Behaviours

Negative Automatic Thoughts

Physical Symptoms

Emotions

To put the model into words, something happens which acts as a TRIGGER for a NEGATIVE AUTOMATIC THOUGHT which gives rise to certain unpleasant EMOTIONS which in turn give rise to correspondingly unpleasant PHYSICAL SYMPTOMS so that these three together – negative thoughts, negative emotions, nasty symptoms – prompt the individual to engage in certain BEHAVIOURS to try to deal with them all. This is expressed as a circle rather than a line, because these behaviours, while providing a certain amount of immediate relief from the cognitive, emotional and physical aspects of anxiety, are in the long run ineffective, as they do not enable the sufferer to do what she really needs to do to escape from the circle, which is to challenge the thoughts in the first place and to modify the behaviour accordingly. The model is probably best explained by example:

TRIGGER: I am waiting to cross a road. I look both ways and see that a car is turning into the road, about a hundred yards away.

NEGATIVE AUTOMATIC THOUGHT: If that speeds up on its way down the road and I'm halfway across and I fall over and can't get up and the driver is talking on his mobile phone or something and doesn't see me or is drunk perhaps, he might run me over and kill me.

EMOTIONS: Anxiety, fear.

PHYSICAL SYMPTOMS: Pulse speeds up, butterflies in the stomach, muscles tense.

BEHAVIOURS: I wait until the car has approached and passed, so that the road is completely clear before I cross.

The behaviour is the perfect strategy in the short term, because it lessens my anxiety and ensures that I'm still alive and intact on the other side of the road. It doesn't help in the long term because I have failed to take the opportunity to cross earlier and to learn through experience, firstly, that I do not need to wait until the road is completely clear in both directions before I can cross it safely and secondly, and more importantly, that I can do something that makes me anxious and *bear that anxiety*. As I have not taken this opportunity, all those unhelpful thoughts, emotions, physical sensations and behaviours are free to reinforce each other in life as in diagrams.

In behavioural terms, the trigger – the sight of an approaching car – is a 'stimulus' to which I have become 'sensitized': I am paying it greater attention than it warrants, and as a consequence I am judging it to represent a bigger danger to me than any objective evidence might suggest it to be. This inflated perception of risk makes me anxious, and the anxiety only inflames the situation further. As Ben put it during one of our sessions, 'The thought only seems true because it gives you anxiety and anxiety makes thoughts seem truer than they really are.'

The CBT approach is, in the first instance, to help the patient understand the nature of the problem, by explaining the cognitive-behavioural model, as I've tried to do, and then to work with the patient to figure out what her own problematic triggers, thoughts and behaviours might be. At the first session, Ben asked me to begin keeping a journal in which I would record my negative automatic – or 'hot' – thoughts alongside the situations which had triggered them. When I came back with my first, long list, he began to help me see my habitual reactions in terms of the model, something I've tried to do here with the thought CAR – CROSSING – SQUELCH.

Once he was sure that I had understood how the model worked, Ben set me a series of tasks. The aim of these was to breach the vicious circle at its behavioural and cognitive points. On the cognitive side, I was to try to counter each 'hot' thought with a 'fair and realistic thought'. So, if the hot thought were something like, 'X hasn't replied to my email because I've inadvertently upset her and now she hates me and will never speak to me again,' I could counter it with, 'If X hasn't replied to my email *so far*, it is most likely nothing to do with me, but because she is away, too busy or too upset for some completely unrelated reason to answer it.' These thought exercises were recorded on tables with the following headings: 'Situation', 'Hot thought', 'Emotions %', 'Realistic thought', 'Emotions %'. Under the percentage headings I would record what CBT practitioners call 'SUDs', with SUD standing for Subjective Unit of Discomfort, a self-administered measurement of the intensity with which an individual feels any given negative emotion. If the thought that I have offended X and she hates me now makes me – by my subjective reckoning – 70 per cent anxious and 80 per cent sad, then the hope would be that, after thinking and writing the realistic thought, I might record myself as feeling merely 30 per cent anxious and 20 per cent sad, which would be, once again, a demonstrable result – or, at any rate, a result expressible as a percentage, which is a start. Personally, I've never liked SUDs: whenever I have to use them, I become horribly preoccupied with the question of whether I'm rating the intensity of my emotions accurately enough; it's a bit of an unwelcome distraction.

Alongside these thought-challenging exercises, I had to perform a series of behavioural 'experiments'. Mostly, I remember crossing a lot of roads in places and at times where it didn't seem 100 per cent safe to do so, in order to establish empirically that I wasn't going to die in a freak road accident as a result. This modification of my road-crossing behaviour would be beneficial in two ways: firstly, it would give me empirical evidence with which to challenge my exaggerated risk assessments; secondly, by confronting again and again the stimulus to which I was sensitized, and not avoiding it, I would become 'habituated' – the opposite of 'sensitized' – to that stimulus and my anxiety would diminish as a result. This is a technique called Exposure and Response Prevention, in which the patient feels the fear, does it anyway, feels the fear diminishing, and discovers through experience that, after sufficient exposure to the feared stimulus, the anxiety will begin to tail off of its own accord. It's not just logical: it's *physiological*.

We also began to address what lay behind my negative thought habits, using a method which Ben refers to as 'schema focus' in his first letter. Feeding into the cycle are the patient's schemata – their patterns of apprehending themselves, other people and the world in general – which are informed by their 'core beliefs'. These beliefs may be partly the product of early experience, and this will be acknowledged by the therapist, but these early experiences will not be the main focus of the treatment, as they may be in other forms of therapy. I remember that we touched on my experiences in primary school, and discussed how they could have led to something like the following core beliefs:

I am bad, and deserve bad things to happen to me.

People cannot be trusted.

The world is not a safe place.

If you feed these into the CAR – CROSSING – SQUELCH cycle, you can see that I deserve to be run over, that I have no reason to think that the driver cares about my safety, and that it is in the nature of reality that, every day, thousands of helpless souls are squelched into road slime and nobody cares.

As Ben wrote in his second and final letter to my GP, after a six-week course of treatment, the approach produced rapid and observable results:

> Her self-rating questionnaires have all reduced in score. She is now able to challenge automatic thoughts more effectively and normalises her changes in mood. She has been confronting her avoidant behaviour whilst out (confronting her thoughts of being more at risk than she actually is) . . .
>
> Treatment has also helped her to look at past issues and has resulted in core beliefs based around the idea that everything that she believed she excelled at has been simply put down to academic capacity. We have explored a broader sense of self whilst putting into perspective developmental issues . . .
>
> We therefore have not arranged to meet again. She tells me that she is reducing her Prozac under your monitoring and is on 20mgs every other day and is not suffering any ill-effects.

I could cross roads by myself now. I had dared to Google the Married Man and found plenty of virtual evidence that he was alive and didn't have AIDS. I had discovered through practical real-world experiment that if I joined Friends Reunited, no one who knew me at school would send me angry messages telling me how horrible I had been and how much they still hated me. I had testified, on paper, that I was not ten years old any more and that the world, and I, had probably changed a good deal since then. I was happy enough to reduce the Prozac again, as I was appalled by the thought of becoming dependent on a drug as well as on other people. At the same time I was having more and more baby thoughts, and a pregnancy on antidepressants seemed far too risky to contemplate.

I had talked to Ben about my baby thoughts, and the fears about pregnancy and childbirth which had begun to take up so much of my ruminating time. When I met with my supervisory board at the university a few months later, I told them about my very real intention to have a baby, and cited this as the main reason why I could not cope with the prospect of the extra year's field research, which one member of the board told me I would need to make my thesis at all credible. The board member responded that babies and PhDs were by no means mutually exclusive. My supervisor said to me after the meeting that he wouldn't worry, that in his opinion the research I had already done was sufficient. But what the board member had said chimed in too neatly with my own fears about my work; now I knew for certain that I couldn't face my thesis any more, that I had ceased to believe in it or be excited by it months or even years ago. My methods weren't valid and I was far from reliable. I threw the whole thing over.

It was a great relief. I wouldn't have to face the work any more and I wouldn't have to travel to supervisions any more. And as I had finished my CBT with Ben, I wouldn't ever again need to take taxis to an insalubrious part of Cambridge after dark and then wait outside for a taxi to take me home afterwards. Life was better all round.

Risk

36. I imagine catastrophic consequences as a result of absent-mindedness or minor errors that I make.

The Padua Inventory

––––––––

Mothers were careful to avoid any upset, but unfortunately many of the old wives' tales persisted and new ones developed along the way. Things that were believed to be damaging to the unborn child were very difficult to dodge: birthmarks were considered to be the result of the sight of something frightening during pregnancy; harelips caused by the sight of a hare; and green eyes from seeing a snake.

Petrina Brown, Eve: Sex, Childbirth and
Motherhood through the Ages

There is an awesome fecundity to OCD: all the time it throws out new shoots, new runners – new compulsions, new obsessions. It is as stubborn and prolific as Japanese knotweed. A new obsession can generate from the tiniest seed: an offhand remark, a ten-line news item, a passage in a book. Here's just one example: I went through an Iris Murdoch phase in my early twenties, and one of the books I read was *An Accidental Man.* In one particular scene, a character – I think her name is Charlotte – takes a bath. Rather foolishly, she balances an electric heater on the side of the tub; it is plugged in; it falls into the bath and she is electrocuted. I sincerely wish I had never read that book: ever since, when my OCD has been particularly bad and I have stepped into a bath, I have been tormented by the image of a live electrical appliance falling into the water, with fatal consequences.

Rather neatly, my OCD was at its most fertile when I was pregnant, and one of my most powerful obsessions, the one that would drive me back to the doctor's surgery, and back onto medication, was triggered by something a builder said.

It was February 2003. I was well into the second trimester of my second pregnancy, and we decided to get some work done on the house. We wanted to put a downstairs loo in before the baby arrived; our boiler was coming to the end of its life and needed replacing. The builder we chose came highly recommended and when he came round to give us a quote, he seemed to sweat trustworthiness from his very pores; he fairly reeked of the quality. He discussed the work to be done in a clear and methodical manner, asking the right questions, explaining all the ways in which he could head off potential problems and save us money.

We were so pleased with him that we took him upstairs to see what he had to say about our loft. It had been converted into two tiny rooms by previous owners. They had been very keen to do everything themselves and so had left a legacy of convoluted pipework, redundant wiring and this cramped and ill-lit loft conversion.

Before we even reached it, he was horrified: to reach the two loft rooms, we had to climb two flights of stairs that ran across the middle of the house, and the first of these flights, from the ground floor to the first, could only be accessed from the dining room. This meant that nobody in either loft room could leave the house without crossing another room, which meant, he said, that there was no safe exit in case of fire, which meant that the loft conversion was illegal, which meant that no reputable builder would even think about putting in bigger windows or replacing the plasterwork unless we first had the lower flight of stairs moved round ninety degrees. Did we have a fire exit? No, we didn't. Did we have any fire doors? No. Did we not, at least, have communicating fire alarms? No. Why then, the loft was a fire trap! He looked shaken, as if a conflagration were already taking place in his head.

To the best of my knowledge, the loft rooms had been in use, one way or another, for twenty years and in that time nobody had died of anything in either of them, but the builder's anxiety communicated itself to me and took a powerful hold. The room at the back of the loft was – and at the time of writing, still is – my office, so I spent a great deal of time in it. I had felt very secure in there, tucked up under the roof beams, but now I realized that I was working in a death trap. I was a highly vulnerable pregnant woman sitting at a desk in a death trap.

I had a good idea as to how the fire might start: it would be the portable electric heater that would do it. This heater was nothing like the more primitive one that had done for Charlotte in her bath. It was a shallow upright metal box with no exposed elements, and never grew so hot that I couldn't touch it, but I knew that none of this would matter in the terrible event. The door to the room was at one end, and inevitably one day I would find myself in the corner furthest from it. On that day, the furniture would happen to be grouped in a particularly unfortunate way, with my upholstered desk chair pulled up next to the wooden writing desk under the window, and the heater standing just behind the desk chair; the heater would then be positioned between the chair and a wooden bookshelf loaded with flammable paper. There would therefore be no way that I could leave the room without touching the desk, the chair, the bookshelf or the heater itself. If – when – the heater came into contact with the back of the chair long enough to set the upholstery on fire, all that wood and paper would go up in an instant, leaving me – remember I'm in the furthest corner – trapped, unable even to reach the phone point with the spare phone, because that was in the *front* of the loft.

I could not relax and settle down to work until I had figured out a foolproof escape route. I guessed that once the chair had caught fire there would be a brief space of time – a minute, perhaps – before the desk succumbed, so that if I noticed the fire quickly enough I would be able to climb onto the desk, crawl across it without touching the chair, climb off the desk and then slip out through the door. If the fire had already taken hold behind the chair but not in front of the chair then I would have to consider climbing out of the window. This might not be too dangerous as the window opened out onto the sloping roof above the bathroom. If I stepped carefully onto the roof I could skid or roll down it until I got to the edge, where I could drop onto the lower sloping roof over the kitchen. From there it would be another short and easy drop onto the ground, and safety. I reckoned that if I could manage not to fall off the first sloping roof, the baby and I would probably both be all right.

So I had my plans, but I still wasn't satisfied. Schools and offices had fire drills to check their procedures, so I thought that perhaps I could reassure myself by having a fire drill of my own. Obviously, I couldn't test out the window option – that would just be silly – but I could at least see how feasible it was to try to climb across the desk without touching the chair. I arranged the furniture as it appeared in the worst case scenario – first making sure, several times, that the heater was switched off. I stood at the corner of the desk, put my hands flat on its leather top and lifted my left knee.

At least I tried. I am a small woman with short legs, who would find it hard to mount a desk from the floor at the best of times, but on that particular day I was doubly handicapped, firstly by my growing pregnant bump and secondly by the maternity skirt I was wearing, a long, tapering denim number that hobbled me, and which I would soon discard. I put my foot down, arranged my hands slightly differently, and tried again. But it was no good; I couldn't get enough leverage to get myself up. I tried again, lifted my knee for the third time, and leaned forward. It was at that moment, in my loft, as I leaned on my writing desk in impractical French maternity wear with one knee slightly raised, that it suddenly occurred to me that I was going mad. I put my foot back on the floor.

It wasn't really all that surprising that I should end up trying to mount my desk, bump and all, in a tight maternity skirt. Quite apart from anything else, everyone expects pregnant women to go a little mad: anxious, emotional, weepy, vague. The mum-to-be literature warns women about this, that it's a huge life change, that you might need to mourn the loss of your pre-baby carefree self, that you might well be apprehensive about how you will shape up as a mother, that you might be upset to find yourself getting fat. They suggest that you might find it helpful to talk to somebody about this, or to have a bubble bath. You must remember that your body has undertaken an enormous task, that you are bound to notice the strain and that, most importantly of all, mind and body alike have been thrown off balance by a massive onslaught of HORMONES.

Some books list the hormones for you and tell you exactly what they do. A couple of them – oestrogen and progesterone – will already be familiar to you as the regulators of your monthly cycle, but in pregnancy, their levels rise enormously, as they have a huge range of new tasks to perform between them: suppressing menstruation, increasing temperature and breathing rate, relaxing muscles, helping the breasts to produce milk and strengthening the uterus. They are joined by other hormones, such as relaxin, which unlaces the body ready for childbirth, and oxytocin, the broody hormone, which will stimulate the contractions when the time comes, assist with the production of milk and make your eyes mist over whenever you see a really tiny pair of socks. In the second and third trimester, some of these hormones are secreted by the placenta, a whole new organ which the mother's body generates in the first trimester, uses for the other two and then expels after the birth. Your blood volume will increase while your brain volume – for better or worse –

does the opposite. Parts of your body may darken. Your hair may get thicker and shinier or, alternatively, start to fall out. You may go off sex, or want it more. Some women find that their pelvic tissues soften too much, and they develop symphysis pubis dysfunction, making it painful to walk. Many women report the most vivid and peculiar dreams. A few are troubled by excessive saliva.

Meanwhile, the world seems to change around you, and it isn't just your hormones making you imagine things: all of a sudden, society at large has obtrusive, disabling OCD. One of the main ways in which OCD presents itself to the sufferer – as opposed to the observer – is as an overwhelming sense of personal responsibility, particularly where possible harm to the self or others is concerned. The moment a woman conceives, she becomes responsible for seeing that no harm comes to her child and no one allows her to forget it. (A recent – and notorious – article in the *Washington Post* [32] took this even further, drawing on a government report on the health of women of childbearing age to suggest that all such women should regard themselves as permanently 'pre-pregnant' and limit their activities accordingly.)

Drugs and cigarettes are out, for a start – not a problem for me. Neither was the advice that I should drink only the occasional glass of wine, as I could never hold my drink anyway. I was given a list of foods to avoid, such as pâté and unpasteurized cheese, as these could harbour listeria. I was also told to avoid eating liver (because of vitamin A) and swordfish (because of mercury) along with pre-cooked foods, ready meals, bagged salads and pre-packed sandwiches, just in case. I was told to wash my hands after touching the cat because of the risk of toxoplasmosis. I did my best to follow this advice to the letter, agonizing over every tiny choice. I dutifully took my folic acid

32. *Washington Post,* 16 May 2006

for the first few weeks to reduce the baby's chances of developing a neural tube defect. I rested, as I knew I should. I slept, as the books advised, on my left side, so as not to restrict the flow of blood to the womb.

While I took care of myself and my unborn child, we were carefully monitored, measured, checked and surveilled. At my 'checking-in' appointment, the midwife gave me a folder of notes which was to contain information about my health, any previous pregnancies, my marital status, my occupation, my lifestyle – anything regarded as relevant to the pregnancy, which seemed to be just about everything. On a regular basis, she measured my bump and listened to it. An ultrasound machine allowed the hospital staff to see inside my body and inspect the baby's for defects. My blood was checked to make sure that I was immune to rubella, which I'd already had, and also to see if I was carrying syphilis, which I knew I hadn't had. At eighteen weeks I took a 'glucose challenge' test, which sounds like a sponsored fun run but which actually involves the consumption of a bottle of Lucozade followed by the production of a precisely timed urine sample. It's a way of screening for gestational diabetes. Not all hospital trusts bother with it. Unfortunately for me, mine did: I hate Lucozade.

There is something about screening tests that feels strangely familiar to someone who suffers compulsions. While I do understand that there are clinical reasons for all the various ultrasound scans, blood tests and examinations which are routinely offered to – or imposed on – women ante-natally, it also seems to me that they are rituals, attempts to ward off the anxiety that seems to follow pregnant women about like a malignant cloud. But like compulsions, they only serve to feed it.

But then, why should we expect a few tests to hold out against such ancient, possibly animal terrors? Pregnant women used to be menaced by jealous spirits and malevolent gods; now they are frightened by statistics. No risk is considered too slight for a good headline. No wonder it took me so long to recognize how aberrant my thinking had become.

If any pregnant woman was going to wind up trying to escape a notional fire by climbing onto a writing desk, there was always, in retrospect, a good chance that that woman would turn out to be me. By this time, I had been struggling with anxieties of one kind or another for as long as I could remember, and had always found it difficult to face the prospect of risk. It was hard to get me on a plane, hard even to get me across a busy road. Pregnancy and birth, I knew, were a mother and foetus steeplechase in which you might fall at any fence. I knew this with painful certainty because, a few months before my second pregnancy, I had lost my first.

In early 2002, I finally put my limping PhD out of its misery and we agreed to start trying for a family – or, at least, to stop trying to prevent one. Of course, I was terrified: of the possibility of failure, of childbirth, of becoming an awful, damaging mother, of giving birth to somebody who might inherit their mother's capacity for making a misery out of things. On the other hand, I had always assumed that I would have a child, could not imagine life without a child, and there was a relief, of sorts, in giving way to a biological imperative, something so much older and deeper and wider than my own fidgety, changeable reasonings. I might not be able to finish a PhD, but at least I could fulfil my animal purpose. So we put our contraceptives away in a drawer, and two months later I was pregnant.

A couple of weeks after my positive test, I began to bleed, so I was sent to the local maternity hospital for an emergency ultrasound. That first time, we saw a tiny blob with a heartbeat: a 'human bean', as Chris put it. A week later the bleeding stopped. Another fortnight later, it started again. At the next emergency ultrasound, the foetus was a tiny homunculus already, waving its skinny limbs at us. The bleeding got worse, stopped, started, got worse again. We trekked back and forth to the early pregnancy unit and, when that was closed at the weekends, to the gynaecology ward. I made panicky phone calls in the middle of the night to bored-sounding nurses. There were more ultrasounds, examinations, blood tests, careful speeches from midwives and doctors who couldn't promise anything. On 29 June, I wrote this entry in my notebook, trying to make sense of how I felt, as I contemplated a possible full nine months of unstable, bleeding pregnancy:

> This fear – there must be those who live in this state constantly, for months, years at a time – if their town is under siege, if they've had a bad diagnosis – how can they? After a while does it become normal, simply how things are? Does it become something else, some terrible white noise always in the background?

When the pregnancy had first been confirmed, we had booked a private nuchal fold ultrasound, for extra reassurance. By the time we turned up for the appointment one evening in early July, I was bleeding more heavily then ever. I had also been in pain on and off for two days. In fact, I was in considerably more pain than I was prepared to admit, but something of what was going on must have shown in my face, because as soon as he saw me, the foetal medicine consultant asked what the matter was. I told him about the bleeding and the pain. When he took a look with his machine, he showed us a womb cinched in the middle, as if it were being squeezed by an invisible fist. Its cervix was full of blood, but the baby was still there, clinging on, with a beating heart. 'You have a fifty per cent chance of miscarrying,' he said and suggested that we postpone the nuchal. Outside his office, the midwife who worked with him told me to go home and take some painkillers, the stronger the better. 'But surely I can only take paracetamol?' I asked. 'I wouldn't worry about that now,' she replied, with unbearable kindness.

We took a melancholy cab home, then phoned my mother to tell her what the consultant had said. She said she'd drive up straight away. While I was waiting for her to arrive, I squeezed out something that looked like a big chunk of liver and the pain, abruptly, stopped. So that was it, then, I thought. The doctor at the out-of-hours surgery couldn't see anything for blood, but was inclined to agree with me. She sent me to the gynaecology ward, where I spent a night having my blood loss examined and failing to sleep. Next morning, a porter wheeled me at terrifying speed to the ultrasound department for one last viewing. Astonishingly, the baby was still there, heartbeat and all.

I was taken back home again. I went straight upstairs to rest, and fell asleep almost straight away, only to be woken soon after by intense, burning pains, more powerful than any I'd had before. In five minutes, I flooded one sanitary towel, then another. On the way back to the early pregnancy unit, on the back seat of my mother's car, with one last excruciating contraction, it was finally over.

The doctor who operated on me – to remove the remaining 'conception products', as they were now called – told me that it was best to wait two periods before I tried to get pregnant again. My husband insisted that we followed this advice to the letter: the miscarriage had left me thin and anaemic, in need of building up. I had all sorts of new fears about my body and how violently it might fail, but at the same time, all I wanted was to be pregnant again. To be suddenly without child felt like an outrage. I felt picked on, persecuted. I lost any sympathy I had ever felt for the teenage mothers pushing their babies around the shopping mall, and snarled at my husband about how they smoked and swore, how they packed their children into buggies and ignored them, how they plied them with sugary drinks in bottles and ruined their teeth. I went on and on and on at him. I think we were both very relieved that I fell pregnant again so quickly.

Between pregnancies, I had changed GPs. I chose my new doctor for her obstetric training, made an appointment to go and see her, sat down next to her desk and burst into tears. I told her all about my miscarriage, my past bereavements, my bouts of depression. She listened carefully. When I had finished, she said that I clearly didn't cope with loss very well and that she was going to refer me to the midwife counsellor at the maternity hospital. Then she asked how I would feel about taking antidepressants again, given that I was hoping for another pregnancy. I said I didn't know. She said if I wanted to make a properly informed decision, why didn't I go onto the Internet and research the risks?

The Internet is a hypochondriac's best friend, so I didn't need any encouragement. When I had a look online, I discovered that while there were no confirmed dangers from fluoxetine (Prozac) during pregnancy, there had been some reports of increased risk of miscarriage in the first trimester, and a few more reports of babies being born with withdrawal symptoms after their mothers had taken fluoxetine in the third trimester. It turned out that precious few medicines were officially deemed safe for pregnancy: if they cross the placenta, which most would, then the foetus would receive a concentrated dose of whatever its mother had taken, and could suffer a variety of nasty consequences as a result. Of course, I already knew about the 'thalidomide babies' with shortened limbs who had been born to mothers who had taken that drug during the first trimester.

Thalidomide was a known 'teratogen' – literally, a 'creator of monsters', a phrase that called to mind those old folk beliefs about foetuses imprinted with the horrors that their mothers had seen. There was no evidence that fluoxetine could lead to the birth of malformed offspring, but then, there didn't seem to be all that much evidence about fluoxetine one way or another. There is a serious methodological problem where studies on the use of drugs during pregnancy are concerned, which lies in the fact that it is not ethically possible to do a proper prospective study, a double-blind trial, with a control group – what sane mother would agree to take a substance, in the interests of science, solely in order to see whether or not it would harm her child? The scientific papers I saw had tentative and provisional conclusions, as scientific papers tend to do, and these conclusions usually included a sentence to the effect that, in each individual case, possible risks to the foetus had to be weighed up against the mother's need for treatment. Faced with all this uncertainty, I did some weighing up of my own, and turned the doctor's offer down.

This book has given me the perfect excuse for – I mean to say, has *necessitated* – further research into all kinds of health issues. I have been very busy feeding terms into search engines, downloading entries from citation indexes and going on frenzied hunting trips to the periodicals shelves of specialist libraries. I have entered, among other combinations, 'mental illness + pregnancy', 'obsessive-compulsive + miscarriage', 'anxiety + effects + on + foetus'. Some research has been done into the incidence (new cases arising) and prevalence (all cases reported, whether new or ongoing) during pregnancy of anxiety disorders in general, and obsessive-compulsive disorder in particular. The researchers' conclusions, of course, are as tentative and provisional as they have to be, but, taken together, they do suggest to me that anxiety disorders, including OCD, are far from uncommon during and after pregnancy; also that women who have previously suffered from depression or severe premenstrual tension are particularly vulnerable; that changes in the levels of gonadal hormones – oestrogen and progesterone – play a part; that although some OCD patients may find their symptoms are alleviated during pregnancy, others will experience a worsening of symptoms, or the appearance of new ones; that the experience of miscarriage may put certain woman at risk of developing OCD.

Nobody has developed any treatments especially for pregnant women with OCD or its sister ailments. If a pregnant woman is to be treated, it will be in the usual ways: by antidepressant medication, almost certainly one of the selective serotonin reuptake inhibitors such as fluoxetine, which are considered to be the safest and most effective drugs for such patients. She may instead – or additionally – be offered a course of cognitive behavioural therapy. As expected, the papers' authors all sound a note of caution about the prescribing of drugs to pregnant women, but it also seems that leaving a highly anxious woman *untreated* could prove harmful to her unborn child. As a recently published review of the medical literature puts it:

> Recent findings indicate that symptoms of anxiety are common during pregnancy and the postpartum period and that maternal symptoms of anxiety during pregnancy are associated with adverse fetal and developmental consequences. Over-activity of the maternal neuroendocrine system has been implicated in negative health outcomes seen in fetuses born to stressed or anxious mothers. Fetal exposure to elevated levels of hormones (particularly cortisol) may contribute to premature labor and delivery. Maternal exposure to stress and anxiety may precipitate the release of catecholamines that can result in maternal vasoconstriction and ultimately a limitation of oxygen and vital nutrients to the fetus. The exposure of the fetus to maternal stress and increased levels of adrenal hormones therefore has possible consequences for fetal central nervous system development and specifically glucocorticoid brain receptor development.[33]

33. Lori E. Ross, PhD, and Linda M. McLean, PhD, CPsych, 'Anxiety Disorders during Pregnancy and the Postpartum Period: a Systematic Review', *Journal of Clinical Psychiatry,* 67:8, August 2006

Stress and anxiety have the effect of reducing the blood supply to the womb, which in turn restricts the supply of food and oxygen to the foetus; at the same time, the foetus will be exposed to high levels of stress-related hormones such as cortisol, and this can help to trigger premature labour and birth. In other words, the old wives were right: you should never frighten a pregnant woman.

When I was frightened by something, I could at least take my fear to the midwife counsellor. By the time I went for my first appointment, I was already pregnant, and she continued to listen to me, answering my incessant and tortuously detailed questions with great patience, for the best part of my pregnancy. Many of my questions, unsurprisingly, had to do with miscarriage and its causes. Even though I had been told by doctor after doctor that most miscarriages were 'independent events', in which either foetus or placenta had developed in such a way that the body could only reject it, I could not get the soap opera theory of miscarriage out of my head: a woman is pushed over/falls down the stairs/has a terrible row with her partner/is in a car accident/gets drunk one night with the girls and as a direct result clutches her abdomen, screams and promptly miscarries just before the closing credits.

I was particularly concerned that I might be raped. During the first few months of my pregnancy, the so-called 'Trophy Rapist' was at large in the south-east. Nobody knew what he looked like, as he attacked from behind, threatening his victims with a knife or a fist if they tried to look at his face. He always took a piece of clothing or property from them, hence his name. Many of his victims were schoolgirls but he attacked grown women too. He seemed to have no preference as to age or type, but one thing was consistent: he attacked in wooded areas. He lurked always in the Home Counties, in woodland, waiting for his meat.

In those same few months, I had a part-time temping job at

the maths department. My route there included a short walk down a footpath which was fenced on one side and wooded – ever so slightly and thinly wooded – along the other. It was a straight path, not very long and anybody passing down it was visible from one end to the other. I was rarely the only person using the path, and I only used it in daylight, but it was, just about, a wooded area and it was, almost, in the Home Counties, so I would always scurry along it, looking over my shoulder. I knew I wouldn't see him, though; there would be rapid footsteps, a sudden whiff of cigarette smoke and alcohol, then an arm round my neck, a hand over my mouth and that would be it: 'Trophy Rapist Attacks Pregnant Woman.'

The midwife counsellor knew of this slightly wooded path and often cycled past it, so I enlisted her help as I tried to assess the exact dimensions of the threat. Did she think there was enough cover for a man to lurk in the bushes? What if he became bold, attacked in the daytime? When she cycled past, how many people were usually on the path at one time: one? Many? None? Was the whole length of the path visible from the main road that she was cycling on? Might an attempted attack be spotted from the road? From the maths department? From the houses alongside? And, say I was unlucky and was raped, would the rape hurt the baby? Would the baby become infected with HIV? Could I possibly lose the baby that way?

A railway worker was arrested and charged in early December, which put paid to any specific anxiety I might have had about being raped in a certain place by a particular rapist, but my general sense of vulnerability did not abate. When I took my shower or bath after my husband had set off for work in the morning, I always locked the door of the bathroom from the inside, so that no psychopath who might happen to break into the house while I was washing myself could burst in and catch me at my most defenceless. The villain who stalked my thoughts was always the same: his facial features were blurry, as if he had been made out of plasticine, but I could always picture very clearly his great bulk – of course he was a huge man, who could overpower me in seconds – and his navy knitted skullcap, as worn by the men who had hammered at the walls of the glass houses I had inhabited in my pubescent nightmares. I was awake now, and much older, and I understood how absurd and exaggerated my fears were, I understood that the risk of being attacked at random in one's own home in broad daylight was negligible, but the scenarios I conjured up seemed to have some kind of independent malevolent power. I was terrified by my own imagination, and locking the door was my attempt to placate it. It was a compulsion.

Locking one door couldn't accomplish much, though, when my imagination and its horrors followed me everywhere. When I left the house, I walked with great care, a hand over my bump in case it should get knocked by something – the corner of a briefcase, perhaps, or a wire shopping basket – in such a way that the baby sustained an injury. Crossing any road was a horrible ordeal, every time. I could not walk by the river without wondering how long it would take a foetus to drown inside me, should I fall in. I could not look at a staircase without picturing myself falling down it. Every morsel of food I ate was a choking hazard. There are women who feel that the baby is completely protected inside them, that it only becomes exposed to the world and its dangers after the birth, but I did not feel like a safe place for a baby to be; instead I felt painfully brittle, as if I were made out of matchsticks and tissue paper. I started at another temping job after Christmas, but the walk to the office terrified me so much that I jacked it in after only one day.

Much later, I would read about the Japanese ritual of *mizuko kuyo*, in which a mother would ask forgiveness of the spirit of her miscarried or – more commonly – aborted foetus, while asking the *mizuko jizo*, the saint who cared for such children in the other world, to help her lost child on its way. After abortion was legalized in Japan in the 1970s, a portion of the inevitable backlash took the form of terrifying images of vengeful *mizukos* (aborted children) menacing their mothers, perhaps injuring or killing any subsequent children *in utero*. Some temples were thus able to make a good deal of money out of the guilt, grief and fear of women who'd had abortions, by performing these propitiatory ceremonies and charging for them.[34]

While I couldn't help being horrified by the way this mythology had been used, I found the images themselves deeply compelling. The idea that a pregnancy might be haunted by an earlier, thwarted one made sense to me. Certainly my two pregnancies, which were so close together, overlapped in my imagination. A dream I wrote down in my notebook illustrates this very well.

> I dreamt that I was lying on a bed in a hospital ward. My abdomen was cut open, and the baby, tiny in a white sac, and attached by the umbilicus, was laid on the sheet next to me, its heart visibly beating. [30/12/02]

I remember telling the midwife counsellor about this, and about the sense I had in the dream, that I could nurture the baby to term in this way, if only I were to remain on that bed, lying on my left side, absolutely and perfectly still.

Of course, it wasn't possible to remain completely motionless in my waking life. Although I had been able to give up working, I still had to leave the house to go to the shops or to see friends, and inside the house I still had to face the stairs I could fall down, the bath I might drown in, the knives I could cut myself with, the gas hobs which could set my sleeve alight

34. Helen Hardacre, *Marketing the Menacing Fetus in Japan (Twentieth Century Japan – The Emergence of a World Power)*, (University of California Press, Berkeley and London, 1997)

242

and the food which might choke me. When I thought about my state of mind, I was reminded of a picture I had seen in some book I had been shown as a schoolgirl; there was an article about phobias in the book, illustrated with cigarette card-sized cartoon panels, each one captioned with the name of the phobia it depicted. At the bottom of the page, as a kind of visual punchline, was a picture of a man who had squashed himself into the corner in the room, his legs pulled up to his chest, arms clasped tightly around his knees; little whizz lines around him showed that he was shaking; sweat poured down his face and his eyes popped. The caption said: Pantophobia – fear of everything.

In March, when I was six months pregnant, I finally told my doctor about the pandemonium in my head. She watched me as I gibbered on about how anxious I felt all the time, how terrifying it was just to negotiate the aisle of a busy shop, how I was afraid to go on trains because they might derail, how I hadn't really given myself much time to recover from the miscarriage, had I? How hard it was to cross roads, how I couldn't travel to London because of terrorism, which was absurd because hadn't I once commuted day after day, years before the IRA ceasefire? I don't know what I expected her to say after that, but I do remember that when she said the word 'medication', I was utterly stunned. As I had come to understand it, psychotropic medication was only offered to pregnant women as a last resort, and it simply hadn't occurred to me that I could ever be that ill. Until that moment, I had always seen myself as just sane enough: I might be neurotic, but at least I always had insight.

I backtracked, said how important it was to me to protect the baby, how I couldn't take unnecessary risks. I'm no Howard Hughes, and don't normally suffer from obsessions about contamination, but that changed while I was pregnant: I had sat one lunchtime in the maths department canteen, hoping nobody would notice that I was inspecting each little forkful of my chilli con carne – I wanted to make absolutely sure that every last cubic millimetre of mince had been cooked through properly. I was reluctant to take paracetamol, which was allowed; reluctant to take so much as a sip of white wine. How could I reasonably be expected to take a serious, psychoactive, prescription-only *drug*? But rather than praising me for my responsible attitude to my foetus, my doctor came as near to losing her patience as I have ever known her to do – and she's often been pushed. Listen, she said, you are *not well*. Anxiety is *bad for the baby* and if you carry on like this, you will *not be fit to look after it* when it arrives. That was persuasive: I agreed to take the medication.

The doctor approached the business cautiously, speaking to a psychiatrist who specialized in obstetric mental health, then coming back to me with a prescription for the safest, 'cleanest' drug available: an SSRI called citalopram, which I was to take at a low dose for the foreseeable future. I had the sense – surprisingly, in retrospect – not to go surfing for citalopram horror stories while I was still pregnant, but I downloaded some information on citalopram and pregnancy just the other day and found more articles warning of the risk of 'neonatal withdrawal syndrome' for babies who had been exposed *in utero* to SSRIs in the third trimester. The reported symptoms listed in the articles included irritability, constant crying, shivering, increased tonus, eating and sleeping difficulties, convulsions, respiratory distress, cyanosis, apnoea, seizures, temperature instability, hypoglycaemia, vomiting . . .[35] When my newborn son was examined in the post-natal ward, after a long labour and an emergency C-section, he was found to have a low temperature and hypoglycaemia, and did not feed easily, but whether this had anything to do with the citalopram, as opposed to the traumatic nature of his arrival, to my incipient, as-yet-undiagnosed hypothyroidism or to any number of other factors I couldn't

35. See the article 'Citalopram Hydrobromide' on www.rxlist.com; also 'Citalopram in Pregnancy and Breastfeeding' on www.obfocus.com

even name, is impossible to say. I can say for sure, though, that he has turned out to be a remarkably happy child – and he certainly doesn't get it from me.

The citalopram did not remove the anxiety – one can't knock out an elephant with a glockenspiel beater – but it did take the edge off it, so that I was able to move about more comfortably, within the small compass I allowed myself. I started going to the local coffee morning group, began to make friends among the local mothers, went shopping for the baby's things. A good twenty-week scan had given me some confidence, and I was aware, as each week passed without incident, that my baby's chances were getting better and better: twenty-eight weeks was the 'viability' threshold; at thirty-three weeks my pregnancy manual told me that my baby 'has an excellent chance of survival if it comes out now'.[36] I relaxed, somewhat, and was even able to write – a little.

The focus of my activities and anxieties now switched to the birth. While I watched my bump grow and waited for the big event, I had the antenatal classes to occupy me. We took two courses – one run by a small local charity, and one at the NHS, to familiarize me with the hospital and its ethos – and I was an appalling little swot at both of them. All the way through my pregnancy, I binged on information, as if childbirth and motherhood were two more dissertations for me to research. My questions to the midwife counsellor continued, but there were also books to read, and the Internet to trawl. The independent birth teacher, at least, encouraged this approach, and handed out wonderful things at her classes: a diagram to show which hormones were released at which point in labour; information sheets about the reasons for each intervention, and their attendant risks; we could even become acquainted, if we wished, with the local hospital's policy on

36. Kaz Cooke, *Rough Guide to Pregnancy and Birth* (Rough Guides, London, 2001)

every single aspect of perinatal care. I looked through the hospital's statistics on interventions, types of delivery, morbidity and mortality with the midwife counsellor. I discovered and followed exercises which would minimize the chance of a posterior – and more difficult – birth. I produced a splendidly detailed birthplan, complete with plenty of conditional verbs to show that I understood how unpredictable the whole process was. I knew about the C-section performed on a goat in seventeenth-century Switzerland. I knew that pethidine, an analgesic used in labour, had been developed by two scientists working for I.G. Farben during the Nazi era.

If maternal researches made any difference to birth outcomes, I'm sure I would have had one of the easiest deliveries in medical history. But they don't, and neither did they assuage my fears. When we were shown around a room in the delivery unit, so nakedly a hospital room full of hospital equipment, so obviously waiting to be filled with screams and splattered with blood, I was horrified. Next day I wrote:

> Last night saw the Delivery Unit at the hospital. The strength of my reaction took me by surprise. The woman pushing in the next room didn't throw me at all, but I *hated* the room. The hospital-ness of it, a room such as one might have chemo in, I thought. A room full of horrible memories. One of those too-high, slablike, hospital beds in the middle (which, OK, one can push to the side), facing a wall with a ghastly, bland example of tea-towel art on it. A door to the right leading to the hospital-smelling hospital corridor, with people in scrubs pushing equipment down it, and a window on the left with a view of the car park. My gut feeling was, 'I DON'T WANT TO BE HERE!' All the grieving ghosts of miscarriage, family illnesses, family deaths. I came home and cried, and cried for grief and anger today, morning and afternoon. What shall I do? [1/5/06]

At least I could console myself with the thought that I hadn't disgraced myself too much in the classes; I never cried or ranted until we were safely back home, and never once had I asked the only really compelling question, the one that goes: what if we die?

Harm

56. I sometimes have an impulse to hurt defenceless children or animals.

The Padua Inventory

———

No one can do *everything* right – not even a mother.
Arlene Eisenberg, *What to Expect the First Year*

Birth-planning, researching, exercising – it was all a distraction, really, from that unaskable question. All I truly wanted from the birth was that the baby and I would emerge from it alive. Secretly, I also hoped that my child's birth would be like mine – quick and early – but I wasn't counting on it, which, as you'll already know, was just as well. My son was a term baby, and his birth took many hours, a birthing ball, a birthing pool, an artificial rupturing of membranes, several monitors, countless lungfuls of gas and air, a sampling of blood from his scalp, three midwives, a spinal block, a small army of obstetricians and, ultimately, a scalpel. None of this bothered me much: the baby was stuck, and by the time they took him out he had his cord wrapped twice round his neck and my placenta was abrupting, so there was never any question in my mind, then or since, that the C-section was necessary. My only regret is that I was listening when the midwife told me and Chris in the recovery room that she'd heard the obstetrician saying they'd gone in 'just in time'. Yes, I certainly could have done without that.

After some-length-of-time-or-other in the recovery room, the baby and I were wheeled into the post-natal ward and Chris went home to sleep. We stayed there for a few hours, the boy squeaking and snuffling in his plastic box and me flexing my reawakened feet under the blankets and wondering when they would let me move and pick my child up. A paediatrician came by at some point to do his routine examination; he told me that the baby had low temperature or low blood sugar or maybe both or something else and that they would get a baby-warmer down from the transitional care ward. Then I was told that the equipment couldn't be spared and we were being taken up. As my bed and I were being pushed into our new slot, a group of midwives and nursery nurses gathered at the foot end and asked me which formula I preferred ... Did you get that? I said, THEY ASKED ME WHICH FORMULA I PREFERRED.

Unlike the emergency Caesarean, which I had, deep down, been expecting all along, this came as a shock, an absolutely appalling shock. As I said in the letter I wrote to the ward manager a few months later:

As I had always intended to breastfeed my son exclusively, on demand, until he was six months old, I was completely taken aback by this question, and was devastated to be asked it. Nothing I had heard in the ante-natal classes, let alone in the breastfeeding workshop, had prepared me for a situation in which formula would be given to my baby without my being asked how I wished to feed him first. Although I could not answer the question satisfactorily, I was able to explain that I intended to breastfeed, and would therefore be grateful if [my son] could be given his formula in a cup rather than a bottle ... After this, [he] was taken away from me, his mother, without my permission, and given his very first meal by a nursery nurse, an event I found more distressing[37] than anything I had experienced during the labour.

37. In the interests of fairness, I feel I should add at this point that if I could spend my life with a tube of gas and air shoved down my throat, there is almost nothing in the world that could distress me *at all*. Does anyone know where you can score some?

To anyone living outside the new mother/new baby bubble, this must seem like an absurd overreaction, a plum example of middle-class maternal preciousness; indeed, when I look at this paragraph now, I feel quite embarrassed by it. Take a look at the same incident from inside the bubble, though, and you can begin to understand why I was so upset, and why, in the following months, I remained so stuck in my upset that my health visitor suggested I write the letter, if for no other reason than to help me move on.

Another new mother, who like me was having trouble breastfeeding, and was having to supplement with bottles of formula, said to me wearily one day that to bottle feed was, among all the other dreadful things, 'a social faux pas'. We were both a few months into motherhood by then, and heavy with shame. Well, of course we were: we'd met at Active Birth classes; we were educated, left-leaning, middle-class women, a poet and an artist respectively; we believed in natural birth, breast milk, and not allowing the Man to use the occasion of your baby's birth to sell you shit you didn't need – like environmentally polluting scented babywipes, for example, or disposable nappies, or evil corporate *formula*. It was about doing right by your baby, right by the planet, and also about showing you hadn't been duped. Pity the poor, disadvantaged, ignorant women who gave birth on their backs full of drugs, then stuck a disposable on their baby's backside and shoved a bottle into its mouth. They didn't have access to the information that we had; they couldn't afford the classes; they didn't have the social reinforcement you need to breastfeed.

I was so much luckier than they: I'd been drinking in the reinforcement long before I was even pregnant. My relatives breastfed; my friends breastfed; I read newspaper and magazine articles about research that showed me how, all the time, they were discovering new and different ways in which breastfeeding was wonderful. Then, when I was pregnant, I joined the NCT and they sent me more literature along similar lines; I learned from various online sources that formula was not only inferior for the child but risky too, as unlike breastmilk it could never be completely sterilized, and what's more, your child would have few defences against all the pathogens paddling around in it because he would not be getting the benefit of the antibodies that his mother would have been able to dispense daily from her naturally germicidal nipples. I also learned that a woman's risk of breast cancer decreased in proportion to the length of time she spent breastfeeding. This is all true as far as it goes, but it doesn't follow that if you don't breastfeed, your child will die of septicaemia and shortly after be reunited in the family vault with your own cancerous body. And if you are better at assessing risk than I was, you'll appreciate that.

The reinforcement reached its antenatal crescendo with the NHS breastfeeding workshop. We all watched a video which showed us how great things were in Norway, which apparently leads the world in maternal nourishment. Look: here is the sophisticated bar/restaurant, all woody and glassy and Scandinavian; here are the beautiful tall folk in evening dress, milling about with their drinks and their gravadlax;[38] here is the woman sitting on the lovely designer chair with her evening gown half open, and, as the narration says, 'nobody blinks an eyelid if *junior* has some supper too'. Never mind that it wasn't like that here, that our mothers and aunts – bless them – might say things like 'my milk was too thin, you see' or 'they're much too big: you'll suffocate the baby' or 'no more than ten minutes each side' or 'isn't there some room where you can do that?' We knew better now, we knew that nobody's milk was too thin, that the baby's demand would stimulate the perfect level of supply, that human babies had prominent noses for the sole evolutionary purpose of not getting suffocated by oversized tits, that

38. Or is that Swedish? Never mind.

if you kept the baby on long enough to get to the creamy, nourishing hindmilk, then baby would get all he needed for the first six months, that it was just a matter of getting a good 'latch' and they had the counsellors to show us how, that once we had the latch and the supply and demand thing sorted, we'd be away and could breastfeed, discreetly, anywhere, even in the most sophisticated of wood and glass dining venues.

The midwives explained to us that it would take a few days after the birth for the milk to 'come in'; however, we would from the start produce a yellowish liquid called colostrum, which would begin to give the baby the benefits of our mature immune systems, and would provide enough incentive for the baby, who would be born with a couple of days' worth of fat in reserve, to establish a good sucking habit. We were not to worry about the baby losing a little weight – that was normal – and it was best, in this early period, if we didn't let anyone come between us and the baby with formula. Except, they didn't add, if the staff consider the baby's temperature, blood sugar and fat reserves too low; in which case, they didn't advise, you might like to consider which brand of formula you prefer.

Or perhaps they did add something like that, and I just chose not to hear them. It was probably at the workshop that I learned that cups were less prejudicial to successful breastfeeding than bottles. So my son was fed by cup, at two-hour intervals, and the feeds marked on a schedule. A day or maybe a couple of days after, a nurse thought she detected signs that his blood sugar level had dropped sufficiently to put him in immediate danger, so he was given a lumbar puncture, dosed with intravenous antibiotics and fed by tube for twenty-four hours; then it was back to the cups again. I was told not to pick him up between feeds, as his temperature could be better regulated by the heated cot. Chris came in on each of the five days that we spent on the ward, and learned to cup feed, and to change nappies. I wouldn't go near the cups, because I was still working to my own strict version of the breastfeeding workshop agenda, and didn't want him to take any food from me that wasn't my own. I tried to attach him at every feed, sometimes with a staff member helping or hindering me; I breast-pumped like fury, I cried buckets and fidgeted irritably with my surgical stockings. By nightfall, I was so exhausted that I could only wheel him to the nursery for a few hours, and trudge back to my bed, half grateful, half resentful. I was resentful because he was mine, and I wanted to take charge of him, to be his mother; I was grateful because I knew that I was weak, and anxious, and incompetent, and he had to be better off with anyone else in the world than me.

It was such a relief, after being discharged, that there were still other people around: proper adults who could guarantee the baby's safety as well as my own. There was Chris, for a start, who had learned how to cup feed and nappy change, and, unlike me, didn't appear to be afraid of carrying the baby up and down stairs, or over hard surfaces; for a day or two a week, my mother was there too, and she had also given us some money to hire Carrie, a post-natal doula, to help a few hours a week. They all pitched in, and left me free, when I wasn't holding the baby, to tend to my milk and tear-supplies, and recover from the wound infection which my doctor had diagnosed a couple of days after leaving hospital. In a perverse way, it was quite satisfying to be able to add 'puerperal fever' to the list of child-bearing complications I might have died of a hundred years ago.

Ben had encouraged me to challenge my fearful thoughts about the dangers of childbirth – and crossing roads, and travelling, and leaving the house, etc. – by asking myself how often real catastrophes actually happened. 'Have you heard of anyone dying in childbirth?' he might have asked. 'Do you know anyone who's been hit by a car in broad daylight? Been involved in a plane crash? Died of an undiagnosed ruptured appendix?' I'd found the technique useful for a while, but now I was faced with the absoluteness of my new son's helplessness and vulnerability, and my fears for him had their very own, monolithic, unarguable Thusness.

Much as it had during pregnancy, the world seemed to agree with me about the necessity of constant fearfulness. The nurses in the ward had taken care to warn me about not allowing a feed to slip back, because then the next feed would slip back, and the next, and the next, and before you knew it your poor baby would be starving. And don't forget to sterilize everything you use to feed him. We left the hospital with a sheaf of leaflets about sudden infant death syndrome and the importance of regulating the baby's temperature at all times. He couldn't regulate it himself yet; he couldn't hold his own head up; he couldn't control his movements or focus his eyes. He could neither perceive nor avoid danger. According to the developmental psychologists, he wouldn't even be able to distinguish fear from any other state of arousal. According to the psychoanalysts, the processing of baby's emotions was, for the time being, also my job.

Our household was not like the more traditionally arranged textbook ones; the father did everything he possibly could, and we both did our best: we kept up with the feeds, bought a microwave steam sterilizing unit which always seemed to be on, changed him regularly, put him into bodysuits and took him out of bodysuits and then put him back into them again; we followed the SIDS-prevention guidelines to the letter, keeping him in our room but not in our bed for the first six months, and always putting him down to sleep on his back, with his feet to the foot. When he fell asleep after feeding, half across my lap and half across my big triangular breastfeeding cushion, I remembered all the stories I'd heard about how easy it was to smother a tiny baby, and made sure to adjust everything whenever he stirred, just in case. If his little nose wound up pressed into the cushion for a few seconds, or he flailed about and dragged a muslin over his head for a short moment, or someone stepped over rather than round him when he was lying on his sheepskin, I would screech, 'I/You/It could've KILLED him!' I probably wasn't very good at the emotional processing bit.

The first three months in a new mother's life are sometimes referred to as 'the fourth trimester'. This is partly a nod to the length of time it takes for a woman's body to recover from pregnancy and birth, to make the transition, anatomically and hormonally, back to a non-pregnant state. At the same time, it is a way of acknowledging the necessary intensity of her physical relationship with the baby during this period, while he in his turn makes the transition from life inside someone else's body to life outside. He has a tiny stomach still, and needs frequent, regular small feeds; he panics, and cries, and only those things that remind him of the womb – being held closely, or swaddled, being rocked – can comfort him. He can't help but make constant demands on his carers, and he makes them outside office hours, and after bedtime, and at all hours thereafter, and his mother is sleep deprived, and very often his father too, and this drives them both mad.

All new mothers go through this. All prospective mothers will have been warned by midwives or relatives or friends that they will, for some or all of the time, be exhausted, and anxious, and feel alone and inadequate and quite, quite overwhelmed. To take the edge off this, there are mother and baby drop-ins, and lunches with other mothers met at antenatal classes, and postnatal coffee mornings. These can be a wonderful source of support, shared tips and advice, commiserations over broken nights and blocked milk ducts, that kind of thing. I was very fortunate to live in an area with an exceptionally good NCT coffee morning group, which was full of charming, interesting and funny people, many of whom had older children and so were able to provide a calmer, post-neonatal perspective on matters. I discovered that, like dogs, babies enable you to meet all those neighbours you'd always wondered about. The local streets, the park, the shop round the corner became abundantly peopled, and friendly with it.

When the company consisted of new mothers only, there was a far edgier atmosphere. I'm sure the sleep deprivation had a lot to do with this; that, and the fact that every new mother is secretly terrified, firstly, that she is doing everything wrong and secondly, that everyone else isn't. This means that any admission of difference in mothering practice, no matter how tiny, which comes up in conversation, has to be followed by at least five minutes of excuse-making, shrugging, self-deprecation, justification and counter-justification; otherwise, there's a real risk that at least one party present will feel all judged and criticized and will need to go straight home and spend two hours crying into a rancid muslin.

I couldn't see inside these other women's heads; I couldn't tell you whether I felt more or less judged than any of the rest of them. What I do remember very clearly, and very painfully, is the way I experienced my feeding problems as the social faux pas my friend had described. I seemed to be surrounded by women who could do it like they did in the Norwegian breastfeeding video, any time, anywhere; some of them even complained that they had *too much* milk, that their breasts leaked all over the place, and that it was so easy and comforting for their babies to feed from them that they despaired of ever getting them to take a bottle – it was a terrible bind, being so indispensable to one's offspring.

I thought that I would have given anything to have problems like theirs. For the first few weeks, I had hoped that, if only the baby and I could get our 'positioning' right and I pumped frantically enough, I could 'get my supply up' and we could get rid of the formula and the cups and the nipple guard and the triangular breastfeeding cushion and then I would be shoving my baby up my T-shirt in coffee shops with all the other girls. I was – in the colloquial sense – obsessed: the notebook I kept at the time is full of reports on volume, flow and consistency, made while simultaneously writing and pumping. It didn't work. At my son's nine-week check-up, he was pronounced underweight and we were told to increase the supplemental feeds. To help this, and to make life easier for Chris, who was still lumbered with most of the cup feeding, we switched to bottles, which the poor hungry baby took to immediately. My breasts were obviously harder work, and he became more and more reluctant to try to feed from them. Early in the autumn, the baby and I both got nasty colds and that was that: I remember turning him towards my breast and watching in horror as my son's face passed in the course of a second from smiling through blank and bewildered to distressed and enraged. I phoned the NCT breastfeeding advice line and they could only tell me that, if a baby decided to go on 'feeding strike' like this, there was nothing I could do.

I cried for a day or two, then picked up a bottle; the baby smiled at me around the teat. We were friends again, and, as I explained to anyone whether they had asked for an explanation or not, I would always give him the bottle with my expressed milk in it first, and I planned to keep expressing for another three months – at least. I'm making myself sound paranoid, but actually there were a fair number of people who did seem to want explanations. When I performed my first post-natal poetry reading a few weeks after the feeding strike, and included some poems about my recent pregnancy in the set, a woman came up to me in the interval, announced herself as a midwife and asked me straight off if I was breastfeeding. I told her, there in the theatre lobby, as people queued behind her to get their books signed, that my son had recently refused the breast but that I was still expressing, and approval was bestowed.

The first months of our son's life were hard for Chris too.

Of the two of us, he was almost certainly the more sleep deprived. He has always been a light sleeper, and infants tend to be noisy, so he found it very difficult to share a bedroom with our snuffling son. He didn't have the benefit of oxytocin, the 'ahh' hormone, which helps the new mother to sleep after – and sometimes during – night feeds, whereas for several months I was capable of nodding off in the middle of a sentence. And when I was asleep, which, to him, I seemed to be for an indecent amount of time, I was, apparently, snoring like a buffalo. And while I was asleep and snoring, he would be up, with the boy on his lap, giving him his supplementary feed and trying to soothe him back to sleep. As nobody had told either of us that small babies can sleep with one eye open, he would sometimes be up for hours. And then in the morning, before he could get away to work, he would have to help me and the boy out of bed and settle us into the living room, because I was too nervous to carry our son downstairs. It was no wonder that sometimes, when I threw him a drowsy glance from my pillow at night, his face was scribbled all over with exhaustion, resentment and despair.

I could see that he was suffering; I could see that he thought I was being selfish and lazy and that he couldn't understand why. I didn't understand why either, and couldn't explain to him how everything – feeding, changing, making decisions, leaving the house, talking to people – emotionally and physically, felt every day nearer and nearer to impossible. It happened at a creeping pace, this paralysis, and I was barely aware of it myself: it was just part of the general, post-natal misery of life, along with the complete absence of libido (because of lactation), continual thirst (also down to the lactation, presumably), constant migraines (stress, anxiety and sleep deprivation), insidious weight gain (because of sitting around too much? Not taking the baby out on enough walks? Eating as if I were breastfeeding properly when really I wasn't?) and muscle aches (also my fault for not exercising perhaps?) I could see Chris was suffering, but I didn't seem to have it in me to relieve his suffering, or even comfort him; I didn't even have it in me to take care of myself. We were a pair of lost causes, and, by some tacit agreement, we were concentrating our last remaining resources on the baby.

Late in October, I visited my doctor to get a repeat prescription for citalopram, and to discuss my possible familial breast cancer risk. She took my concerns seriously, and arranged for a preliminary screening interview for me. Then she asked, 'Do you mind if I take a look at your neck?' She palpated it, and was able to confirm her suspicion that what she had seen from halfway across the room was indeed a goitre, an enlarged thyroid. I'd have an imbalance one way or another, she said, and took a couple of phials of blood then and there. I think I burst out laughing: I'd spent half my life so far wondering if and when I'd get cancer like my mother, or Crohn's like my great-aunt, or coeliac's like my uncle, fearing that I'd caught AIDS, quaking in my flat-soled shoes every time I had a slightly numb finger in case I was developing multiple sclerosis, and in all that time, in all my anxious cross-questioning about who had had what, I'd somehow failed to identify my father's family's weakest point. My grandmother had undergone a thyroidectomy; my cousin had developed hyperthyroidism; following my father's death, my brother had suffered from stress-induced thyroiditis for over a year. And now it was my turn.

The thyroid is part of the endocrine, or hormone-secreting system: a butterfly-shaped gland that sits low down in the neck, just in front of the windpipe. Its function is to produce two hormones: thyroxine, known as T_4, which has four iodine atoms, and triiodothyronine, or T_3, which has three. Although they are two different substances, they are usually referred to together as 'thyroid hormone'. The thyroid secretes the hormone into the bloodstream, which distributes it around the body. As the

Thyroid Sourcebook I bought that month puts it, 'It is one of the basic regulators of the function of every cell and every tissue within the body, and a steady supply is crucial for good health.'[39] Broadly speaking, if the thyroid overproduces, and you have hyperthyroidism, everything speeds up; conversely, if the thyroid underproduces, then the patient is hypothyroid, and everything – pulse, digestion, metabolism, reflexes, all of it – will have slowed down. Symptoms of hypothyroidism include, among others, fatigue and lethargy, a constant thirst, creeping weight gain, depression and anxiety, poor concentration and memory, and muscle cramps. In women, it leads to heavy menstrual periods, and is often first suspected because of this. As I had not yet had my first post-natal period, and was already diagnosed as suffering from depression and anxiety, my hypothyroidism was easily masked.

To diagnose hyper- or hypothyroidism, you take a blood sample from the patient and then measure the level of 'free' T_4 present in that blood, along with the level of the thyroid-stimulating hormone (TSH), which the pituitary gland secretes in order to prompt the thyroid to produce its goods in whatever quantities the body may require. In a hypothyroid patient, therefore, you would expect TSH levels to be elevated. If you have a T_4 level of between 11.5 and 22.7 and a TSH level between 0.4 and 4, then your thyroid would appear to be functioning normally. When the doctor phoned me with my results she explained this to me, and then told me that my T_4 was 3, while my TSH had come in at over 100. It seemed probable that my thyroid had started to underperform about halfway through the pregnancy, and had been deteriorating ever since. She put me straight on to a 'starter dose' of 50 mcgs of synthetic thyroxine per day, and referred me to the local endocrinology clinic. I referred

39. M. Sara Rosenthal, *The Thyroid Sourcebook* (Lowell House, Los Angeles, 4th edition, 2000, p. 4)

myself to the Internet and the nearest branch of Borders.

Among the new pieces of knowledge I acquired was the fact that it is not uncommon for women to experience transient hypothyroidism post-natally (and that this is often misdiagnosed as post-natal depression). At first, I was hopeful that this might be the case with me, but my doctor told me that with my test results, and family history, it looked quite certain that my hypothyroidism would be permanent. I would depend on medication for the rest of my life. 'Goodbye, whole body, whole life,' I wrote, 'such as you ever were. From now on, my body will have to import one of its most essential regulatory hormones from a pharmaceutical manufacturer.' On the positive side, I added, the diagnosis explained all the disquieting changes I'd been noticing in my body and in myself:

> the fatigue
> the depression / 'low mood'
> the intolerance of cold
> the parched throat
> the onset of creeping weight gain
> the anxiety
> the dry skin
> the irritability
> the muscle aches
> the loss of leg hair
> the constipation
> the daily migraines
> the short-term memory problems
> the 'brain fog' / difficulty in concentrating.

As the health visitor put it, I have indeed been 'wading through treacle'. I just hope that medication alone shrinks the goitre. What with that & the weight – and OK I know it probably seems a lot only to me, I feel like I don't know my own image any more, my own body, its processes, its bound-aries. How do I manage such a body? feed it? dress it? regard it? I'm dressing down, avoiding mirrors.

In another entry I said that I had gone, in a matter of days, 'from young, slim and healthy to old, fat and medicated'. This, as I was discovering, was not that rare an experience post-partum. The usual cause of permanent hypothyroidism is Hashimoto's disease, which is an autoimmune condition: the body's own defence systems mistakenly identify its thyroid tissue as alien, attack and then destroy it. Like autoimmune conditions in general, it is more common in women than in men, and is not uncommonly triggered by pregnancy. In the weeks after my diagnosis, I learned that at least two women I already knew had developed the condition post-partum. Meanwhile, my best friend, who had given birth to her second child in August, had suffered two strokes and been diagnosed with an autoimmune blood-clotting disorder. I had also recently come across a woman who had given birth to her first son in May, and been admitted to hospital three months later, unable to move, suffering from what turned out to be a rare form of rheumatoid arthritis.

In answer to the question: Who is vulnerable to auto-immune disorders? my *Thyroid Sourcebook* replies:

Women who are either pregnant or have just given birth are particularly vulnerable to autoimmune disorders. During the first trimester, and in the first six months after delivery, the risk of an autoimmune disease is at an all-time high in a woman's life. During the first three months of pregnancy, the body is naturally more fatigued because it is busy providing nutrients (including iodine) for the growing fetus and adapting itself to the pregnancy in general. In fact, pregnant women are naturally iodine-deficient for this reason. Pregnant women are also immune-suppressed to avoid rejecting the fetal tissue. The immune system may then 'rebound' to an aggressive state, causing an autoimmune thyroid disease. [pp. 47–8]

I didn't remember reading anything about this before the birth, and nobody had told me about it either. And as they hadn't warned me that I might become hypothyroid after the birth, they hadn't gone on to tell me that, if I did, it would most probably affect my milk supply. That, at least, had been no fault of mine.

Now that I knew I was ill, I became aware that I felt ill, deeply ill, down-to-the-bones ill. Early one evening I found myself standing in the middle of our living room holding our son and sobbing, 'I can't do this any more! I can't do it! I can't!' I might have asked my mother to come up for a couple of weeks, but she was away on holiday, so we phoned a nanny agency and asked if they might send us some temporary help. Alison arrived with her nineteen-month-old daughter, Saskia; they took to my baby straight away, and he to them. They would take him off my hands for two days a week for the next year, and I would spend the last of my inherited money paying them to do it. I felt hugely relieved to be able to put my son into such a safe pair of hands – a safer pair, I felt, than mine – but the relief was shadowed with a sense of failure, and a jealousy so intense it was almost physical: '. . . no sooner have I given [the baby] to Alison, than I yearn for him back again, even though I don't feel up to it, not at all. Once more he recedes from me. He was slowly anyway, as I was slowly sinking, & Chris was doing more and more . . . And [he] seems to look at *me*, me in particular, more & more. He's so trusting, & so beautiful, & he smiles beautifully, showing/making two little apple cheeks. How I want to be his proper mother.'

Compared to other new mothers, 'I feel that I'm trying to mother in some universe parallel to the one they're inhabiting.

One with darker, denser matter. How could I ever begin to explain?' It was 'time to break into poetry', now that I had two baby-free days to do it in:

Love

Sickness came to baffle love,
exhaustion to unravel love.

Some let pity overwhelm them;
others are stirred to practical love.

Your mother is not adequate.
She has to buy and bottle love.

As fast as we can spoon it in,
you piss and puke and dribble love.

Did I ever smile like this,
beaming my uncritical love?

With such unstable chemistry,
we struggle to assemble love.

The hypothyroidism explained my physical symptoms. I hoped it might explain all the mental goings-on as well, the prey-animal anxiety, the morbid thoughts, the way my view of my baby was obstructed always by cobwebby curtains of fear. I hoped that, as my thyroxine dose was raised and my TSH came down, I would no longer have any reason to suspect that Evil was a real presence in the world, and that there was some particular weakness in me that meant I had to struggle not to be possessed by it.

Cognitive psychologists use the term 'thought-action fusion' (TAF) to refer to two kinds of beliefs which are noticeably common among obsessive patients: firstly, that one can 'tempt fate', and make a bad thing more likely to happen by thinking about it, and secondly, that to have a thought about doing something bad is somehow tantamount to doing it, so that the thought, whatever it is, is every bit as 'immoral', or 'evil' as the act itself. Ben, the cognitive behavioural therapist I had seen a few years earlier, had been fond of reminding me that 'thoughts are just thoughts': the appearance of a mental image of a lorry crushing my skull did not in any way increase the risk of my skull's being crushed in the real world, no matter how vivid and distressing I found it. I must have forgotten his telling me this, or ceased to believe it, or perhaps never believed it in the first place, because when certain images came into my mind, say of my stamping on the baby's neck, or dashing his brains out against the wall, or gouging out one of his beautiful blue eyes, or pushing his buggy under a bus, or pressing a pillow into his face, or holding him under the bathwater until he drowned, or throwing him out of his bedroom window, or stabbing him, or dousing him in boiling water, or any number of other terrible things, I knew with certainty that these were evil thoughts, and that I was an evil mother, capable of the most evil things.

Nothing helped. Knowledge of my own established patterns of cognitive behaviour prior to giving birth didn't help, and neither did my psychoanalytically informed understanding of the unavoidable violence of the human psyche, and of the effect the unprocessed emotional outbursts of an infant could have on the 'unanalysed' parts of its mother. If anything, my psychoanalytical leanings probably exacerbated my distress, as they made me inclined to discount – to almost overlook – my complete lack of any conscious desire to harm my child. That the images were present in my mind, meant that I harboured an unconscious 'wish' to carry out the actions they depicted; that they were so immediate, so vivid, had to mean that that wish was so powerful that all my defences and resistances were struggling to keep it in check. I had been taught that the 'unconscious wish', in the Freudian sense, is a slippery concept, something far more ambiguously and ambivalently and subtly held than the kind of wish which a fairy godmother grants in a pantomime, but that didn't help either. My wishes were evil, as straightforwardly evil as the spurned wicked fairy's desire that a good and beautiful baby should grow up to prick her finger on a spindle, and languish, in some kind of enchanted vegetative state, for a hundred years.

No, they were more evil than that the wicked fairy is only doing what is expected of her, but a mother is expected above all to protect her child from harm. A mother who desires to harm her child is an *un*mother, an *anti*-mother, the mother in opposition to whom all good mothers are defined. My proper place was in the back of a Black Maria as it drove away from court, the angry crowd spitting on it and shouting into branded microphones that there went the most evil woman in Britain, that they should bring back hanging, and that if I were ever mistakenly released from prison they would do their best to hang me themselves.

I think I knew – although of course it didn't help – that what would make the righteous mob parents so animated was their fear of their own violent thoughts. Violent images, thoughts or impulses directed towards babies are so common that even the most bland of mainstream childcare manuals give them a token mention. As psychologists Ross and McLean put it in their paper 'Anxiety Disorders during Pregnancy and the Postpartum Period':

> The prevalence of such intrusive thoughts across diagnoses and in healthy community samples suggests that at subclinical levels, they may be a normal feature of new parenthood. Evolutionary theories propose that these thoughts may be adaptive in that they may cause the parents to be vigilant in protecting the infant from potential harm.

266

It's a fascinating idea that something that feels so abnormal could be not only a normal experience, but an 'adaptive' one. I found it very comforting too; when I read the paper, I highlighted it. I had been convinced that, even if other people had thoughts of harming the child, they could hardly be as violent, vivid or simply as *numerous* as mine were. In my case, the thoughts were a sign of my essential unfitness for motherhood, and I was afraid that if I confessed them to my health visitor or GP, I would lose my child. This was my own private struggle with the Dark Side, and I would have to face it alone.

> Whether or no the compulsive tendency expresses itself in thought or action the patient persists in regarding himself as evil. It is characteristic of him that he tends to reject the reassurances one offers. He is unimpressed by soothing statements that these are only symptoms. Such emollients ease for the moment, then the pain returns. Often he believes that his thoughts are of the devil. The best that he will allow is that he is bad or mad. It is as though the obsessional patient is a battleground between good and evil and that he recognises himself as such.[40]

Asking for reassurance about the evil thoughts could be risky, so my chief strategies on the battleground were rumination and avoidance. The rumination wasn't so bad; it just meant that I spent rather a lot of time completely dead to my surroundings, while I followed another crucial but tangled line of thought. My son didn't move in any direction until just before his first birthday, when he figured out how to bottom shuffle backwards, so I wasn't putting him in any danger while I went off on my inner wanderings. It was the avoidance that made life difficult,

40. Arthur Guirdham, *Obsession, Psychic Forces and Evil in the Causation of Disease* (Neville Spearman Ltd, London, 1972)

or, at any rate, rather restricted. The responsibility of keeping my child safe had weighed heavily on me from the moment I suspected that I was pregnant with him, but while he remained inside my body, I'd had no choice but to take the lion's share of it. Now that I was no longer carrying him, I could find ways of easing the burden.

I could ease it by leaving the house as little as possible. As far as the baby was concerned, the ABYSS extended all the way to the front door, and I needed all the courage I could muster just to wheel him round to another mother's house, or to the local shops, what with all the hard pavements and roads and potentially clumsy or malevolent human beings standing between the door and our destination, not to mention all the opportunities to commit acts of involuntary infanticide along the way. Wheeling him into town was one long nightmare; taking a bus into town was an impossibility as it had been during pregnancy. Changing him outside the house was out of the question, because if I didn't throw him onto a hard floor I might fail to prevent him falling onto it. If I walked past an HGV, I felt as if we were both being pulled under it. If I even thought about pushing the buggy alongside the river, I immediately pictured him sinking into it, buggy and all.

Inside or outside, I could get some measure of relief by sharing responsibility, or passing it over altogether. As Alison took the baby out and about with her for two days a week, I didn't have any need to pressure myself to take him out much on the days I had him. Sometimes, I accompanied her on trips out, and then I felt a little safer. Similarly, if the baby and I went out with my mother or Chris or another, calmer new mother, I could relax a little.

Inside the house, there were other ways to delegate. Alison had already brought up nine small children; she was an expert at introducing solids, so I let her take the lead with that task, and make sure that my child learned to pass tinned mush from the front of his tongue to the back and then swallow it down without choking to death. Chris could carry the baby up and down the stairs. Chris could bathe the baby so that I didn't run the risk of drowning him accidentally or involuntarily but murderously. Chris could provide reassurance about whichever thoughts I felt safe enough to share with him. Chris could put the drops in the baby's eyes when he contracted conjunctivitis. Chris could get any necessary medicines into him orally too. Chris could hold him when he had his vaccinations. Chris could easily have throttled me, and easily escaped conviction.

I could not so easily hand over the jealousy I felt, or the sense of failure. As a consolation, I kept one task to myself, and rocked the baby to sleep every night before we took him upstairs and put him down in his cot. Sometimes, I would stand up with him, singing and rocking, for half an hour or longer: it was my substitute for what I really longed to do, which was to feed him to sleep. After a year of this, my health visitor suggested, gently, that it might be time for him to learn to go to sleep by himself. 'It's a ritual,' she said, 'a habit, and you can replace it with another one.' We bought a plastic star that played Brahm's lullaby and projected a light show onto his bedroom ceiling, and used that instead. It felt like a second weaning.

When I call that first year to mind, I always get a picture of myself sitting in the living room looking at my son in his bouncy chair while he sleeps or watches a Baby Einstein video or maybe chews one of his toys. I know how inaccurate this must be, because I have the notebooks, the poems and even the short story to prove it. I also have the article which the Poetry Society commissioned while I was still in the post-natal ward, and which I wrote, quite insanely really, as soon as I was out of the hospital. Shoved into the back of a filing cabinet are the notes I made for the evening course I taught that winter, and payslips from the Open College of Arts, for which I was doing the occasional bit of distance-learning tuition. That was also the year that I joined, and then began to chair, the local maternity services liaison committee, because I hadn't managed to put my post-natal experiences behind me, and joining a committee seemed the most positive way of dealing with them. All this work brought in next to no income, and some of it – like the teaching – I almost hated, but most of it had been offered to me, and I still had a vestigial Party Girl to placate, so I took it, and felt ill, and did some of it badly.

I had an idea for a novel too: it would be about a woman with a new baby who was going mad. Of course it would. The woman wasn't going to be exactly like me, though, because she would suffer from severe post-natal depression, whereas I hadn't. Truly I hadn't: the health visitor had administered the Edinburgh post-natal depression scale at the appropriate time, and I'd checked out just fine.

Round about my son's first birthday, I went to the University Library to do my research on PND. I searched through the catalogue for suitable material and ordered a few books to be brought up to the Reading Room. One of them was the second volume of a collection of essays called *Motherhood and Mental Illness*; it was subtitled 'Causes and consequences', and was edited by an R. Kumar and one I.F. Brockington. I flicked through it, and on page eleven, under the heading 'Other disorders occurring in the postnatal period', I found the following passage:

Disorders of the mother-infant relationship
Obsessive thoughts of hostility to the infant

Mothers with an anankastic [i.e. obsessive] personality may experience intrusive and distressing thoughts about their babies, including impulses to inflict bodily harm. Button, Reivich and Kan (1972) described 42 patients with 'obsessions of infanticide' in a review of 605 consecutive admissions and 712 outpatient referrals to Kansas Medical Center (3.4 % of psychiatric referrals). These thoughts coexist with a normal mother–infant relationship, though they may cause distress, and may lead to some avoidance of contact with the infant.

Then they cited a case history about a woman who had

these thoughts – evil thoughts blaming him for things which have happened, swearing at him, e.g. 'bloody baby.' She was considerably distressed by the thoughts, but otherwise well. The nature of these thoughts as obsessional phenomena was explained to her, and she was advised to label them as 'stupid irrational ideas', not to feel ashamed of them, but rather to react with amusement at the tricks her mind was playing on her. This helped her a good deal. The thoughts worried her less and became less frequent.[41]

And I thought, Oh.

41. R. Kumar and I.F. Brockington, *Motherhood and Mental Illness* (Academic Press, London, 1982)

Brain

35. My brain constantly goes its own way, and I find it difficult to attend to what is happening around me.

The Padua Inventory

———

Brain: an apparatus with which we think that we think.

Ambrose Bierce

I've told the library story so many times now that it's refined
down into an image of me running then and there from the
Reading Room, across the river, round the corners of a college
or two and straight into the GP's surgery, but my journal entry
makes it sound almost as if I blurted the thing out by accident.

4/8/04

Went to Dr this morning ... there was a letter waiting telling
me that my TSH was low & my dose needed reducing. When
I went today I wound up telling her about my SCARY
THOUGHTS & she doubled my Citalopram dose &
referred me to a psychiatrist with a view to longer-term CBT.
Knowing one's OCD is preferable to suspecting it. She said
I'd done very well to have a baby at all considering what I was
dealing with. Wldn't've dared tell her if I hadn't come across
my symptoms exactly in a post-natal illness book – when I
told Mum I'd feared social workers she laughed like a drain.

The doctor didn't laugh. She did tell me, though, that in her
opinion I was not a danger to my child. The next time I saw her,
my health visitor said exactly the same thing. The truth – and

it's a very important truth, which is why I'm going to risk repeating myself here – is that OCD sufferers are at a very, very low risk of carrying through what they believe to be their criminal, perverted or evil impulses. Crimes are not usually committed by the over-conscientious, and the distress that accompanies these violent intrusive thoughts is a more reliable indicator of that sufferer's characteristic behaviour and values than the thoughts are themselves. They were not, as I had feared they were, the deepest and truest parts of me. They were obsessional thoughts, symptoms of an illness; therefore my doctor increased my dosage and spoke to a psychiatrist about them.

She sent me a note a few days later to say that the psychiatrist had 'agreed with our plan of increasing the citalopram for now'. He wasn't worried about me, though, and suggested that she postpone referral for a month at least, and see how I got on with the higher dose. In the meantime, I self-medicated with books and web articles. The more I learned about OCD and other OCD 'spectrum' disorders, the more I found to attribute to them: the glass penguin, the fear of losing my shoes, my ruminations in the past unreal conditional tense, the AIDS fears, the difficulty finishing essays, the slow note taking, the hypochondria, the preoccupations I'd had with the shortness of my legs and the imagined unacceptability of my nose – so much. The Os in my OCD were easy to identify and I had certainly had plenty of them. It took me longer to figure out what my Cs might be. Depending on one's point of view, I might not have had any at all; some of the writers of books and websites talked about a variety of OCD which they called 'pure O': obsessive thoughts, no compulsions as such. Compulsions are classically defined as rituals, mental or physical, which must be performed in a particular way in order to ward off the anxiety generated by the obsessive thought which usually precedes them. Hand washing and checking, of locks or switches, are the obvious examples, but compulsions can also take the form of touching, counting, making lists, saying or writing a certain phrase over and over again, thinking a 'good' thought to neutralize the 'bad' one, walking through gates or doorways in a certain fashion or a certain number of times – any act can become a compulsion, if it is compulsively performed. I wasn't into washing my hands, or making lists, or counting, or touching. Instead, I responded to my obsessions with rumination and avoidance. So, did I have pure O?

Not according to Fred Penzel, an OCD expert whose book was one of the first I read. 'A compulsion,' he reminds the reader, 'is basically anything mental or physical that you may do to relieve the anxiety resulting from obsessions. The truth is that many sufferers either fail to recognize many of their own obsessions or mistake mental compulsions for obsessions.'[42] My ruminations, which I tried to use to neutralize my obsessions, could be seen as compulsions. As could one of my most annoying traits – my constant reassurance seeking. It was a great relief to be able to file that under the 'symptom' heading: it made it easier to resist the compulsion to drive everyone mad by doing it.

When I returned to the doctor a month later, I was, as she wrote, 'only slightly better', but I did have a lot of research to share with her. One of my more exciting findings was that my disgusting, perverted self-harm habit, which I had so often tried and failed to find in any of the literature about 'cutting', was actually an OCD spectrum disorder, had a couple of names of its own – dermotillomania, or compulsive skin-picking – and was not unlike trichotillomania, its hair-plucking cousin. I wasn't the only person in the world who did it, it didn't mean I'd been abused and forgotten it, it had nothing to do with sadomasochistic sexual impulses, but it was a real condition, with

42. Fred Penzel, *Obsessive-Compulsive Disorders: A Complete Guide to Getting Well and Staying Well* (Oxford University Press, 2000, p. 54)

symptoms, and, like the OCD, an entity separable from myself. That was perhaps the greatest relief of all.

This morning, I dropped my son off at school, then I went into town and did some shopping, then I went to get my right ear syringed. When I got home, I read the newspaper I'd bought in town, then I phoned a friend and talked for half an hour while my Internet connection was down. Then I rebooted and got the connection back again. Then I phoned up the National Insurance helpline and requested a form for a new card, because I'd lost my wallet with the card in it. Then I took a look at my Facebook home page, which had nothing of significance on it. And then it was time for lunch. Now I've had lunch, I've checked Facebook again, and my email messages, and there are no more excuses to avoid this chapter. Avoidance is such an enduring symptom with me that maybe it would be more honest to call it a character trait.

The trouble with writing, the trouble always with writing, whether it's poetry or philosophy essays or psychoanalytic studies, dissertations or memoirs, is that you fear in advance – or rather, you *know* in advance – that whatever comes out on the page is bound to fall short of the fuzzily luminous piece of perfection that you plan to write beforehand. In order to write anything real, you have to kill that luminous potential, and erect something concretely disappointing in its place. It's like Milner said: one of the necessary conditions of creativity is the ability to bear the disillusionment which an encounter with one's real-world, unidealized products inevitably brings.[43] If you can get through that, you have a something, which is better than a nothing, be it ever so luminous.

I wanted to write something incredible about OCD and the

43. That is to say, although it is a very good poo, and Mummy knows you're proud of it, it's still a poo, it's smelly, and she's going to have to flush it now.

brain at this point, something comprehensive yet concise, something which would be comprehensible and interesting to the general reader without oversimplifying the science behind it. I've had this perfect chapter in my head for so long: I've prepared for it, I've read books with 'brain' in the title, I've surfed and resurfed, I've spoken informally to a researcher from the brain-mapping unit at the local hospital, I've borrowed half a plastic brain from a friend of mine who teaches neuroscience – it's on my desk right now and I can't take my eyes off its cortex, which is implausibly pink and appears to have been sculpted out of petrified blancmange . . . Anyway, I've tried. I want you to know that I've really tried, but I haven't been able to turn myself into Jonathan Miller in the space of twelve months. I've let myself down, I've let my publishers down, I've let the OCD research community down, and most of all, I've let you, the readers, down. Now I've got that out of the way, I can carry on with what I meant to do today.

For a long, long time, as I've said, the mainstream view of OCD was the psychoanalytic one: deep unconscious conflicts, repressed sadism, fixation at the anal stage of development, potty training traumas, etc. Freud's French contemporary Janet, who had a better feel for the condition than Freud ever did, was left untranslated and, at least in the Anglo-Saxon world, largely ignored. Even though it was generally acknowledged that OCD symptoms were largely resistant to psychoanalytic treatment methods, no rival theory or treatments emerged to replace them. Then, in the last few decades of the last century, things finally started to change.

Within a few years of each other, two new treatments emerged, one psychological, one biological. A number of psychologists on both sides of the Atlantic began to apply behavioural techniques to the treatment of OCD, a form of exposure and response prevention in which the patient was encouraged to expose themselves to the stimulus that triggered their obsessions, and then try to prevent themselves from resorting to their usual response, which was to perform their compulsions. In this way, they would be able to break their obsessive-compulsive cycle and allow themselves to experience the anxiety associated with their obsessions, rather than fore-closing on it by neutralizing it with a compulsion; this would enable them to become habituated to the thought and its accompanying anxiety, and so the thought would be revealed for what it was – just a thought, no more – and lose its power. Studies were done which found that this kind of treatment, addressing the mechanisms of OCD symptoms rather than the causes, was proving to be more effective than psychodynamic forms of therapy. Behavioural approaches could not help all of the patients all of the time, but they gave new hope to many.

Elsewhere in Europe, researchers were investigating possible medical treatments for OCD. In the late sixties, a Spanish psychiatrist, Lopez-Ibor, reported that a tricyclic antidepressant called clomipramine, administered initially to treat the depression which accompanied OCD, had been found to be helpful in relieving the obsessive-compulsive symptoms themselves. Following this, doctors at the Karolinska Hospital in Stockholm carried out a more systematic test of the drug. Judith Rapoport, who would later write *The Boy Who Couldn't Stop Washing*, was a former student at the hospital and was visiting at the time of the clomipramine trial. When she returned to the States, she and her colleagues at the National Institute of Mental Health obtained a special licence to use the drug in their research into OCD. Initially, they were sceptical.

> I confess that my group and I started the study not at all confident that the drug would work. But after a few years, we were converts. Our patients did not improve when they took placebos (sugar pills that look like the drug but have no effect) or when they took another antidepressant. But when

they were on Anafranil [the trade name of clomipramine], most did improve. The thoughts grew weaker. They were able to fight off the urge to carry out ritual activity. For some it was the end of a nightmare.[44]

Although clomipramine is an older drug than fluoxetine or citalopram, a second-generation tricyclic, as opposed to a third-generation selective serotonin uptake inhibitor (SSRIs), all three drugs, along with others in the SSRI group, are known to relieve obsessive-compulsive symptoms. Clomipramine works differently from the later drugs, as it is known to affect the levels of another neurotransmitter, norepinephrine, but it also acts on the serotonergic system by inhibiting the reuptake of serotonin into the presynaptic neuron, so increasing its availability in the brain, and promoting better transmission between neurons. Following the success of these drugs in OCD treatment, researchers were able to hypothesize that one of the mechanisms – if not the main mechanism – behind the symptoms of OCD was biological, a result of a disorder of the serotonergic system. According to this hypothesis, serotonin reuptake takes place prematurely in the obsessive-compulsive brain, thus preventing effective electrical transmission between the cells. If this happens across a large enough number of cell junctions, the brain will not function as it should. I have taken both citalopram and fluoxetine, and have found that they both relieve my OCD symptoms. Anecdotally, I can vouch for the correlation.

Further support for a biological view of OCD came from the development of brain-imaging techniques, such as positron emission tomography (PET), single-photon computed tomography (SPECT) and magnetic resonance imaging (MRI). These enable researchers and clinicians to measure relative levels of activity across different areas of the brain, and to track

44. Judith L. Rapoport, *The Boy Who Couldn't Stop Washing* (Penguin, New York, 1989, p.11)

278

changes in these levels across time. Over the last twenty years or so, there have been a number of studies which have used imaging techniques to compare patterns of brain activity in OCD sufferers and non-suffering controls. The brains of OCD patients have shown characteristic patterns, with higher than normal levels of activity in two particular areas: the basal ganglia, a small cluster of structures in the middle of the brain which, among other things, enable the individual to coordinate their physical movements, and the orbito-frontal cortex, which sits above and behind the eyes, and helps to regulate 'such things as anxiety, impulse control, meticulousness, personal hygiene, perseveration, and the starting and stopping of behaviours' [Penzel, pp. 396–7].

Much of the research in this area was undertaken by a research group at UCLA, lead by Jeffrey Schwartz, who came up with the 'brain lock' theory of OCD. This hypothesis offers an explanation of what might be going on in the brain when SAUCEPAN – HOT – OUCH! fails to turn itself off. It suggests that there is a problem with the pathway between the orbito-frontal cortex, a particular basal ganglia structure called the caudate nucleus and two further regions: the thalamus, which relays signals between different parts of the brain, and the cingulate gyrus, a part of the brain's limbic system, which processes emotion. If my hand strays too near a hot saucepan, the orbito-frontal cortex will register that something is amiss and send a signal – you could call it a 'worry signal', an 'error message', or, if you like, an 'alarm' – to that effect to the thalamus; this stimulates the nerve cells in the thalamus, which start firing away and send powerful signals to various other areas of the brain, prompting the cingulate gyrus to initiate a worried feeling and all the physical sensations which come with it, and causing the orbito-frontal cortex to interpret the various bits of sensory input, the signals and sensations and signs of arousal – 'I've got a very unpleasant feeling . . . Why? It must be because my hand is about to be burned' – and initiate appropriate action: *Jump to it! Take your hand away NOW!*

So, either you've registered that your hand is indeed about to get burned, and you've pulled it away, or you've realized that, in actual external fact, your hand is nowhere near anything hot and so there's no real need to be alarmed. At this point, the caudate nucleus, which acts as a gate, or filter, or valve, or checkpoint – choose your metaphor – and determines which of the brain's innumerable flickers of thought or impulse are significant enough to be relayed to the conscious mind and acted upon by it, steps in, switches off SAUCEPAN – HOT – OUCH! and enables the brain to direct its attention elsewhere. You have that 'just right' feeling now; the sequence is complete and you can get on with the rest of your life.

Unless you have OCD, however, in which case the caudate nucleus is a little sleepy or maybe not quite assertive enough, or perhaps a little indecisive or wishy-washy about what it allows through, and so the orbito-frontal cortex, the thalamus and the cingulate gyrus just keep on screaming at each other SAUCEPAN – HOT – OUCH! SAUCEPAN – HOT – OUCH! even when you've pulled your hand away, or realized that the cooker is in fact switched off or you can see perfectly well that you are, say, in the departure lounge at Malaga Airport with your entire family and that therefore neither you nor anyone you love is any danger of coming into contact with a hot saucepan. But as you are at that very moment deeply concerned and anxious about the danger from saucepans, you feel compelled to resolve the matter, to act in some way – your brain is nudging you in that direction – so perhaps you tap the seat in front of you five times to ensure that no one is ever burned by a saucepan, or you turn to your long-suffering spouse and start a discussion about the dangers of hot saucepans so that you can get some reassurance, or alternatively, you sit there and you ruminate about it. And by obeying the promptings to action which arise out of this repeating pattern of faulty messages, you further reinforce the pattern. Your body is in the departure lounge, and you are conscious of this, but as far as your orbito-frontal cortex, your cingulate gyrus and your thalamus are concerned, you're stuck in the kitchen, and the gas hobs are hot. They've made each other hysterical, and now they won't listen to reason.

Schwartz has developed a self-treatment method informed by this model, and has published his method in a self-help book, *Brain Lock* (1996). What is crucial to this method is the patient's ability to 'relabel' and 're-attribute' their obsessions and compulsions, so that she can come to understand them as arising from a malfunctioning organ – the brain – and in doing so detach them from her self, from her own intentionality and her own agency. As a sufferer, I find something very appealing about this view: it's not my mind, it's my body; my eye teeth were impacted, my thyroid conked out and now it turns out that my brain is on the fritz, and maybe always has been. The thing is, although we – by which I mean, my GP, my husband, my friends, the writers of textbooks for professional readers, the authors of memoirs for general readers, the newspapers, the BBC website, the Royal College of Psychiatrists, the government, the World Health Organization and I – talk of mental illnesses as 'illnesses', in the same way that we might talk about Hashimoto's disease, or influenza, or cancer, I'm not at all sure that, down in our gut of guts, we're really entirely convinced. I know I'm not. Can you link the symptoms to a known pathogen? Can you see anything through a microscope? Can you point to anything at all? Perhaps when we call these experiences, or patterns of behaviour, 'illnesses' with 'symptoms' we are doing so only by analogy with the proper diseases, the cancers and the influenzas. So, are they illnesses, really, or do they belong to some other category? Attention-getting strategies? Sulks? Tantrums? Lame excuses? Character faults? Moral weaknesses? Do I feel unconvinced, because I know, deep down, in my gut of guts, that I'm to blame for my suffering, that I chose my suffering, and that, if I wanted to, I could choose to lay it aside?

But if it's my brain, an organ, and here's the physical evidence – the MRI scan, the PET scan – to prove it, then my suffering has been visited on me, from outside, and I didn't do it, I didn't choose it, and you can go ahead and feel sorry for me now. And I can feel sorry for myself. I've got a disease, and, like cancer patients do, I can 'battle with' it. I can do the best I can despite it. You can all root for me. You can admire me too, if you like. It's a much more straightforward narrative now. It's got a clearly identified antagonist, and a sympathetic heroine.

Now it appears that my tone has been tragically afflicted by another bout of snideness, but I'll try to battle that for a moment, and say that I really do find the brain view very plausible. It fits in well with the way obsessions feel. The thoughts are, as the literature says, intrusive: they are experienced as coming from the outside. An obsession[45] is like a bully or a nag, standing too close to you, gesticulating in front of your face, shouting into your ear. You know they're shouting nonsense, but you'll do anything you can to appease them because you find what they're doing to you, all the bullying and the nagging, so unbearable. You feel in two minds, only you can see that one of your minds, at least, has lost it.

In my experience, depressive thoughts are quite different from obsessions, not only in content but also in form. It isn't only, as I said in the chapter entitled 'Sin', that they are past rather than future orientated; sometimes they are future orientated, but without the anxious uncertainty of the obsessive rumination, that is, you are certain that you can predict the future, and that the future is going to be shit. Everyone I love is going to die; I myself am going to get old and getting old is horrible; over time, more bits of me will stop working and the

45. The word 'obsession', by the way, derives from the Latin verb *obsidere*, 'to besiege'.

exterior bits will look worse and worse; at the end of that nasty process, I'll die; the world is full of suffering; there is no discernible point to any of this. I can find plenty of evidence in support of the first five statements and no good reason to doubt the sixth. I am always entirely in agreement with myself when I think along these lines. I've tried cognitive behavioural therapy for this, but it couldn't get much of a purchase.

I can see that I would be better off without these thoughts, that by allowing them into my mind again and again, and letting them run their course, I am helping myself to suffer. I appreciate that all this death business, as Larkin said, is 'no different whined at than withstood'. I can even believe that, if I managed to change my thinking habits – because they are habits – in this regard, I might well be physically healthier, because habitual thoughts have a way of working themselves into the body, its posture, its sleep patterns, its digestion and its appetites. I can't argue with them, though, and I can't stop noticing that we are living in time, that everything changes around us, that we lose much as we go along, that in the end we lose everything, and I can't see this as anything but irredeemably sad. I could never accept an explanation of these thoughts that was purely biological: they come out of the thinking, philosophizing, essentially human part of me – my *mind*, the part that writes the poems.

By contrast, I have no trouble at all in accepting that my obsessions might emerge, without any philosophical justification, out of the disordered activity of an animal brain. I'm thinking again about the 'fixed-action patterns' I touched on in 'Habits', the compulsive skin picking that I always felt was so senseless and seemed to come from a mute part of me. There are disorders in animals, such as canine acral lick, which have been thought to resemble OCD spectrum disorders, and so shed further light on their nature. Ethologists, who study animal behaviour, have also observed certain dysfunctional fixed-action patterns in some animals, which look, on the face of it, very similar to the compulsive behaviours of human OCD sufferers. The ethologist Konrad Lorenz kept his greylag geese in the house with him. He noticed that one of them always walked in a particular way when she returned home.

> At first she always walked past the bottom of the staircase toward a window in the hallway before returning to the steps, which she then ascended to get into the room on the upper floor. Gradually she shortened this detour, but still kept on heading toward the window before turning around and heading up the stairs.

One day Lorenz forgot to let her in at the usual time. By the time he opened the door for her, darkness was beginning to fall. Eager to get in, she ran through the door, went straight for the stairs, and began to climb them. Then, as Lorenz tells it:

> Upon this, something shattering happened: Arriving at the fifth step, she suddenly stopped, made a long neck, in geese a sign of fear, and spread her wings as for flight. Then she uttered a warning cry and nearly took off. Now she hesitated a moment, turned around, ran hurriedly down the five steps and set forth resolutely, like someone on a very important mission, on her original path to the window and back.
>
> This time, she mounted the steps according to her former custom from the left side. On the fifth step she stopped again, looked around, shook herself, and performed a greeting behaviour regularly seen in Graylags when anxious tension has given place to relief. I hardly believed my eyes. The habit had become a custom which the goose could not break without being stricken by fear.

Quoted in Rapoport, *The Boy Who Couldn't Stop Washing*, pp. 217–18

So, the argument runs: a greylag goose, unlike a human being, but like the vast majority of animals, has only a repertoire of inborn fixed behaviour patterns at her disposal. When these patterns are activated inappropriately, the resulting observable behaviour closely resembles that of a human patient in the grip of OCD; therefore, it seems plausible that what we are seeing in OCD might be evidence of what Rapoport calls 'built-in patterns', which normally lie dormant in us but reveal themselves in OCD, and which 'document some stored knowledge that serves an ancient purpose. Cleaning, avoiding, checking, and repeating relate to the most basic preoccupations of cleanliness, safety, aggression and sex' [p. 218]. If OCD really was something that we shared with other animals, if our brains really did function and malfunction along similar lines, then this would be a great gift to OCD-related brain research, for the practical reason that living human brains are not generally available for invasive manipulation and investigation, whereas, rightly or wrongly, there are large numbers of living animal brains whose owners have been reared for that very purpose.

To recap: on the brain side, we have OCD's response to drugs which are known to alter neurochemistry, distinctive patterns of activity as revealed by brain scans, this patient's subjective sense of the 'rightness' of the brain model, anxious geese, and dogs who groom too much. There's also Tourette's syndrome. In the same way that, in the popular imagination, OCD is the one where you wash your hands too much and check the oven, Tourette's syndrome is the one where you involuntarily swear. In reality, coprolalia is a relatively unusual symptom of Tourette's, which (in Penzel's definition) is what you have if you are unlucky enough to suffer from both chronic vocal tic disorder and chronic motor tic disorder. A tic is 'an intermittent, repetitious vocal utterance or motor movement'. Tics are not voluntary: a sufferer may be able to hold some of them back for a certain amount of time, but tics are always driven by very powerful urges, which are experienced physically, so that until or unless they are performed, that person will be in intolerable discomfort, which can only be relieved by carrying out the tic, and carrying it out till it feels 'just right'. Trying to suppress a tic is like trying to hold in a sneeze.

Tics can be simple, which are relatively easy to diagnose as such, or complex, which may be harder to identify with any certainty. Simple tics on the vocal side may include grunting, sniffing, clearing the throat and squeaking; simple motor tics include eye blinking, grimacing, head turning or shoulder shrugging. Coprolalia is classified as a complex vocal tic, as it involves recognizable language. Also in this category are echolalia, the senseless repetition of words or sequences of words just heard, and palilalia, the increasingly rapid repetition of words or phrases. Like complex vocal tics, complex motor tics consist of sequences of actions, and more closely resemble intentional behaviours such as jumping, smelling or touching objects, touching other people, or self-harming behaviours – in his memoir *Busy Body* (2006), the musician Nick van Bloss describes how he is impelled to punch himself, hard, in the stomach. Of course it hurts. The jerking and tensing of muscles which tics involve make pain – sometimes the most terrible pain – another feature of Tourette's.

Van Bloss, like a significant number of 'Touretters', also experiences many obsessive-compulsive symptoms. Sometimes compulsions, with their repetitive, ritualistic quality, are hard to distinguish from complex motor tics. Sometimes, a distinction can be drawn in terms of the patient's experience, in that whereas the discomfort preceding a compulsion is mental, that preceding a tic is physical, or sensory, but in practice, it is not always easy to separate the two. Tourette's syndrome can be classified as an OC spectrum disorder, and something like 20 per cent of those with a 'classic OCD' (again, according to Penzel) also qualify for a diagnosis either of Tourette's, or of one of the other tic disorders. That there may be a genetic link between the two is suggested by studies which have shown a high rate of OCD and/or tics in relatives of TS patients, and a high rate the other way round.[46] Following these findings, it has been argued that Tourette's syndrome, and at least some cases of OCD, may be different expressions of the same underlying problems.

These underlying problems would have to lie in the brain. Tourette's syndrome is understood, quite uncontroversially, to be a brain disorder, not a mental illness. From a neurochemist's point of view, the two disorders appear different at first sight, as the Tourette's brain has difficulties with dopamine levels, rather than the OCD brain's struggle with serotonin. On the other hand, the dopaminergic and serotonergic systems are known to interlink; sometimes Tourette's patients with obsessive symptoms respond to SSRIs, and sometimes OCD patients respond to another group of drugs called dopamine blockers. And then there's the matter of faulty wiring. In the Tourette's brain, apparently, there's a certain pathway between the basal ganglia and the orbito-frontal cortex that just doesn't function as it should . . . Is it possible, could it be possible, as some have suggested, that OCD symptoms are produced through the same mechanisms as physical tics?

It's a tidy notion. I took it and I ran with it. I read somewhere, and agreed wholeheartedly, that the skin picking could be classified as a complex motor tic. So could my pacing. Then there was the pulling-my-hand-down-my-face thing – remember that? – in primary school. And the hair chewing, which I don't do any more. And the cheek biting, which I do. And the way the end of my nose is always itching so that I'm always not-quite-voluntarily rubbing it (a 'sensory tic', that would be). I read a list of 'Tics Tic's Tixs Tix's' on a site called

46. Dan J. Stein and Eric Hollander, 'The Spectrum of Obsessive-Compulsive-Related Disorders' in *Essential Papers on Obsessive-Compulsive Disorder* (New York University Press, New York and London, 1997)

www.tourettes-disorder.com and found I either had done or still do the following: animal sounds (I sometimes miaow back to cats and on one occasion cawed back to a crow before I'd had a chance to stop myself), hopping, skip stepping, chewing on clothes, nose wrinkling, stammering and toe scrunching. Sometimes I start running before I know what I'm doing. When I think a distressing thought, I shut my eyes very tightly to make the tension go away, and this is so automatic that it's hard to say whether it's willed or not. I remembered a conversation I'd had with my father and my brother after I'd inadvertently danced across the living room once and been embarrassed, and we'd laughed about how we, all three of us, did these 'involuntary movements' – that was the word my father used – from time to time.

You could make something of all that, or you could choose to leave it be. I'm aware that there is a certain absent-mindedness in most of the actions I've described, and absent-mindedness is not the same as involuntariness. Some people are just fidgets. And when I compare my experiences to those of someone like Van Bloss, it seems a little ridiculous, not to say insulting, to suggest that I understand what it's like to suffer from real, fully expressed, diagnosable Tourette's. For a time, though, I made quite a lot of it. I also noted that Tourette's and OCD can sometimes be found scudding across the pages of books and websites in a loosely formed conceptual cloud along with attention deficit disorder and various forms of autism. I recognized in myself some of the characteristics of sufferers from the second two, in particular 'sensory sensitivity': I'd always found noise and crowds intolerable; like my father, I also hated rough fabrics, hard seams and having to swallow pills. It was a hardware fault; I just couldn't process certain stimuli. All my problems and I, I supposed, were the products of a slightly tragically but fascinatingly abnormal brain.

*

I saw the consultant psychiatrist in October. The waiting area in psychiatry outpatients was ever so much nicer than the cattle-processing plant at the endocrinology clinic, where the queues were long and the nurses behaved as if thyroid dysfunction was something you were being sent down for. There were calm green walls and pot plants, the reception staff were pleasant and there was a general air of tranquillity about the place, as if the very walls understood that the patients here were fragile, and required some delicate handling. It felt like a good step up in the world.

The psychiatrist came to fetch me. He didn't shake my hand. I couldn't remember if all the other doctors I'd met in my life as a patient had shaken my hand or not, and wondered if the not shaking hands was a psychiatry thing, in order to preserve sound doctor–patient boundaries. Perhaps he thought that I might, as an OCD suspect, have anxiety about contamination and so didn't offer his hand, or maybe, on some unconscious or at the very least subconscious level, he had anxiety about mind contamination through contact with the known-to-be-mad.

When we had sat down in his office, he explained that he would need to take notes throughout the consultation, and, if I remember rightly, apologized for the lack of eye contact that this would entail. He lifted his pen, and I began the usual recital of what he refers to, in his letter to my GP, as 'a long history of anxiety, depression and obsessional symptomatology'. He asked about my family history, and alludes in his letter to 'affective disorder' in some members, and 'some obsessional features' in others. He mentions the bullying at school, my 'chequered career' and my miscarriage, but notes, on the plus side, my 'reasonably' happy childhood, good relationship with my husband and son, and the fact that I was continuing to write. My writing certainly was going extremely well at the time: I had so much fantastic material.

The letter moves on to consider my psychiatric history: the

'mood disorder' which had first shown itself in my early teens, and my pubescent habit of unplugging appliances and taking extra care on the stairs; the more recent intrusive thoughts and the twenty-year skin-picking habit. The treatments are all there too: the various bouts of counselling and psychotherapy, the fluoxetine and the citalopram. When he comes to his own diagnosis, he describes what he sees as 'a rather complicated picture', which includes features of OCD, as well as 'dysthymia and generalised anxiety'. He adds that I am sometimes 'more significantly depressed'.

Not long afterwards, Chris and I changed life insurance providers, and I had to get a copy of the psychiatrist's letter from my GP for the insurance people to inspect. They also needed to know which drugs I was taking long term – fluoxetine and thyroxine – and how much of each. When I saw the letter, I remember picking up straight away on the term 'a rather complicated picture', and saying to Chris how that wasn't really a term you wanted to see in a psychiatric diagnosis. The insurance company must have agreed, because my premiums went up quite a lot.

They might have gone up for another reason. It wasn't as if the psychiatrist had said anything about a lowered life expectancy, either to me or to my doctor. At the end of the consultation, he told me that the good news about OCD was that, if you had insight, the symptoms did improve somewhat with age, as you got used to managing and working round them. He thought that I should continue on the citalopram for the time being, as I had made a 'partial improvement', but added that it might be worth going back to fluoxetine if, as the letter has it, 'the picture [you know, the complicated one] deteriorates at all'. He also agreed with my GP that the patient 'might benefit from psychological treatment directed at her obsessional symptoms'. He didn't say so in the letter, but I remember his telling me that my several difficulties might well continue to wax and wane, and it was quite probable that I might need to return for 'top-up' courses of this treatment from time to time. For now, he was referring me back to psychological treatment services.

Behaviour

18. I have to do things several times before I think they are properly done.

The Padua Inventory

Through hard work and determination, the symptoms can be controlled or in some cases largely eliminated, and you can maintain a normal life.

Fred Penzel, Obsessive-Compulsive Disorders

It had been three years since my first visit to psychological treatment services, and much had changed: they had moved into new premises, and I had a new diagnosis. Last time, I had been referred by my GP, but this time, it was a psychiatrist who'd sent me. As a genuine nut straight from the office of the certified nut doctor, I took it for granted that they would offer me treatment. I was hopeful of a good offer: fifteen sessions at least. And it was almost Christmas. I arrived in a buoyant mood.

This is not in any way a how-to book, but allow me to pass on just one piece of advice: if you are seeking treatment, never go into a mental health assessment in a buoyant mood; if you suspect yourself of being in a buoyant mood on the day, think hard about all the things that make you most depressed or anxious, and if that fails, take yourself off to the lavatory, lock the door and hit yourself somewhere where it really, really hurts. Because if you don't, there's a real risk that they'll tell you that you don't need them, and send you on your way.

To put it bluntly, the psychologist said, I was too well for them: here I was, writing, getting out with my child, 'functioning', as she said in her letter to the psychiatrist, 'reasonably well', and there they were with dozens of people stuck halfway up their one-year waiting lists who could barely leave their houses. I'd had plenty of therapy already. I'd had cognitive behavioural therapy, and clearly understood how it worked and how to use it, so she really couldn't see how they could possibly add anything to my understanding of my problems and how to treat them. My skin looked perfectly normal to her, I was choosing to pick it rather than to do something else, and I needed to think about why I was making that choice. As to my other problems, what I needed to do now was to apply the understanding I already had and push myself into doing the things that I feared – bathing my child, travelling with my child, travelling alone. I felt myself compelled to agree that their resources were scarce, that I had got into the habit of playing the sick, helpless one in my relationships, that there was no avoiding the hard behavioural work which no one else could do for me, that I could not expect to be happy all the time, and that there was, as she put it, 'no substitute for suffering'. There was no need to agree – because she didn't say so – that I was a spoiled, middle-class therapy junkie who was wasting her valuable NHS time and probably my GP's as well, but the thought was in the room somewhere.

She was tempted, she finished, to offer me nothing, but just to give me 'a push in the right direction', she would refer me to the local primary care service for a brief course of behavioural treatment. I accepted gratefully, and left, feeling not so buoyant.

By the way, the advice above applies only to those seeking treatment on the NHS: in my experience, if you believe that therapy will help, and you can pay for it yourself, you'll very likely get it.

By relying on the testimony from the psychiatrist, I had made a serious tactical error in my quest for treatment. I had forgotten that professionals prefer to make their own minds up, to assess what walks into their offices on the day, and I had forgotten, too, that they do this largely by looking for external signs, behaviours. In order for them to believe that you are depressed or anxious, you need to act the part. What they are asking from you is that, to borrow a phrase from my five-year-old son, you 'show me the face of how that feels'. Show your sad, scared face – don't try and save it. Where resources are scarce and waiting lists long, you'd best leave your dignity and self-restraint outside the consulting-room door.

A few months ago, someone sent me a copy of a new book, a cultural history of obsession by an American academic, Lennard J. Davis. In a section on self-help books and memoirs, he writes that: 'The very nature of self-help books, particularly first-person ones, is that they trace a heroic path from a low point of disease and disorder to a high point of triumph over despair.'[47] I had thought that I was getting to that triumphal point: I'd had the 'eureka' moment in the library, I'd finally found a couple of clinically defined concepts – obsessive-compulsive disorder, compulsive skin picking – that offered an explanation for certain bewildering, frightening and shaming parts of myself, and allowed me to attribute them to something other than myself, to a bodily organ, my brain. Now all I had to do was to obtain the treatment to which that officially dysfunctional organ entitled me and then I could begin, at least, to manage my symptoms, to claim my life back from my adversaries – my compulsive skin picking, my OCD.

As Davis points out, wider medico-historical narratives of OCD also tend to follow this kind of 'heroic path'. This was the story I told in the last chapter, where I traced the progress of OCD from a poorly understood disease, wrongly thought to be rare, and with a poor prognosis, to a condition which is now treatable, has been revealed to be common, and is well on the

46. Lennard J. Davis, *Obsession: A History* (The University of Chicago Press Ltd, London, 2008)

way to being explained. It's the brain, so the story goes; it's the dysfunctional basal ganglia, it's the abnormal serotonin system. It's physical. Family studies suggest that it might even be inherited (we just haven't found the relevant genes yet). So what can you do? You medicate. You pin your hopes on trans-cranial magnetic stimulation, a brain research tool which looks as if it might, maybe, one day, be an effective treatment. You look to the drug companies to keep funding that research, to keep the big, expensive scanners running.

That's our straw man built, now let's give him a good kicking. The first kick is a fairly gentle one, a friendly tap from the neuroscience side. When I had put myself in the straw man's place, I had found it tempting, for many reasons, to see myself and my problems in terms of this simple equation: BRAIN = DESTINY. I was born that way, I had grown up that way, and, if left unmedicated, that is the way I would always be. It's a static picture: OCD is written into the body, is stable across time in the individual, and – if you apply this to the bigger picture – stable across history too. My brain is like Samuel Johnson's brain and St Ignatius of Loyola's brain and Martin Luther's brain and Hans Christian Andersen's brain and all those other brains which have been posthumously diagnosed in the last few decades.

First of all, even if you accept that a certain proportion of human brains have been addled by OCD since prehistory, there is no need to conclude that these brains can do nothing to help themselves. It has long been accepted that a developing brain, a child's brain, is partly shaped by nurture. More recently, as recounted in triumphal narratives such as Norman Doidge's *The Brain that Changes Itself*, researchers in various fields of neuroscience have found more and more evidence that the brain retains this 'neuroplasticity' – the capacity to reshape itself – into adulthood. This is why and how practice makes perfect, this is why and how we develop habits; it also offers us the means of breaking them. Jeffrey Schwartz's behavioural self-treatment method for 'brain lock' is based on this idea: once the patient has relabelled her invasive thoughts as OCD and re-attributed them to a fault in her brain, she can then refocus her attention, so that, for example, every time she finds herself thinking that she might stab her child, she can think of the music playing on the radio instead, or attend to her washing-up, or pick up an absorbing book, and *not* perform her compulsion, ruminate or run away. Schwartz describes this technique in terms of the patient's performing a 'manual gearshift' in her brain, which, if performed consistently enough, will, over time, enable the patient to bypass her obsessive-compulsive circuit, rather than get sucked further into it. It's a matter of habit: the less you perform your compulsions, the less you want to. It's also a matter of rewiring the brain, and to make this clear, *Brain Lock* has before and after scans of patients' brains prominently and colourfully displayed on its cover: *You can change your brain!*

Well, maybe you can. Certainly, if your usual patterns of thinking and behaviour change, the picture on the scanner will change too. That much we know: that much has been observed. What nobody could claim to know, at this stage, is what the relationship between the changed nature of the mental activity and the changed levels of activity in different parts of the brain actually consists in. It's like the sadness and the serotonin levels: it could be that certain patterns of brain activity cause OCD; on the other hand, it could be that what the scans are showing is the brain's *response* to the anxiety generated by certain mental events, by obsessive thoughts, as it is 'desperately trying to calm a system which is under pressure from too much anxiety'.[48] When it comes down to it, a brain scan can show a researcher which regions of a particular brain happen to be metabolizing glucose at a given moment, and that is all. I don't know if

48. David Veale and Rob Willson, *Overcoming Obsessive Compulsive Disorder* (Robinson, London, 2005)

Schwartz would agree with this, but I have read and heard several OCD experts who work with a cognitive model of the disorder saying that nothing of any clinical use has yet come out of those big scanning machines. This is in spite of the fact that an awful lot of money has flowed in. Science moves pretty slowly; speculation and conjecture run on ahead.

When advances are made, they often seem to happen accidentally, or at least *incidentally*. Take pethidine, for example, which was discovered to be a powerful painkiller by two scientists who were looking for a spasmolytic. Sometimes, what starts out as a drug's side effect can end up as its main therapeutic purpose. Iproniazid was originally prescribed to treat tuberculosis; when so many patients taking it grew so cheerful that the effect had to be more than coincidental, one of the first effective antidepressants was born. I've already told the story of how clomipramine emerged as a treatment for OCD only after it had been prescribed to patients to treat the depression that accompanied their OCD, and was then found to ease obsessive-compulsive symptoms in some of the patients who took it. We know that clomipramine, and many other newer drugs, act in such a way as to reduce the reuptake of serotonin throughout the brain; we also know that if you give these drugs to people who suffer from OCD, a certain proportion of them will show, or report, a reduction in the severity of their symptoms. That, again, is all we know.

It's all so tantalizing – the lit-up brain patterns, the response to a drug that is known to act on a particular system, the resemblance of certain obsessive human behaviours to certain animal ones, the prevalence of OCD among Tourette's sufferers – and it's undoubtedly fascinating, but on closer inspection, all it amounts to is a bundle of correlations, 'links', 'associations', 'similarities'; nothing causal; little proved. It is perfectly possible – maybe even probable – that the obsessive-compulsive symptoms which Nick van Bloss experiences come from a completely different source from the ones which have been plaguing me, and are expressive of an entirely different disorder.

And as no research has yet shown any relationship between brain activity and chemistry – or indeed any other factor – on one hand and the content of particular obsessions on the other, it is also by no means certain that I am suffering from the same condition as someone who washes her hands ten times an hour, that she has the same affliction as the man who keeps stopping his car and getting out to check that he hasn't run over anyone, or that his underlying pathology is in any way similar to the woman living next door to him who can barely move through her front hall because she's spent the last seven years compulsively hoarding her junk mail.[49] The causes may well be quite different in each case – and that's 'causes' not 'cause'. Veale and Willson describe OCD as arising from a cocktail of various psychological, biological, and social factors.

> The ingredients and quantities that make up the cocktail in the glass will be different for each unique individual, and they also mix in different ways . . .
>
> One day there will be an adequate model of OCD that integrates biological, psychological, and social factors, but a lot more research needs to be done before we arrive at it. For the present, when anyone tells you '*the* cause' of your OCD, don't believe them; the combination of causes for each person is likely to be unique, with different factors all interacting in a complex manner. [p. 42]

OCD is a mental illness, an illness of the mind. I do not know how the mind and the brain are related, and neither does anyone else. Let's leave it at that.

49. Having said this so confidently, there does seem to be some new evidence that suggests that the impulse to hoard arises out of a distinct part of the brain, but I'm not going to interrupt the flow of my argument just for that.

My GP was not at all happy that I had been bounced by psychological services, and tried to find some alternative sources of support for me. She got in touch with a local mental health charity, who were able to offer me help through their befriending scheme. My son was my priority: it was all very well to hobble my own life with my avoidant habits, but I had and have no right whatsoever to keep him so confined; he was getting bigger and more curious all the time, and he needed his world to expand with him. I asked if somebody might accompany us on trips out, and for the next few months, every fortnight or so, a very pleasant and interesting woman would pick me and my son up, and we would go into town together, either on foot or in the dreaded bus. I was lucky to have this help, and lucky too in my friends, who strapped my son's car seat into their cars alongside their own toddlers, and took us all out to harrowing out-of-town supermarkets and terrifying playparks. Back home, Chris continued to put up with me. I think that the boy must have caught a nasty cold sometime in February, because I found this conversation in my notes:

'How will I know if he develops meningitis during the night?'
　'Why would he develop meningitis overnight?'
　'Well – why wouldn't he?'
　'How would you tell if *I* developed meningitis during the night?'
　'I – don't know.'
　'Well you'd better stay awake all night then, hadn't you, just in case.'

You can learn a lot about OCD by examining this little exchange, not about the *causes* of OCD, but about the kind of beliefs and thinking habits which, along with compulsive and avoidant behaviours, are understood to maintain it. The cognitive behavioural model of OCD focuses on these beliefs and behaviours. I have already touched on most of these elsewhere, but, following on from Veale and Willson, for quicker reference, here is a list:

Avoidance and Safety-Seeking – I refer you to the discussion of road-crossing dilemmas in 'Dependence', in which I considered the theory that the only way to avoid being run over is never to cross the road when you can see a moving car; as the behaviour informed by this belief has kept me safe up till now, I am reinforcing the belief every time I engage in the behaviour.

An Inflated or Exaggerated Sense of Responsibility and Magical Thinking – A belief that one has the power to cause or prevent bad events from happening, and that, therefore, one has the responsibility to prevent them. In the meningitis conversation, I am working from an assumption that I can prevent my child from becoming ill, that it is therefore my responsibility to prevent my child from becoming ill, and that I should try to do this by anticipating every possible scenario, and then ruminating about it. If my child falls ill, it has to be my fault, because I failed to do enough to prevent it. 'Magical thinking' refers to the superstitious thinking behind some people's OCD symptoms, such as the compulsion to touch every lamp-post one passes in order to keep one's family out of danger. Of course, many people without OCD have their little superstitious habits, just as many of them also have a habit of worrying, that is of seeking to avert all possible disasters by anticipating them in advance. In political terms, this belief in the magical power of foresight is known as the 'precautionary principle' and is the reason why you can never find a rubbish bin in a railway terminal, or leave your baggage unattended. It will not, however, prevent a suicide bomber from sitting down next to you on the bus and detonating his backpack. You could try never travelling on a bus, but that doesn't mean you won't get cancer.[50]

The Over-Importance of Thoughts – It is perfectly normal to experience intrusive thoughts and images, and equally normal for these to be taboo in nature; you would only be abnormal, say Veale and Willson, if you *didn't* have them. These thoughts are not the problem: the problem, for the OCD sufferer, is the importance she attaches to them, the meaning she ascribes to them. In 'Harm', I talked about one aspect of this, 'thought-action' fusion, the belief that a bad thought or image, such as the thought of stabbing one's baby, will not only lead to a bad action, but is a kind of bad action in itself. This kind of belief can have a distinctly moralistic tinge, and can turn a young student's fleeting, completely normal thoughts about what it might be like to have sex with her tutor into evidence of the twisted, disgusting perversity of an exceptionally dirty girl. Some people with OCD believe that the presence of the thought indicates that they could have done the terrible action already, only they don't remember it: 'How can I be sure that I haven't stabbed a baby? The image is so immediate, so terrifying. Maybe it's a memory of something real?' For the OCD sufferer, an intrusive thought is not just some bubble of a thing that rises up to the top of your head and then pops without trace; these thoughts carry real weight, they are responsible for them; they can and should control them. These attempts at control, are, of course, self-defeating. Whatever you do now, don't think of a white bear, I said – don't! Stop it! No white bears! No white bears! NO. WHITE. BEARS!

---

50. For a fuller discussion of what I think of as 'Macro-OCD', see *Risk: The Science and Politics of Fear* by Dan Gardner, or Joanna Bourke's *Fear: A Cultural History* (Virago, London, 2006)

Overestimation of Danger or Risk – This is something which OCD has in common with other anxiety disorders. How likely was it that my son's cold would develop into meningitis? That I would inadvertently step in front of a van at the next pelican crossing? That I would set my desk chair on fire, be unable to put it out, be incapable of escaping and burn to death in the loft? That I would skid on the kitchen floor with a knife in my hand and accidentally stab my husband in the heart? If you are in the habit of attaching great importance to these thoughts, and to paying more attention to them than to the evidence outside you, then this is likely to bias your answer.

Intolerance of Uncertainty – But I have to be *absolutely sure* that my son won't develop meningitis, not tonight and not ever, or the matter cannot rest.

Perfectionism – I spent the best part of a day writing this paragraph over and over again, but I still couldn't get it completely right so in the end I just deleted it.

Attention, Bias in – The lion's share of this will be focused on anxiety, and on the signs of dangers which seem to justify it. You don't see the kitchen, because you've already zoomed in on the saucepan.

Interpreting Ambiguous Information – If my son has pain in his neck, I'd better assume it's meningitis, even if there are no other symptoms – just to be on the safe side.

Anxiety, two habits and one attitude that make it worse – Awfulizing: It's vile! It's dreadful! It's the worst thing ever! Catastrophizing: And it's going to be the death of me! That is, if the advanced, untreatable cancer that's making my stomach hurt doesn't get me first.

Low Frustration Tolerance – What I'm demonstrating, apparently, when I call the feeling of anxiety 'unbearable'. If the anxiety is something you believe you can't bear, you'll do whatever it takes to make it go away as quickly as possible, or even to stop yourself feeling it in the first place.

So now you know you all this, you understand the cognitive and behavioural underpinning of your obsessions and compulsions, but no amount of understanding, by itself, will make them go away: even the most rational thoughts are nothing more than thoughts, and they can bring nothing about. Thinking about getting better is not the same, unfortunately, as getting better. The lessons you need to learn – that anxiety is not the worst thing in the world, that thoughts are only thoughts – can only be learned through experience. You need to start crossing busy roads, using the big knife in the kitchen, taking your baby to the supermarket, and handing in imperfect copy. You have to allow your bad thoughts in and let them follow their course.

When I interviewed Dr Veale, he asked me if my obsessional symptoms had gone. No, I said, they were still there: I just 'kind of swatted them away'.

'Welcome them,' he said. 'Welcome them. Don't fight them – just let them be there.'

I thought about this for a moment. 'Yeah. Well, my child – who is four and a quarter – will lie down on the floor and I'll think, Ooh – I could stamp on his neck! – and then I think, Yes I could, but I won't.' And I laughed.

Then Dr Veale said, 'Well, you could do that, or you could imagine in your mind a nice little picture of stamping on it, and blood going all over the place, *and the blood all over the place!*'

I laughed again, but first I screwed my face up as tight as it would go. I wish there were another way, a less painful way, but, as things stand, there really is no substitute for suffering. And you can't get anyone else to suffer for you either. For any practical purposes, both the problem, and the means of dealing with it, are in your mind. We speak of the mind as something you can make up, something you can change. It is both the source of our agency, and subject to it.

On 13 May, the clinical psychologist at the primary care services wrote to the psychiatrist, and to my GP, to tell them that I had commenced my course of treatment with her the previous day. She reminded them that the psychologist who'd referred me had thought that 'a brief, focused course of treatment targeting [my] significant avoidance behaviour would be most helpful'. The treatment would, therefore, focus on improving my self-confidence and reducing my avoidance behaviour in relation to my son. She added that I had asked if we might focus on my skin picking: 'It became apparent that although her skin objectively looks fine, she is extremely concerned that other people will think her skin is "disgusting" and thus hides it as much as possible.' Since my skin objectively looked fine, and since reversing an ingrained habit like skin picking was very difficult, and would take far more sessions than we had available to us, she suggested that it might be more helpful to 'objectively assess' how other people reacted to my appearance, and to work on reducing my anxiety about the issue.

I agreed, although I failed to see what was so objectively fine about the way I looked. Especially when I was sitting opposite one of the most beautiful people I'd ever come across in real life: flawless skin, fine bone structure, perfectly symmetrical features, etc., etc. I didn't and never would look like her; therefore I disgusted myself, but I made an effort, for the sake of our therapeutic alliance, not to hold this against her. The following weekend, I bought a couple of sleeveless tops. I wore them a few times and noted that nobody around me threw up. Then I stashed them away in a drawer and managed never to wear them again, or buy anything else sleeveless. (All right, some of my sleeves are shorter than they used to be, but that's as far as it goes – most of the time.)

At that first meeting, my symmetrical psychologist drew me a diagram to show how my anxiety, if I could only stay with it, would trail off by itself. Then she asked me to come up with a hierarchy of tasks that made me anxious, with the least stressful at the bottom and the most terrifying at the top, using SUDS as a rating system. I came back the next week with the following table:

Percentage	Activity
100	Taking a train with my son alone with changes.
90	Taking my son to Lammas Land [a play area across town] alone.
85	Taking my son by bus to the Botanics alone.
85	Crossing the road holding my son's hand alone.
80	Taking a train with my son alone with no changes.
80	Walking with my son on reins by water alone.
75	Walking with my son holding his hand alone.
70	Taking a train with my son with someone else with changes.
70	Flying with my son and someone else.
70	Taking my son into town on reins alone.
65	Taking my son on the bus into town alone.
65	Crossing the road with my son on reins alone.
65	Walking with my son holding his hand with someone else.
65	Crossing the road holding my son's hand with someone else.

65	Taking a taxi with my son alone.
60	Walking with my son on reins in the street alone.
60	Walking with my son on reins by water with someone else.
55	Flying alone.
55	Taking my son to Lammas Land with someone else.
50	Taking my son into town on reins with someone else.
50	Crossing the road with my son on reins with someone else.
45	Taking my son to the Botanics with someone else.
40	Taking a train with my son and someone else with no changes.
35	Walking to local shops with my son on reins alone.
30	Taking my son on the bus into town with someone else.
30	Taking my son somewhere in someone else's car without Chris or Mum.
20	Walking with my son in the buggy into town alone.
10	Walking with my son in the buggy along the main road alone.
5	Walking with my son in the buggy to local shops alone.
3	Local shops alone.

I was quite pleased with this as a piece of work: it was neatly presented, its numbers meticulously calculated, and I felt that the repetition gave it a certain incantatory power. The psychologist was pleased too, and we were able to use it to set some realistic goals for the next fortnight: I would take my son, who at twenty-two months had only just begun to walk, on the bus into town with someone else – I already had my befriender lined up for this – and I would walk to the local shops with him. On reins. Alone. I completed my homework, ticked the items off the list, and at the next session agreed to move up the Ladder of Fear (as she didn't call it), and tackle the two items I'd rated at 50 per cent.

We only had six sessions together, and the highest tick on the list is only at 60 per cent: 'Walking with my son on reins by water with someone else.' This was during an *in vivo* session the day before his second birthday, when I met the psychologist and her student on Jesus Green, and we took my boy down to the river. We stopped at the top of a flight of concrete steps which led down from the path to the water's edge and I was told to take my son by the reins and start walking down them. We stopped at each step, the psychologist would ask me to rate my anxiety as a percentage, then we would chat for a minute or two and she would ask again. The percentage fell each time. At the conclusion of the experiment, I was crouching right next to the Cam with my son on reins beside me, pointing out ducks and driftwood. Later that session, I even took him off the reins – once we were safely back on the path – and we fed the ducks together. It showed, if nothing else, that these things were physically possible.

In the three and half years since the *in vivo* session, I have taken care of many of the more fearful items on the list, but, if I'm honest, this probably has more to do with my son's growing all the time older and less acutely vulnerable than anything I've managed to do through deliberate therapeutic effort. I now cross the road holding my son's hand alone (85 per cent) every day, with no more than about 30 per cent anxiety most of the time, and I can do this because crossing the road with a five-year-old is a completely different activity from crossing it with a toddler.

Then again, habituation does help – practice makes possible – with everyday tasks. The longer, more complicated, less regular trips, however, remain as abyss crossings. Last summer, I took a train with my son and my husband with changes (70 per cent) – and a boat too – when we travelled to the Isle of Wight for a holiday. Our son was perfectly easy to manage on the journey, but my anxiety wasn't: too many trains, too many platforms, too many gaps between trains and platforms, too many people milling around making dangerous crowds on the platforms . . . Still, I did it, and there's nothing on the list about not being a pain in the arse on the train with my son.

That's it, I'm afraid: the most effective way to treat your OCD symptoms is, rather ironically, to make a to-do list, rate the items on the to-do list and then work up it, ticking as you go. It's stressful to accomplish, and transcendentally dull to write about. I've always found the common-sense language of CBT to be rather disappointing, distinctly lacking in the colour and drama that makes psychoanalysis so attractive to read about and to engage in. I've been in the habit of seeing this as a flaw, but lately I've been coming to think that maybe the flatness of it is the point. If I look at the cognitive behavioural model of OCD with a poet's eyes, the picture that emerges is of a person who is suffering from hyperbole, and perhaps an over-excitation of the metaphorical: it's not a thought but a PREMONITION; it's not an impulse but the DEVIL'S PROMPTING; it's not a spot, but a DISFIGUREMENT; it's not anxiety but TERROR; it's not a mistake but a FATAL FLAW. When I think about a journey, it's an abyss. When I see an HGV coming towards me after dark, I see a stampeding monster, bearing down on me with flaming eyes. It's not a realistic way of seeing things; it's just not *proportionate*.

But then, as I've said, no one expects normality from a poet. We have something of a propensity for mental illnesses of all kinds, and female poets especially. I've seen it referred to as The Plath Effect. Psychoanalysts, psychologists, psychiatrists, psy-folk of all kinds have filled libraries with their efforts to figure out what the exact relationship between poetry and madness might be. Some suggest that there is a certain mental lability that predisposes a person to both: if you have it, chances are that you will turn out to be creative, or mad, or some combination of the two. Others see the making of poems not as a symptom, but as an ingenious attempt at self-cure, a kind of symbolic healing. I have seen research that suggests that, rather than there being a sharp distinction between poetry-as-art and poetry-as-therapy, the formal working-through of the poem on the page brings about a corresponding working-through of a problem in the psyche. Difficulties with emotion and experience are trans-formed on the page into difficulties with form, and as you find a solution to these, an acceptable compromise between the experience or thought you are trying to express and the means available to express it, there is a sense of real physical and emotional release. I say 'you' here – I mean 'me'. And how do I know when I've finished a piece of writing? Well, I don't for sure – that is to say, I don't know *objectively* – but when I get that certain feeling, that release of tension, that sense of a task completed, I know it's time to stop.

Losses

29. After doing something carefully, I still have the impression I have either done it badly or not finished it.

The Padua Inventory

Some obsolete psychiatric diagnoses: phrenitis, melancholia, dancing mania, Scythian disease, oneirodynia, neurasthenia, nostalgia, spasms, monomania, hysteria, sexual inversion, nervous exhaustion, railway spine.

Then the certain feeling wears off and you realize you haven't finished after all: there's still something to add, or cut out, and maybe just *tweak* a little. Take hoarding, for example: I've only touched on it in passing, and it deserves more space than that.

Although it is usually included in lists of OCD symptoms, compulsive hoarding is seen by some as a quite distinct and separate category within OCD, and by others as a separate disorder altogether. Hoarders are far less likely than other sufferers to acknowledge their problem, or to seek help, and when they do, the medical and therapeutic treatments currently on offer are less likely to have any noticeable or lasting effect. They feel justified in their gathering and stockpiling of conventionally worthless things, in some cases even when they can no longer sleep in their bedrooms, cook in their kitchens, wash in their bathrooms, or open their front doors. The point they will make, to anyone who asks, is that you never know when you might want a thing, so you had better keep it, because if you throw it away, then it's lost to you, and what will you do then? Anything might be valuable, and therefore, it is safest to assume that everything is.

In his section on compulsive hoarding, Penzel includes 'an offshoot' of the behaviour, a hoarding of less tangible things, such as 'names, faces, facts or events'. This group of hoarders are concerned that they might miss or forget things. Like material hoarding, which may involve only one or two specific categories of objects, such as newspapers, lint, or string, the compulsions of those suffering from the offshoot disorder are often confined to one category of facts.

> One sufferer I met had actually memorized all the names and complete specifications of all the world's fighter aircraft, which he then had to keep studying daily in order not to forget the information. The thought of forgetting any of these facts caused him great anxiety. In addition, he had to save a very large library of books on the subject and constantly keep it updated as new types of aircraft were manufactured. He would read them repeatedly and drill himself on the facts. [Penzel, p. 247]

Yet another group have compulsions to hoard memories and experiences, not the kind of significant ones that most of us would expect to commemorate with cards, parties and photographs, but quite trivial experiences, often, again, in one particular category. One woman Penzel treated tried to hoard all her eating experiences, as she was never sure, for example, if this particular apple might be the last she'd ever see or eat, so naturally she would want to commit it fully to memory, just in case.

I wouldn't call myself a pathological hoarder. I can happily throw all kinds of things away: packaging, newspapers, magazines, junk mail, worn-out clothing, knackered toothbrushes, blunted razor blades, food past its use-by date, last term's school newsletters, broken plastic coat hangers, tins of dried-up paint –

I've chucked them all out, and I've enjoyed doing it. Other things are harder to part with. I find it almost impossible to throw a book away, but then I am a writer, so I genuinely might need to look something up at some point (and so what if I live half an hour's walk away from a copyright library – that's half an hour I'll never get back). Anyway, what some call hoarding, others might call building a library.

So, I can justify my books. I believe I justify them in a perfectly rational way. I believe that I can also justify my hanging onto every notebook I've ever used, all the letters and drafts of poems which other writers have sent me, and every draft of everything I've ever written, on professional grounds. For a start, I couldn't have written this book without them.

But ask me why I find it so hard to throw away any of my son's old toys, books, drawings, paintings, scribbles or flaking collages without Chris's help, and the rationalizations run out. My first thought is always that I can't make these decisions for this other person, and I imagine him looking for his lost things and not finding them; I'm aware, even as I think this, that my job as a parent is precisely that, to make decisions for another person, and also that my son is more likely to forget, rather than miss, what he doesn't see every day. So, I have to admit to myself that I want to keep his old things for my sake, because they represent those earlier versions of my son, the obsolete versions, and it's these – the baby, the toddler, the three-year-old, the four-year-old – that I can't bear to lose.

Most of the things that I hoard represent lost or absent persons in some way. Like the horcruxes in the Harry Potter books, they do not just represent other souls, but are containers for pieces of those souls, which I feel myself responsible for keeping and preserving. Anything written by another person, whether they are a writer or not, comes into this category: sitting in my office are letters and postcards I've kept since I was a teenager, and autograph books signed by my classmates in primary school. I find it almost impossible to throw old photographs away, even if I have three copies of the same image, and this is especially true if that image has my son in it. To throw away a photograph of someone is to signal to some supernatural force somewhere that you wish that person dead, whether you really do or not. Throwing away a photograph is tantamount to manslaughter.

You'll have guessed that I'm something of a memory hoarder. Sometimes, I'm a fact hoarder too, though I prefer to call it 'research'.

Whether it is a species of OCD or not, hoarding has this in common with other compulsive behaviours: it doesn't work. A thought resisted will come back redoubled; a checked lock will only have to be checked again; all children grow older, and the day will come when everyone who ever was, is or will be in a photograph will be gone. Uncertainty, change, decay and death – you can't wash, check, avoid, touch, count, pick, groom, arrange, step, jump, dance, reread, rewrite, confess, reassure or think them away. Accept them, or paralyse yourself.

For a start, if I can't accept that I'm going to have to begin this paragraph in an unsatisfactory way, I won't be able to begin it at all. I just caught myself picking my skin, which is something I still do when I get a bit stuck. It's not as bad as it was, but I haven't been able to stop. I still find myself hideous, and now I have ageing to worry about too. It didn't help that, a few weeks after I finished my treatment with the symmetrical psychologist, I discovered that my hair was falling out: I had developed alopecia areata, another autoimmune condition. That loss wasn't permanent, but it did leave me with another topic to obsess about, and another thing to check.

Early in 2006, I had strep throat, then sinusitis, then another bad cold on top of that. I told my GP that I was asking myself how many decades of this I was prepared to put up with, the illness, the inevitable deterioration. She switched me from citalopram to Prozac, and referred me back to psychological services. This time, I had a more sympathetic assessment, and I began a new course of CBT the following January. I'd started work on the book by then, and wrote about the cycling I was doing as part of my homework. I'm sorry to say that didn't last. The therapist's and my efforts to make me feel better about ageing, by counting the number of attractive and well-dressed mature women I saw walking down the street in one afternoon, or interviewing my mother and her friends about how good they felt about themselves, didn't really do much either. Of course, I didn't want to disappoint my therapist, so I pretended that it did at the time. We also looked at the high standards I set myself. The therapist asked me to write down my rules for living. For the first time in my life, I did so, and saw how harsh they were, how they contradicted each other.

My writing should sell, or I'm a failure, but if I write for money, I will have no integrity.

I should do my best to stay thin, while bearing in mind that only trivial-minded women think about these things.

I should be a perfect and ever-attentive mother to my son, without being the kind of reactionary betrayer-of-the-sisterhood who allows her husband to support her.

I read them out to the therapist and realized, again for the first time, that they were entirely laughable. Now that *did* help: I saw, really saw, that my internal legislator was a ridiculous figure, who had never deserved the attention I'd been paying her. When she turns up these days, which she still does, I try not to engage with her too much. I suppose that, in principle, if I made enough of an effort, I could oust her altogether, and even stop my picking as well, but I've been living with these symptoms for decades now, and, to be perfectly honest, the thought of losing them almost terrifies me. What would I do without them? Who would I be then? And what could I blame when I failed?

This course of CBT had begun, as they always do, with the filling in of inventories. When I handed them back to the therapist, I shared my scepticism about them. No, she agreed, they weren't perfect instruments, but you had to use something, and it might as well be those. And as for CBT, no that wasn't magic either, but it was worth trying, because it might be *some* help at least. In a similar vein, when we discussed diagnoses, and my confusion about how many and which ones applied to me, she said that, as she saw it – as *most* clinicians saw it – patients were people who were suffering, who were having certain difficulties with their experience, and even though you had to give some label or other to these, to fill in some boxes, to provide some bureaucratic rationale for the treatment, all that mattered, in the end, was whether or not a person needed help, and whether or not you were able to give it to them.

This is just as well, because diagnostic categories are themselves subject to change, revision and obsolescence. I suffer from OCD; Samuel Johnson, living in another age and a different cultural context, suffered from the Hyps. It is entirely possible that in the next few decades, OCD may also become a defunct disease entity, either subsumed under a wider category, like impulse disorders, or broken up into smaller, more specific ones. Even as I write, the members of the American Psychiatric Association are revising their *Diagnostic and Statistical Manual* again, suggesting the inclusion of new disorders, proposing the dismissal of old ones, and arguing every point.

The compilation and revision of DSM is a Byzantine process, subject not only to the competing views and interests of the clinicians and researchers themselves, but also to those of other groups: the pharmaceutical companies who lobby for the inclusion of newly minted disorders which they claim their drugs can treat, and the American health insurance companies who would prefer to limit the number of diseases for which patients can legitimately claim funding for treatment. There are political pressures too, as 'special interest' groups, voluntary organizations and political activists argue for the inclusion or exclusion of this or that diagnosis. It was as a result of such campaigns that post-traumatic stress disorder came to be recognized as a psychiatric condition, and homosexuality ceased to be defined as such. As well as simply appearing or disappearing, a category may expand or contract, as the lists of criteria for each diagnosis are revised.

I have seen OCD described as an 'imperializing' diagnosis. Since the 1970s, estimations of its prevalence have risen from between 0.05 per cent and .005 per cent[51] to around 2 per cent[52] of the population, a huge rise, suggesting that there are over a million sufferers in the UK alone. The older, more conservative estimates reflected the fact that, until fairly recently, only those too severely affected to hide their condition would have been diagnosed. This group were, and remain, difficult to treat. The difference between the two sets of numbers has been made up by people like me, who are mildly to moderately affected, and who have been found, in many cases, to be responsive to the pharmaceutical and therapeutic treatments which have appeared since the earlier estimates were made. It is not that we respond to treatment because we have the disease; it is that we have the disease, by definition, because we respond to treatment. If Prozac helps you with your shyness, then you have social anxiety disorder; if it alleviates your grief, you've been suffering from reactive depression. It's very much that way round.

There are differences, important ones, between psychiatry as it's practised in America and psychiatry as practised in the UK.

51. Lennard J. Davis, *Obsession: A History* (University of Chicago Press, Chicago and London, 2008, p. 209)
52. Source: the Royal College of Psychiatry's website

If I were in the States, I would probably be on three drugs rather than just the one: my daily antidepressant, of course; a second drug, such as Xanax or Klonopin, which I could use when I needed to alleviate anxiety; then a third drug, perhaps to take the edge off some of the side effects from the other two. I would have a GP, a 'family physician', but I would also have a psy-chopharmacologist (do they even *exist* in the UK?) to visit, and we could experiment together. Maybe I would make an appointment after seeing a television advertisement for some exciting new product or other – 'Why not ask your doctor about . . .?'

I was in America for ten days last summer, and I found these advertisements jaw-dropping. They made me desperately sad, too: they made me think of my brother, who had spent most of his adult life in the States, and who had been diagnosed two years earlier with adult attention deficit disorder,[53] and pre-scribed, for a brief but catastrophic period, with amphetamines to treat it. As he came from the UK, with its socialized medi-cine, it had always been especially hard for him to negotiate the American medical system, with its competing practitioners and institutions, its insurance companies and its huge bills. After our father died, he was physically ill for over a year, and had to undergo expensive tests for every syndrome under the sun before being diagnosed, in the event retrospectively, with tem-porary thyroiditis. He also became very depressed – or grief-stricken, perhaps? – and tried several antidepressants before he found one that suited.

And he couldn't afford to be ill. He had to finish his PhD. Then, when he did finish, and moved to the west coast to take up a post-doctoral position, he had to work, to keep producing, and keep publishing, in order to prove his worth. When the back pain which he had experienced since he was a teenager

53. Although this diagnosis is almost unheard of the UK, it is far from uncommon in the States.

became much worse, the effects on his work, and his morale, were dreadful. The back pain was treated with the first of a number of cortisone injections. He and his wife moved to a town in the Midwest to take up a pair of tenure track positions; the pain kept recurring, and, after a struggle with his insurance company to persuade them to fund treatment with a surgeon he actually trusted, he had surgery on his back.

He still couldn't afford to be ill, of course – he was on the tenure track; he had evaluations every year; he had to work; he had to recruit and manage the staff in his lab; he had to publish. His wife was in the same position. They had a baby daughter, and together stepped off the tenure track for a year, which, again, they couldn't really afford to do – but had to. It was some time around her first birthday, if memory serves, that he was diagnosed with ADD.

After the brief but catastrophic period, he came off the amphetamines. He changed psychiatrists, and changed his therapist too. I couldn't tell you which, if any, medications he was taking after that, because he never told me. Neither, for the same reason, could I tell you what he'd been given to understand was wrong with him. Maybe if I had been a more willing traveller, and had been prepared to take the time away from my home, and force myself on to the planes, to see him in person, we might have had a few proper conversations, and he might have told me then. He did suggest, over the phone, on more than one occasion that Chris and our son and I might like to come over and visit, to, you know, 'just hang out?' It always sounded like a casual suggestion, not as if he was desperate to see me, but just as if, you know, in that ascending American way that my brother used to finish his British-accented sentences, it would be nice? I thought it would be nice to see him too – I missed him – but the thought of travelling on all those trains and planes and automobiles to the Midwest with a small child and then dealing with the jet lag on top of that, and then having to do the whole journey again in reverse made it seem quite impossible. I just hung on and hoped that he and his wife would decide to take their daughter on a visit to the UK, thus relieving me of the responsibility for travel. Stupid, selfish woman.

In spring and summer last year, I would often entertain fantasies of taking a plane or two by myself and arriving unannounced on his doorstep, so that we could have our proper talk and I could find out how he was, really. I hadn't heard from him in a while, and our last conversation had been strained. There was something in the tone of his voice that suggested he'd rather not have to talk to me, or anyone else from his UK family, not even over the phone, that he wanted, and needed, some space to think away from us, but I felt, in my gut of guts, that I should go and see him face to face, or otherwise – otherwise what? I stayed in the UK, and worked on 'Avoidance', and described my Unbearable Feeling as if I had no particular reason for it. Then my uncle phoned to tell me that my brother had taken his own life. And so I had to make that trip, with my mother, in the end.

After some toing and froing, Bloodaxe accepted my second poetry collection in the summer of 2006. I was all poetried out again, and thought I might try and write a novel. I'd written a few short stories in the previous year, so it seemed like a reasonable ambition. All I needed was a decent idea, one for which I could sustain my enthusiasm for more than a couple of months. How about, I thought, a novel about a woman with OCD and her long-suffering husband? So I started to make notes, writing down lists of intrusive thoughts, memories of conversations, that kind of thing. Then I tried to change the central characters, to make those alterations that writers use to distance their fictional creations from the real-life people whose attributes they've ripped off to use as their starter ingredients. That's when I got stuck, and it occurred to me that I hadn't seen too many

319

OCD memoirs. Depression, yes; anorexia, plenty; self-harm, getting there; OCD, not too much. It was inevitable that someone was going to write one at some point, so, I thought, it might as well be me.

And yet . . . I really wanted to write a novel. Novels were what proper writers wrote, and to write a memoir instead seemed, by contrast, like a failure of imagination, of creativity. It was a lesser form, I thought, and a narcissistic form at that; it was an act of unadulterated exhibitionism, in a way that even the most autobiographical poem, with its ritual clothing of rhythm and imagery, somehow manages not to be. I was concerned, too, about the morality of writing about all the people who had been involved in my life but happened not to be me, or to have chosen to have themselves depicted in someone else's book.

I had lunch with a friend of mine, a novelist and self-proclaimed life-writing sceptic, and confessed that I was thinking of writing an OCD memoir, a piece of mad lit. She thought about this; it might be worth doing, she said, if it were done well enough. She could let me get away with it, she added, as long as I promised – *promised* – that I wouldn't give it a redemptive ending. So I promised, and now here's the ending, the real ending.

A couple of weeks after my brother died, I had a dream about him. I was at one of the innumerable dream versions of my mother's house, when the phone rang. She picked it up, listened, and turned white. 'It's your brother,' she said.

I told her to give the phone to me, took it into the downstairs toilet, and locked the door. Then we had one of our normal, bantering conversations, and laughed together, entirely as if nothing had happened. We kept this up for five minutes or so, and then there was a pause. I felt something change, in the dream atmosphere, and in me, and then I asked him, 'So why did you do it?'

There was a silence.

'Do *what?*' he asked, as if he really didn't know.

'*You* know,' I said. There was another silence and when he spoke again, he sounded as he had done in our last waking conversation: guarded, offhand, evasive.

'I got distracted,' he gabbled. 'Things were distracting me. Look – I have to go now – 'bye!'

Then he hung up, and I think that's as much of an answer as I'm ever going to get.

A note on permissions

The author and publisher wish to thank the following for permission to quote from copyright material:

The Padua Inventory reprinted by permission of Ezio Sanavio; *Jacob's Room* by Virginia Woolf, reprinted by permission of The Society Authors as the literary representative of the Estate of Virginia Woolf; *Pull Yourself Together!*, reprinted by permission of the Mental Health Foundation; Sigmund Freud © The Institute of Psycho-Analysis and the Hogarth Press for permission to quote from Volumes 9,10 and 16 of *The Standard Edition of the Complete Psychological Works of Sigmund Freud* translated and edited by James Strachey, reprinted by permission of the Random House Group Ltd; 'Developmental Precursors of Depression: the Child and the Social Environment' by Elizabeth McCauley, Karen Paulidis and Kim Kendall and 'Child Depression: Clinical Phenomenology and Classification' by Israel Kelvin and Hartwin Sadowski in *The Depressed Child and Adolescent*, edited by Ian M. Goodyer, reprinted by permission of Cambridge University Press; *Obsessive-Compulsive Disorders: A Complete Guide to Getting Well and Staying Well* by Fred Penzel, reprinted by permission of Oxford University Press; 'What She Said', words and music by Johnny Marr and Steven Morrissey © 1985, lyrics reprinted by permission of Universal Music Publishing Limited (50%), and Warner Chappell Music Ltd (PRS) on behalf of Marr Songs Ltd (PRS) and Bona Relations Ltd (PRS) (50%), administered by Warner Chappell Music Ltd (PRS); *The Second Sex* by Simone de Beauvoir, translated by H. M. Parshley, first published by Jonathan Cape, 1949, reprinted by permission of the Random

Acknowledgements

Thanks, first of all, to everyone at Atlantic, especially Angus McKinnon, Karen Duffy, Sarah Castleton and Caroline Knight; also to Louisa Joyner and my agent, Louise Greenberg. I would also like to thank David Veale for his time, and for answering my questions about OCD; Esther Binns, for answering questions about neuroscience; the health professionals whose contributions to my medical notes have been quoted in the text; Ruth Bell-Pellegrini, for help with permissions; Magdalene College, Cambridge; the Royal Literary Fund; Rowan Pelling, for encouraging me in the first place; my family and friends, for their willingness to be depicted; my husband, Chris, for this and everything else.